P9-DTG-306

NOV 1 4 1983

DATE DUE

Russia and the United States

Nikolai V. Sivachev and Nikolai N. Yakovlev

Russia and the United States

Translated by Olga Adler Titelbaum

The University of Chicago Press
Chicago and London

The University of Chicago Press, Chicago 60637
The University of Chicago Press, Ltd., London

Printed in the United States of America
83 82 81 80 79   5 4 3 2 1

Library of Congress Cataloging in Publication Data

Sivachev, Nikolaĭ Vasil'evich.
  Russia and the United States.

  (The United States in the world: foreign perspectives)
  Translated from Russian manuscript.
  Includes index.
  1. United States—Foreign relations—Russia.
2. Russia—Foreign relations—United States.
I. IAkovlev, Nikolaĭ Nicolaevich, fl. 1946–
joint author. II. Title. III. Series.
E183.8.R9S5713   327.73'047   78–10554
ISBN 0–226–76149–5

*Nikolai V. Sivachev is professor of history at the University of Moscow.
Nikolai N. Yakovlev is senior research scholar at the Institute of Sociology, Academy of Sciences of the USSR. Both authors have published books and articles in Russian on the United States.*

Contents

Foreword

by *Akira Iriye*
Series Editor

This book is a volume in the series entitled The United States and the World: Foreign Perspectives. As the series title indicates, it aims at examining American relations with other countries from a perspective that lies outside the United States. International relations obviously involve more than one government and one people, and yet American foreign affairs have tended to be treated as functions of purely domestic politics, opinions, and interests. Such a uninational outlook is not adequate for understanding the complex forces that have shaped the mutual interactions between Americans and other peoples. Today, more than ever before, it is imperative to recognize the elementary fact that other countries' traditions, aspirations, and interests have played an equally important role in determining where the United States stands in the world. As with individuals, a country's destiny is in part shaped by how other countries perceive it and react to it. And a good way to learn about how foreigners view and deal with the United States is to turn to a non-American scholar of distinction for a discussion of his country's relations with America.

The authors of this volume are well-known Soviet scholars who have specialized in the study of United States history. Their numerous writings, for instance Professor Sivachev's *Government and Labor in the United States during World War II* (1974) and Professor Yakovlev's *Contemporary History of the United States* (1961) have been widely acclaimed in Russia. And yet few American historians and students are aware of these works. Despite the fact that these scholars have written extensively on their country's relations with the United States, most American historians do not appear to have even heard of them. This is regrettable, not only because American historical works are regularly read in the Soviet Union, but also, and fundamentally, because one can never expect to have a full appreciation of binational relationships until one breaks away from a purely uninational perspective. Readers of this book will become aware of the sharply contrasting ways in which past events are interpreted in different countries. They will not necessarily agree with what Professors Sivachev and Yakovlev have written; they may in fact take issue with many of their viewpoints and with the conceptual frames into which they fit historical data. They may feel puzzled and even provoked by the book's description of such events as the United States intervention in Siberia, Russian contributions during World War II, and the origins of the Cold War. They will undoubtedly be struck by what appear to be unusual emphases placed by the authors on certain events. If so, they will then be in a position to understand how each society comes to terms with its own history, and how it imposes meaning on events in order to ensure political and cultural stability. International relations are a complex phenomenon because they involve a multiplicity of symbols and meanings. By knowing something about other peoples' symbolic systems, one arrives at a deeper understanding of one's own society and its interactions with others. Professors Sivachev and Yakovlev have spent many years writing this book, and it deserves to be read and discussed extensively by all those who are interested in coming to grips with the cultural and intellectual gaps that separate countries.

Foreword

by *Rem V. Khokhlov*

In April 1971 the University of Chicago Press proposed to the University of Moscow that a book on Soviet-American relations be written as part of a series of publications under the general title "The United States and the World: Foreign Perspectives."

It was not just coincidence that the University of Chicago initiated this new undertaking—the publication in the United States of a book prepared by Soviet authors concerning the relations between our countries. The University of Chicago was the home of the first important center for the study of Russian subjects in the United States, and it occupies a prominent place in the annals of professional contacts between the scholars of our two countries, historians as well as others.

It seems logical to me, also, that the Press addressed its proposal to the University of Moscow in particular. Ever since the university, which now bears his name, was founded in Moscow by the great Russian scholar M. V. Lomonosov in 1755, it has steadfastly maintained a lively interest in America, its science and its culture. Lomonosov was familiar with the scholarly achievements of the great Benjamin Franklin and valued them highly.

During the American War for Independence the newspaper *Moskovskie vedomosti*, published by the University of Moscow, gave its support to the rebellious colonists and assured its readers that freedom would triumph in America.

Today, when the USSR and the United States are moving into the vanguard of scientific-technological progress, it is especially important that we should be well acquainted with each other's achievements. This requires not only the development of economics, science, and culture, but also concern for the strengthening of the world as a whole.

The late Rem V. Khokhlov was president of Moscow University from 1973 to 1977.

The University of Moscow has always played an important role in the development of science in our fatherland and in the international connections of Soviet scholars in various fields. During the last few decades the scale of its activities in science and pedagogy has expanded particularly.

The University of Moscow now has a school of American studies that embraces the most diverse branches of learning. In the field of the natural sciences, scholars of the university maintain a constant, active, and creative dialogue with their colleagues across the ocean.

The humanities departments of the university are developing programs specializing in American problems. The solution of this problem is furthered by required courses in American history in the secondary schools, by a course in the recent history of foreign countries, and also study of the English language—one of the required foreign languages studied by the majority of students of our secondary schools.

Every year scores of specialists on the United States graduate from the University of Moscow. The history department, for example, graduates a group of ten to fifteen specialists in American studies annually. All students in the history department study the history of the United States in general courses in world history. Most of them also study English so intensively that even if they are not specializing in the United States, they can refer to American literature, study American problems independently, and extend their knowledge in this field in every possible way. About eighty students, many of them not specializing in American history, attended the course in history of the United States given in English by Professor E. David Cronon of the University of Wisconsin in 1974.

The University of Moscow participates actively in the program of scholarly cooperation between our nations that has been developing successfully since the late 1950s. The history department alone accepted seventeen exchange students from the United States in 1972–73, and fifteen in 1973–74. Several departments of our university had forty-one researchers and seven professors from the United States in 1974, each working for a considerable period. Our historians, in turn, along with specialists in other branches of American studies, visit the United States regularly.

We can now say with some confidence that the scholarly exchange has made a great contribution to the improvement of Soviet-American relations, to widening the effectiveness of the principles of peaceful coexistence, and to improved cooperation between our peoples and nations. The proposed book is new evidence of this.

Soviet and American scholars can do much to put an end to the obstacles of the cold war. Great opportunities for further cooperation and rapprochement of our peoples are opening up before historians. This does not mean, however, that they must paint an idyllic picture of the relations between our countries, which have developed along different lines. The saying *historia est magistra vitae* takes on a positive meaning only to the extent that history reflects reality scientifically and objectively.

This is the first time that Soviet history professors have addressed themselves to the American student on such an important question. In this book, along with other general works by Soviet scholars in American Studies, you will find the basic concepts we use in evaluating the relations between the Soviet Union and the United States. I hope that the work will be received with understanding by the American reader.

Preface

We have set no easy task—to write an account of Soviet-American relations for an American audience at a time when the heavy burden of the cold war is just beginning to be lifted from the backs of our two peoples.

Having received this unusual proposal from the University of Chicago Press, and having deliberated for a long time, we sent back an equally unusual reply—we agreed to write this book. The decisive factor in dispelling our doubts was the desire to take what part we could in overcoming the negative heritage resulting from the cold war.

We also realized that to bring together the ideas of American and Soviet citizens on the most critical questions of our interrelations would prove no easier than the docking of *Soyuz* and *Apollo* in space. However, inasmuch as the scholars, engineers, and cosmonauts of both countries have undertaken to work together enthusiastically, why should historians not try to take at least a tentative step in the same direction? It seems certain that the one effort will have a positive influence on the other: cooperation in space exploration is bound to help mutual relations on earth—and, of course, the other way around as well.

We did not set out to please the American reader, accustomed to historical works on this subject written from a methodological and political point of view far different from ours. We should point out, moreover, that the Press did not demand this of us, but recommended that we should feel free to present our own views.

We did take into account, however, that certain facts and positions perfectly familiar to Soviet readers would have to be given more attention in a book addressed to a foreign audience. Thus it seemed essential to say a little more about our side of American-Soviet relations.

The proposed book has been written from the standpoint of historico-materialistic methodology. Underlying the historico-materialistic conception of the historical process is the idea of a regular succession of socioeconomic structures: the primitive communal system, slavery, feudalism, capitalism, communism. Adherents of the historico-materialistic school are called Communist historians, or, after the founder of historical materialism as a science and methodology, Marxist historians. It was V. I. Lenin who made the greatest contribution to the development of the historical ideas of Karl Marx and Frederick Engels. That is why the historico-materialistic ideology may properly be called Marxist-Leninist.

As applied to the present subject, which belongs to the problem of international relations, historico-materialistic methodology requires understanding the nature of an historical period, exposing the motive forces and goals of a nation's foreign policy, determining the class nature of those national interests by which governments are guided, and always taking into account the organic connection between foreign and domestic policy. To be more specific, in the given case, historical materialism requires that we point out both the major differences between the foreign policy of bourgeois and socialist states, and at the same time the objective inevitability of peaceful coexistence between countries with different socioeconomic systems.

No methodology can automatically guarantee a historian success nor secure him against errors, mediocrity, and failures. In the final analysis, the value of any research depends on the ability to grasp the meaning of events in a broad and penetrating way, against the professional background of the scholar. But here we must return again to the importance of methodological principles in historical scholarship and point out that errors in a specific analysis are often predetermined by mistaken, unscientific methodology, and by false initial premises. This cannot be said about a scholar's successes—methodology alone, we repeat, will not assure success.

This book is first of all the result of research done by the two authors, based on primary sources, both Soviet and American. We have also utilized works by Soviet and American historians, striving to show the level that historiography on the given subject has reached in the two countries. Encounters and conversations with Americans in both the USSR and the United States have been very useful. These have helped to throw light on the recent past of our relations, their present state, and how Americans conceive them in the immediate future.

Of special value were conversations with a number of American statesmen; with officials of many government and private institutions in the United States; and with our university colleagues and members of the press. We also want to thank the staffs of all the libraries and archives, whose help was so useful to us, and to the International Research and Exchanges Board in New York City.

Our work was reviewed by the Academic Council of the History Department of the University of Moscow and approved for publication. Every manuscript destined for publication by the University of Moscow Press is subjected to this same procedure. In the course of the review many critical comments were expressed for which the authors are sincerely grateful.

We are aware that only insofar as the work is successful can credit for it be ascribed to the collective body, while the blame for all the shortcomings is ours alone.

Chapters 1-4 were written by N. V. Sivachev and chapters 5-7 and the Epilogue by N. N. Yakovlev.

1

Russian-American Relations, 1776–1917

Imperial Russia Faces the American Republic

If we consider Russian-American relations in three basic dimensions—
(1) direct interaction between the two nations, (2) economic-cultural
connections between the two peoples, and (3) the positions of Russia
and the United States within the system of international relations—we
can say with certainty that during most of the period up to 1917 the
third element was predominant in the relations between our two countries. Within the system of the "concert" of European powers that determined international relations in the nineteenth century, Russia's
most constant opponent was Great Britain, though she often had
conflicts with France, and occasionally with Prussia and Austria. Similarly, during the first hundred years of its existence, the young
republic across the ocean found itself in conflict most often with
Britain, and occasionally with the Anglo-French coalition. From this
stemmed the "balance of powers" policy which played a most important role in Russian-American relations up to the end of the nineteenth century.

The basis of direct Russian interest in America was laid long before
the United States came into being—in the course of geographic
discoveries and settlement by Russian colonists in the northwestern
part of the continent, the area later called Alaska. Subsequently
commercial ties were established,[1] though at first these were only
sporadic.

Communion between Russian scholars and their American colleagues began as far back as the colonial period. This took the form of
the acquaintance of M. V. Lomonosov and other Russian scholars with
the works of Benjamin Franklin. Franklin's reputation in Russia
increased quickly, and by the time the United States became inde-

pendent he was one of the foreigners most highly regarded by Russian intellectual society.

Actual Russian-American relations came into being at the time of the War for Independence—at the time of the first American Revolution which led to the birth of the new nation. Having made its appearance in the fires of war, the American republic at once appeared as an important and complex factor in Russian foreign policy, one that had both positive and negative aspects from the Russian standpoint.

In the eyes of the serf-owning Russian nobility and the Empress Catherine II, the chief undesirable aspect of what had taken place in the thirteen English colonies was that the ''rebels'' had toppled the principle of legitimacy so dear to the czarist system. In Russia itself, the great peasant rebellion led by Emelyan Pugachev (1773–75) had just died down. It was apparent to the members of the court of St. Petersburg that a part of Russian society had reacted to the struggle for independence in the American colonies with an intolerable enthusiasm. Unlike the *Sankt-Peterburgskie vedomosti*, another newspaper, *Moskovskie vedomosti*, published by the University of Moscow, openly took the part of the insurgents and consistently assured its readers of the inevitable victory of the cause of freedom.

Although the publisher of *Moskovskie vedomosti*, N. I. Novikov, was by no means a revolutionary, he welcomed the establishment of civil liberties in the United States and criticized Russian serfdom. At the same time he condemned the American republic's sanctioning of slavery.

A. N. Radishchev, the father of the Russian revolutionary tradition, went much farther than Novikov. In his ode, ''Liberty,'' he openly praised the American Revolution and its leader, George Washington. His *Puteshestvie iz Peterburga v Moskvu* (Journey from St. Petersburg to Moscow) appeared in 1790, and the American story occupies a certain place in it. It was not without cause that Catherine II called Radishchev ''a rebel worse than Pugachev.'' Radishchev called for the overthrow of oppression by the landlord-serfowners, and this, viewed against the background of two revolutions—in America and in France—constituted a palpable threat to Russian czardom. Radishchev welcomed constitutional law established through revolution, but sharply condemned the darker aspects of American life, above all, racism.

All this does not mean that news of the American Revolution marked the onset of counterrevolutionary hysteria among the ruling circles of Russia. Nothing of the sort. The Russian government did not even dream of intervention in Boston or Philadelphia under some pretext such as the protection of the wares of Russian merchants in Alaska. To the court of Catherine II, national interests took precedence over ideological interests, and this meant adherence to the principles of the balance of power. What is more, czarism did not put any obstacles in the way of the mission of Francis Dana, sent to Russia by the Continental Congress in 1781. If it had been more insistent, this mission could have won official recognition of the United States government from the Russian empress. In any case, the mission was not molested by anyone; no one suggested expelling it or regarded its members as "subversive" American agents in Russia. Dana returned home in 1783 in accordance with a decision made by the Congress.

The hostility of the Russian nobility to bourgeois republicanism did not play a dominant role in Russian policy toward America.

From the end of the eighteenth century until 1917, differences between the political systems of Russia and the United States played no serious role in determining the nature of the relations between them. Although noticeably different in political superstructure and in other respects, republican America and monarchist Russia were both exploitive class societies based on private property, and were thus fully able to get along with each other.

As a matter of fact, the ideological antagonism between Russia and the United States proved to be very superficial; ideology was subordinate to real national interests. As it turned out, czarist Russia not only did not enter into conflict with the United States but actually supported the struggle of the American colonies for independence. That is precisely how history regards the Declaration of Armed Neutrality proclaimed by the Russian government in 1780.

In this declaration, the powerful Russian Empire came forward in defense of freedom of the seas for neutrals during wartime. This was a blow against Britain, Russia's chief antagonist, and was of great advantage to the American colonists. Within a short time almost all of the neutral European states subscribed to the principles put forward in the Russian declaration. The same position was taken by France and Spain, which were fighting as allies of the Americans. The Americans, as Lenin remarked, took advantage of "the strife between the French, the Spanish, and the British," fighting "side by side with the forces of the French and Spanish oppressors against the British oppressors."[2] The legitimist solidarity of the British and Russian monarchists was superseded by conflicting vital interests of the Russian and British empires.

The leaders of the American Revolution, viewing the various forces in the international arena, made a sensible appraisal of Russia's position, and the tradition of friendly Russian-American relations was established. Trade relations between the United States and Russia, which began during the War for Independence, became permanent only after the war.

During the last years of the eighteenth century a further rapprochement between Russian and American interests took place under the complex conditions of wartime. A series of important diplomatic steps followed. In 1803 the United States sent Levett Harris as its consul to St. Petersburg, and his mission proved far more successful than Dana's. A year later Thomas Jefferson and Alexander I exchanged important messages in a spirit of mutual respect after Russian assistance helped free the crew of an American frigate taken captive in Tripoli.

In 1808–9 diplomatic relations were finally established. After expressing esteem for Thomas Jefferson and James Madison, the instructions to the Russian envoy to the United States, F. Palen, drawn up in the czar's name by Foreign Minister N. P. Rumyantsev, went on to say: "The political interests of my empire reinforce this friendly attitude. In the United States I would like to find a kind of rival to England. I believe that their own interests impel them, to a greater extent than the powers on the European continent, at least to limit if not to end the pernicious despotism practiced by Great Britain on the seas."[3]

The above by no means justifies the lamentations of Thomas A. Bailey in which that American historian gave way to the momentum of the cold war, asserting, "and the Tsar, as was perfectly natural, exploited us openly in promoting his own ambitions."[4] American statesmen at the beginning of the nineteenth century took an entirely different view. In his State of the Union message on 5 November 1811, commenting on the existence of bad relations with Britain and

France, President Madison contrasted them with the relations with Russia which were based "on the best footing of friendship."[5] This was not just a routine phrase, for a second war with Britain already loomed on the horizon. For Madison's administration it was highly important that Russia, engaged in a difficult war with Napoleon, with Britain as its ally, should not alter its friendly relations with the United States.

As shown convincingly in N. N. Bolkhovitinov's book, *Stanovlenie Russko-Amerikanskikh otnosheniy* (The formation of Russian-American relations), Russian diplomacy found itself in a ticklish position. Russia had to strengthen her newly concluded alliance with Britain and at the same time maintain friendly relations with the United States, then at war with Britain. The Russian government found a solution in a mediation proposal which was eagerly accepted by the United States. An impressive American delegation arrived in St. Petersburg: John Quincy Adams, the first minister from the United States to Russia; Albert Gallatin, the secretary of the treasury; and Senator James Bayard. Although the British refused mediation, the Russian initiative placed them in a more difficult position and gave the Americans a somewhat better negotiating position at Ghent.

The year 1815 marks the end of the formative period of Russian-American relations. By this time political relations had been established between the two sides and had passed through their first tests; lasting economic ties had been established; and contacts had been made in the fields of learning and culture.[6]

The Shaping of Russo-American Relations

Outstanding among the important events during the second stage in the history of Russian-American relations (1815-61) are the conflicts surrounding the colonization of the Northwest and their successful resolution, the conclusion of the trade agreement of 1832, and the agreement on the neutral navigation rights reached during the difficult years when Russia was fighting the Crimean War.

Inasmuch as the development of conflicts between Russia and the United States in the American Northwest coincided with the enunciation of the Monroe Doctrine, this episode should be considered in greater detail. There has been long-standing controversy about the

enunciation of the Monroe Doctrine in world historical literature.[7]
Opponents of Russian-American cooperation have claimed that it was
motivated principally by the threat of the Holy Alliance (of which
Russia was viewed as the primary backer) to the liberation movement
in the Spanish colonies of America, and by Russian expansion in
North America.

So far as the possible intervention of the Holy Alliance in Latin
America is concerned, it has been shown that it was completely out of
the question. The impact of Russian expansion in the American
Northwest on the enunciation of the Monroe Doctrine was more
complex. During the cold war years American historians asserted and
declared categorically that Russia was an age-old aggressor, and that
the Monroe Doctrine constituted a long-term barrier against the
Russians erected with a view to the future. This view has been expressed with special frankness and straightforwardness by Clarence A.
Manning, who asserted that Russians constituted "a constant menace
to all their neighbors." In view of this, he set the goal of "reconsid-
ering the present in the light of the past."[8]

In order to examine the origin of the Monroe Doctrine and objectively evaluate its Russian and British aspects, its motive forces must be
discerned in the scope and direction of the expansion of the United
States, Britain, and Russia on the American continent toward the end
of the first quarter of the nineteenth century. The mainspring of all
the political actions that culminated in the Monroe Doctrine was the
ever-growing expansion of the bourgeoisie of the United States on the
American continent. Encountering or fearing that they might en-
counter opposition in their path, the American expansionists were
prepared to exaggerate the threat to them of European governments so
as to create about themselves the aura of an enemy of colonialism. As
Foster Rhea Dulles wrote: "The strong position that the United States
took in 1823, both in its notes to the Russian government and in the
declaration of the Monroe Doctrine, was directed against largely
imaginary fears."[9]

While the Monroe Doctrine was a product of the bourgeois-slave-
holding expansionism of the United States, paradoxically enough it
was also a positive factor in the struggle of the Latin American colonies
for independence because of the principle of noncolonialization contained in it, as well as the ban on the substitution of one colonial

"sovereign" for another, thereby promoting a national liberation movement in Latin America. The imperalist aspect of the Monroe Doctrine in the relations of the United States with the countries of the Western Hemisphere did not make itself manifest in full measure until much later.

Against whom was the Monroe Doctrine directed? A superficial chronological logic has led many authors to assert that this act was primarily intended to ward off the threat contained in the directive of Alexander I on 16 September 1821, prohibiting foreigners from trading in Russian possessions in the Pacific or even approaching them from the sea beyond a distance of 100 miles from the coast in the area north of the 51st parallel. The conflict between Russian and American interests here was self-evident. Britain and the United States protested, and on these grounds some historians perceived the origin of the Monroe Doctrine in the actions of the czar and saw it as a joint countermove by America and Britain against Russia.[10]

In actuality the Russian expansionist drive in America had spent itself during the first quarter of the nineteenth century, and the American government realized this. It strove to foist the principle of noncolonization first of all on the British government, and not on the Russian.[11] A very weighty argument against viewing the thrust of the Monroe Doctrine as primarily anti-Russian may also be found in the 17 April 1824 agreement on the regulation of Russian-American trade and territorial disputes. This was the first official agreement between our two countries. The czarist government readily yielded on two important questions—it moved the northern boundary of its claimed possessions to the north (to 54°40'), and it agreed to free trade in northern Pacific. In his message to Congress on 7 December 1824 President James Monroe said: "It is proper to add that the manner in which this negotiation was invited and conducted on the part of the Emperor has been very satisfactory."[12] The 1824 agreement thus "obviated any danger of a future Russian barrier to American continental expansion,"[13] which cannot be said about the relations of the United States with Britain and other European states.

Thus, while not denying the existence of conflicts between Russia and America in matters of trade and territory in the American Northwest, conflicts that had not been settled entirely even after 1824, it must be admitted that the Monroe Doctrine resulted above all from the expansionist activity of the American bourgeoisie and plantation owners clashing with the English bourgeoisie, who refused to recognize the principle of noncolonization. The enunciation of the Monroe Doctrine had no adverse effect whatever on Russian-American relations, for it concerned a region that had by that time come to be more indisputably peripheral to Russian territorial interests than ever before.

An important landmark in the history of Russian-American relations was the conclusion of the first agreement on trade and navigation in 1832. In principle the ruling circles of Russia reacted favorably to the notion of an agreement proposed by the Americans. But the American minister, James Buchanan, had to make his way through the complex maze of the Russian bureaucracy before he was able to achieve success. It must be said that he managed to do this brilliantly. When the negotiations bogged down in interminable, exhausting delays in the signing of the agreement, he decided to fight fire with fire and announced that he hoped to present the conclusion of the trade agreement to Czar Nicholas I as a gift on the occasion of his name's day (18 December). This became known, and must have pleased the sovereign (at least that was the opinion of the high court officials); and the Russian bureaucracy demonstrated that when it was necessary to do something to please the authorities, it spared no effort. The agreement was signed in time for the solemn occasion on 18 December 1832.[14]

This economic agreement was mutually beneficial, embodying the reciprocal most-favored-nation principle in trade and navigation. It became possible for the citizens or subjects of each country to enjoy all civil rights in acquiring and disposing of personal property on the other's territory.[15] This was of greater advantage to the enterprising Americans than to the citizens of feudal Russia. American hunters and fishermen especially prospered in the waters of the north Pacific, as did American fur traders in Siberia.

Political relations between Russia and the United States remained friendly, and developed further during the years of the Crimean War (1853–56). During these years Russian-American trade expanded.[16] Russia and the United States entered into their third official agreement with the conclusion of the convention on the rights of neutrals on the seas. This agreement, aimed at the protection of these rights under the conditions of war, was of advantage to both countries, but especially to Russia, then engaged in war against Britain and France on both land and sea. The political interests of the two sides became so close that Russia agreed to the annexation by the United States of the Hawaiian (Sandwich) Islands, while the Americans informed the Russians to learn in time of an attack planned by the Anglo-French fleet against the Pacific ports of Russia.[17]

At this point it is appropriate to emphasize once more that at this stage the differences between the political systems of Russia and the United States did not play a role in determining the substance of the relations between them. Jacksonian democracy and the reactionary regime of Nicholas I were completely compatible. In his first annual message to Congress, President Andrew Jackson referred to czarist Russia as "a steadfast friend," while in his last message he stated that between the two countries "the best understanding exists."[18] Nor did the part which czarism played in the suppression of the 1848 revolution in Central Europe make the American government hostile to it. On the contrary, in a message to Congress on 4 December 1849, President Zachary Taylor, after expressing in passing his sympathy with the Hungarian insurgents, announced that with Russia, as with the other European states, the United States maintains "accustomed amicable relations."[19]

Of course, American diplomats, having come from republican, puritanical families, often found the pompousness of Russian court etiquette trying and felt awkward in that atmosphere. Sometimes curious things happened. For example, at an official reception in a czar's palace, John Randolph, who was no ordinary figure in United States history, addressed the czar with unheard-of democratic familiarity: "How are you, Emperor? How is Madame?"[20] Another envoy, John Dulles, was outraged by the fact that Russian women appeared at receptions and balls with "a most profuse display of the bust."[21] To some degree this must have distracted the envoy from more important matters at receptions, but there were not all that many of those for American diplomats in Russia in those years to be concerned with.

It also must be said that American democracy was not unattractive to the progressive circles of Russian society. The Decembrists, for example, to some extent followed the American example in their plans for future reconstruction of Russia. As one historian noted: "Under the conditions of Tsarism and police rule, the bourgeois-democratic freedoms of the United States might actually appear as almost an ideal, and for this reason it is no wonder that the Decembrists as a rule referred to the American experience in their positive plans. This does not mean, however, that they closed their eyes to the negative aspects of American life. As a rule, the Decembrists sharply criticized the existence of slavery, the extermination of Indians, and many other dark sides of bourgeois reality which they saw in the republic across the ocean.''[22]

Russian society was especially critical of the institution of slavery and racism. This to a large extent explains the tremendous popularity in Russia of Harriet Beecher Stowe's book, *Uncle Tom's Cabin*, which the magazine *Sovremennik* (The contemporary) distributed to all of its subscribers as a free supplement in 1858.

The great Russian revolutionary democrat, N. G. Chernyshevsky, praised enthusiastically the heroic act of John Brown, who went to his death for the cause of emancipation. Chernyshevsky welcomed the victory of the Republicans in the 1860 elections. ''The day when victory was on the side of the party that had Lincoln as its candidate,'' he wrote, ''was a great day, the beginning of a new era in the history of the United States, a day that marked a turning point in the political development of the great North American people.''[23]

Russia and the American Civil War

The period of the Civil War in the United States may be regarded as the third stage in the history of Russian-American relations. During these years it was demonstrated once more that the state and national interests formulated by the ruling classes took precedence over less essential factors, even such factors as the political structure of the society, and the class and group sympathies and antipathies of one nation with respect to the social strata, classes, and movements of another. As in the years 1775–1815 and 1853–56, the policy of balance of power once more came distinctly into the foreground.

One would think that the Russian government, so recently representing serf owners, would have sympathized with American slaveholders, especially since the problem of slavery had begun to be dealt with in a revolutionary way. Nevertheless, St. Petersburg came out, without hesitation, for maintaining the integrity of the American nation, that is, in favor of the Republican, revolutionary North. The Russian government declined a proposal by Britain and France to

intervene jointly in American affairs. Hostility to democracy did not
prevent the Russian envoy, Baron Stoeckl, from displaying moderation
in evaluating the events in the United States. In a dispatch to the czar
he wrote: "The disorganization of the United States as a nation is a
deplorable event from our standpoint. The American federation had
been a counter-balance against British power, and in this respect its
continued existence constitutes an element in world balance."[24]

In its policy with respect to the internal American conflict, the
czarist government followed the concept of balance of power not only
in its traditional interpretation, but also by virtue of one significant
specific circumstance. In 1863 an uprising that had been imminent for
a long time broke out in Poland. Britain and France, continuing their
anti-Russian policy of the Crimean War period, quickly decided to
intervene in the name of "justice." They were joined by Austria, one
of the three principal oppressors of Polish freedom. But the American
government did not criticize Russia, although it doubtless had greater
moral justification for doing so than did the leaders of any other great
nation. President Abraham Lincoln and Secretary of State William
Seward declined the proposals of Napoleon III, the "defender" of
Poland, on the basis of the traditional friendship between Russia and
America. "In spite of Kosciusko and Pulaski, the United States was
forced to become anti-Polish; in spite of Lafayette, anti-French. In
fact, for a time it was even to favor official Russia against the revolutionary Polonism of Alexander Herzen and certain other Russian
friends of republican America."[25]

National interests of the revolutionary bourgeoisie of the United
States forced them to close their eyes to the suppression of the Polish
rebellion by the czarist regime and to take a position friendly to Russia
and opposed to Britain and France. The national interests of land-
owning-bourgeois Russia, on the other hand, dictated a course of a de
facto support of the second American revolution—resulting in the
suppression of the South—because of Russia's conflict with Britain
and France. The policy of the ruling circles of Russia had nothing in
common with the policy of Chernyshevsky and other revolutionary
democrats who contributed to the journals *Sovremennik* and *Russkoe
slovo* (The Russian word.). The siding of the latter with the revolutionary North stemmed from the journals' ties to the revolutionary,
peasant-oriented democratic intelligentsia.

With the United States and Russia highly interested in friendly relations, the dispatch in 1863 of two Russian squadrons to the Atlantic and Pacific coasts of the United States aroused all sorts of rumors and interpretations, the sense of all of which remained consistently pro-American. With this move, the Russian Ministry of the Navy accomplished a brilliant military and political operation. It did not rule out the possibility of a new war with Britain and France, and decided to bring the important parts of its navy out to the high seas ahead of time. As evidenced in the instructions issued by the head of the ministry, H. Krabbe, the commanders of the squadrons were set the task of carrying out offensive actions against the expected enemy.[26] The action of the Russian government made sense from the defensive standpoint as well. It did not want to find its fleet blockaded in Russian ports, as it had happened at the time of the Crimean War. The American pubic was unaware of the content of the secret instructions to the Russian admirals who had anchored on the shores of New York and San Francisco. The Russians were greeted with enthusiasm at the highest levels of the government, as well. Stoeckl, the Russian envoy, informing A. M. Gorchakov, the minister of foreign affairs, of the cordial reception of the Russian sailors, remarked that no such reception had been accorded the British and French ships: "It was not without a degree of envy that the English and the French observed the attention of which our sailors were the object, and they even expressed some displeasure in this connection."[27] Insofar as the visit of the squadrons was regarded as a precautionary measure against Anglo-French intervention, the political significance of this visit did, on the whole, serve this purpose.[28] Together with Gorchakov's emphatic refusal to receive a representative of the Confederacy in St. Petersburg, this served to strengthen traditional ties of Russian-American friendship. President Andrew Johnson in his message to Congress on 4 December 1865, attested to the existence of "the unbroken harmony between the United States and the Emperor of Russia."[29]

From Friendship to Estrangement

The fourth stage in Russian-American relations (1865–98) began with a euphoric friendship but ended with an estrangement that had its roots in imperialism.

In the last third of the nineteenth century Russian-American relations broadened. At the beginning of this period Russia "withdrew" from America, having sold Alaska to the United States for a pittance ($7,200,000). Soviet historiography has refuted the legend that has grown up in American literature according to which the purchase of Alaska in 1867 represented a favor to the czarist government, which is supposed to have sought to get rid of this "superfluous" territory at any price, in return for supporting the North in the Civil War.[30] Although the value of the acquisition was regarded in the United States at that time as not very great, the czarist government had compelling reasons to make the sale. This was due to the weakened position of Russia in northern Pacific, and the strengthened expansionist movement of the United States toward the Pacific. The loss of Alaska had a depressing effect on the Russian public. Foreign Minister Gorchakov, who had long opposed this action, consoled himself only because he regarded it also an anti-British measure.

Gradually the time approached when direct Russian-American interaction was coming to an important factor in working out the policy of the two states with respect to one another, and to the extent that this was so, the question of how this would affect the relations of each of them with other powers became less important than it had been formerly. Evidence of the increased direct relations between Russia and America can be seen from the fact that while three official agreements had been concluded before the Civil War, eight were concluded in the years 1867 to 1900.[31]

We should dwell especially on the *Convention on the Extradition of Criminals*. It was signed in 1887, but ratified by the United States only in 1893. Although the agreement did not apply to those accused of political crimes, it was precisely this which was the basic reason for the heated debates over its ratification. This was the heyday of individual terrorism by the *narodniki* (Russian populists) and analogous anarchist activities throughout the world, and the convention provided for the extradition of criminals who had committed or were planning to commit terrorist acts against the heads of states. In the United States a campaign was mounted against ratification of the convention, of which the most prominent activist was George Kennan, publisher of the newspaper *Svobodnaya Rossiya* (Free Russia). At this time he was widely known in the United States as the author of books and articles concerning Russian prisons. To criticize prisons is a safe cause. It would be hard to find a case in history when the gloomy picture of prisons, concentration camps, exile, and interventionist expeditions did not correspond to reality but proved to be so appealling as to cast doubt on the reporter. And Mark Twain was one hundred percent right when he exclaimed, at one of George Kennan's lectures about the condition of political prisoners in the mines of Siberia: "If such a government cannot be overthrown otherwise than by dynamite, then, thank God for dynamite!"[32]

But it was not only Mark Twain and Walt Whitman and all sincere enemies of czarist despotism who listened to George Kennan. His work attracted the attention of the expansionist circles of the United States, with much greater political results. George Kennan's talent as a journalist and his bold, venturesome acts in Siberia *served* the interests not of "Russian freedom," but of Western Union, of which he was an agent, and of the expansionist forces that nurtured fantastic plans for the construction of telegraph lines and railroads across the uninhabited expanses of Siberia. M. Laserson has called George Kennan "the first American crusader for Russian freedom."[33] He actually was the first. He was followed by a vast cluster, including the "crusaders" of 1918–20 and the present-day supporters of the "dissidents."

From the 1880s one other essential theme intrudes into Russian-American relations: mass immigration to the United States from Russia. This was closely related to the progressing development of capitalism. The direction of the migration was determined by the specific features of capitalist development in the two countries: as a result of the destruction of the feudal order, the superfluous work force was eased out of Russia; it was absorbed by America, for only there was this superfluous work force able to find economic use. In 1870–89 about 250,000 people moved from Russia to the United States, while during the following decade alone the movement amounted to 450,000. In 1861–1900 it was more than 16 percent of the total immigrants.[34] Russian population has played an appreciable role in forming the American nation, especially the working class of the United States and the artistic intelligentsia. The lot of Russians was for the most part unenviable; it has been described with merciless truthfulness by V. G. Korolenko, who visited the United States, in his story, "Bez yazyka" (Without a language), published in 1895. An unenviable fate in the United States did not stop the flow of emigration from Russia. Almost no one returned. The emigrants continued to move to the United States, "carrying with them their grief, their hopes, and their expectations."[35]

At the end of the nineteenth century America for the first time armed itself with the slogan of Russian despotism as a hindrance to good Russian-American relations. Writing about the cooling of the traditional friendship between Russian and the United States, Foster Dulles writes: "In the background of these developments was the ideological conflict between autocracy and democracy."[36] The authors of similar assertions do not stop to ponder the reason why during the period of Jacksonian democracy America was enraptured with the Russia of Nicholas I, and why the great republican Abraham Lincoln regarded the Russia of Alexander II as the friendliest of states, while Grover Cleveland, Benjamin Harrison, and William McKinley, those conservatives and reactionaries, henchmen of the monopolies, had their eyes opened and saw to their indignation that Russia was deficient in democracy.

Such an oversight is even more curious in view of the fact that after the Civil War and the Reconstruction, the Russian democracy no longer regarded the United States as a model of political freedom. After having analyzed all of the articles about America in the two most progressive Russian periodicals of that period, *Delo* and *Slovo*, I. K. Mal'kova came to the conclusion that beginning in the mid-1870s publications on American topics became emphatically critical.[37] As earlier, the journals mentioned the political freedoms in the United States that were absent in Russia. They called attention not only to the traditional prevalence of racism in the United States, but also to something new on the American scene—the dominance of corporations, dictating their will to the country. An article published in the first issue of *Slovo* in 1881 pointed out that "economic and political functions in the United States have been usurped by octopuslike corporations."

Here we approach the true substance of the reasons for the exacerbation of Russian-American relations at the end of the nineteenth century. This was the period when the process of changing free-enterprise capitalism into monopolistic capitalism was going forward at a breakneck pace. Expansion had always been characteristic of capitalism, but with the formation of powerful corporate monopolies, gigantic impulses of imperialistic ideology and policy were created and at the same time the means for their realization. Imperialism in the form of striving to seize foreign territory became such a significant feature of bourgeois society toward the end of the nineteenth century that this notion became the most widely used term on the pages of scholarly and publicist works.

The most profound theoretical explanation of imperialism appears in Lenin's work, *Imperializm, kak vysshaya stadiya kapitalizma* (Imperialism, the highest stage of capitalism), which appeared in 1916. Lenin departed from the traditional superficial interpretation of imperialism as simply expansion, pointing out that this is only one of the manifestations of imperialism. Imperialism is monopolistic capitalism, which capitalism had come to be in the highly developed bourgeois countries toward the end of the nineteenth century. The most important trait of imperialism is the concentration of production and capital to the point where it creates monopolies, which play the fundamental role in economic life and politics. Lenin pointed out as one of the principal features of imperialism the merging of bank capital with industrial capital, and the appearance on this basis of finance capital. He also identified three additional traits of imperialism that are directly related to expansion: the export of capital, unlike the export of goods, assumes especially great importance; international monopolies are formed that divide the world markets between them; the territorial division of the world among a handful of the greatest imperialist powers is ended, posing the question of repartition of the world.

Lenin named American imperialism finance imperialism, thereby emphasizing its economic might. Russian imperialism, along with Japanese imperialism, he characterized as military-feudal imperialism, pointing out that the deficiency in economic strength in these countries is made up for by a monopoly of military power, weakened, to be sure, by economic backwardness.

In the 1890s the United States emerged as the foremost country in the world in industrial production. American monopolies set themselves great tasks of an expansionist nature. An imperialist ideology was developed in the United States that embraced wide segments of the bourgeoisie and even penetrated into the working classes.[38] Even before Theodore Roosevelt, Captain A. T. Mahan became the hero of the imperialist expansionists. In 1895, when the National Association of Manufacturers was formed, more that half of its initial program proved to be devoted to the question of expanding foreign markets.[39]

With the "opening" of Japanese ports and the acquisition of Alaska, favorable starting conditions were created for American penetration of the Far East. United States expansion in this direction had a bearing on Russia in three respects: first, the interests of the two countries collided in China; second, the Americans strove to secure from the czarist government approval for sweeping, even patently impracticable adventurist plans for railroad construction in Siberia; third, American capital began to encroach actively into different branches of the economy throughout Russia. And the American national authorities acquiesced in this. The theme of the protection of American monopolies in Russia even found its way into the annual messages of the presidents to Congress. Grover Cleveland, for example, informed the Congress on 3 December 1894 that he was striving to get from the Russian government "equality of treatment for our great life-insurance companies whose operations have been extended throughout Europe."[40]

The economic opportunities for American and Russian expansion were far from equal: the superiority of the United States monopolies was obvious. But Russian expansion did have certain advantages in the Far East. It rested on greater military strength, and was carried out in direct territorial proximity to the boundaries of Russia established by equitable treaties with China long before the appearance of imperialist plans. In 1891 construction began on the great Siberian railroad, which substantially improved Russia's chances in the Far East and caused great concern among the expansionist circles of the United States.

Thus, the cooling of Russian-American relations came about not because the American monopolists, the "robber barons," were not entirely pleased with Russian prisons after having listened to George Kennan or read his works; or because the czar, whose subjects, under the two-headed eagle, included millions of non-Russian peoples of various hues, was unable to understand fully why Negroes were being lynched in the United States. As William A. Williams correctly states, "far more important pressures were at work to split Washington and St. Petersburg. The forces of American and Russian economic expansion were edging into conflict in the area just south of the Amur River.''[41] Even Foster Dulles, in explaining the conflict as a clash between the ideas of democracy and despotism, remarks in passing: ''More important than this wave of popular resentment toward the Czar's domestic policies, however, a direct conflict in foreign policies had for the first time developed between Russia and America. The scene was the Far East.''[42] Pauline Tompkins in her book brought this out especially persuasively, emphasizing that the exacerbation of Russian-American conflicts in the Far East coincided with ''the gradual waning of Anglo-American antagonism.''[43]

In summing up the development of the interrelations between Russia and the United States in the last third of the nineteeth century and asserting that to some extent they had worsened, a number of qualifications should be made. In the first place, it was precisely the imperialist contradictions that were aggravated. Second, the degree of estrangement should not be exaggerated; the placement of American capital in Russia was still scanty, while the conflict in the Far East by no means led to rupture. Third, the role that Russia played in American policy and the role that America played in Russian policy were insignificant, being far outweighed in importance by the relations of each of these countries with Britain, Germany, France, Japan, and many other states. For these reasons one should not exaggerate the degree and importance of Russian-American conflicts at the turn of the century, inflate them artificially, or dramatize them artificially, as many American historians have done during the years of the cold war.

Between the Spanish-American War and the February Revolution

From 1898 to February 1917 is the fifth period in the history of Russian-American relations. It opens with the Spanish-American imperialist war, which Lenin called the first war for the repartition of the world. It became a turning point in the foreign policy of the United States, which was reflected to a certain extent in Russian-American relations as well. This war not only gave America an important colonial acquisition, but inspired American imperialist ideology and policy with energy, having shown the economic might of American imperialism, and how much it had to lose by delaying the application of its entire force and conceding to its rivals, who had long since given up shunning outright seizures.

Instantaneously the Far East had drawn closer to the shores of the United States, a situation that manifested its effect immediately on the formation of imperialist foreign-policy doctrines. Renouncing the principle of establishing spheres of influence in China, with military encirclement, for two reasons—American capital would have felt cramped in any sphere smaller than the territory of all of China, and at the same time would have found it hard to defend the boundaries of a possible sphere since the military strength of Japan, Russia, England, and Germany was greater here than the American strength—the United States government advanced the open-door policy and equal opportunities in China. Its appearance was possible only as a result of the successful imperialist debut in the Spanish-American War.

The anti-Russian trend of the colonial doctrine of the United States was obvious, although it was addressed in no smaller degree toward Japan and Germany, and to some extent England. By the time that Secretary of State John Hay proclaimed the open-door policy (1899–1900), the Russian government had already noted with attention the increased activity of the Americans in the Far East, which held danger for it. At the beginning of 1898, Nicholas II appointed Count Cassini, "a proven expert on the East," as his new ambassador to the United States. In his instructions to the ambassador, approved in the emperor's own hand, Minister of Foreign Affairs Murav'ev wrote: "From your experience in China, you are well acquainted with the sort of greed that guides the Americans in their commercial and trade enterprises all along the west Pacific coast. There can be no doubt that, being well informed on the nature of these relations, you will distinguish strictly between those enterprises that are desirable for us from ones that are directly harmful to our sphere of influence."[44]

In his first dispatch to Murav'ev on 22 June 1898, Cassini reported: "Not long ago there took place a complete change in the ideas and political principles of this country. Discontented with the past, which had made her rich, happy and respected, she wants to try a future which may very well be fraught for her with many occasions for disappointment and serious hardships. I have no faith in the Anglo-American alliance. The mentality of the Yankee is too practical, too calculating to take matters this far. But so far as the rapprochement that has taken place between the two nations from the day the present war began, there can be no doubt about it, and that alone is enough cause for us to be uneasy.''[45]

Considering that this was his first message, the Russian ambassador displayed great discernment, but he still underestimated the potential of the Anglo-American alliance that was formed on the eve of the Russo-Japanese War. In the first five years of the twentieth century Russian-American relations were cooler than at any time during the entire period up to 1917. The United States took a pro-Japanese position in the Russo-Japanese conflict: from the earliest signs of war up to the conclusion of the Portsmouth Treaty in 1905, the American government brought into full play the principles of balance of power, supporting Japan against Russia. During the time of the Russo-Japanese War a wave of Russophobia rolled across the United States. George Kennan, the ''crusader for Russian freedom,'' who exerted great influence over Theodore Roosevelt and other statesmen, descended to outright racism. He very graciously allowed the Japanese into the club of nations belonging to the ''superior'' race, conceding that the Japanese are ''to all intents and purposes Aryans.''[46]

The outcome of the Russo-Japanese War to some extent smoothed over the conflicts between Russia and the United States in the Far East, but it did not put an end to their imperialistic rivalry in this region. The czarist government, having reached a degree of understanding with their recent enemy, the Japanese, undertook measures to achieve a plan that would bring them into balance against America.

Political tension in Russian-American relations at the beginning of the twentieth century was one of the reasons for the weakness of American investments in Russia.[47] Before the First World War American capital in Russia amounted to 118,000,000 rubles, constituting only 5 percent of all foreign investments. The lion's share of these investments (111,000,000 rubles) belonged to two companies—the International Harvesting-Machine Company (a branch of International Harvester) and Singer (a branch of the Singer Manufacturing Company).[48]

In brief, the economic-political interrelations between the two sides consisted first of all in that the Russians sought to obtain large loans from the Americans, while American businessmen demanded substantial concessions under favorable conditions, mainly in the area of railroad building. Up to the time of the First World War neither side had succeeded in gaining its objective. The czarist government made advances to the House of Morgan, but the admiral of American financiers did not loosen his purse strings, considering the conditions not yet ripe for the intrusion of the dollar into Russia. Morgan, and also the jointly operating group consisting of the railroad magnate Harriman and the head of the finance firm Kuhn-Loeb, Jacob Schiff, in turn, planned to establish control over the Siberian railroad, including its Manchurian branch.

In 1907 the Council of Russian Ministers turned down a proposal to give the Americans the railroad concession.[49] This helped Jacob Schiff and the other leaders of American expansionism to realize more fully the insufficient development of democracy in Russia and under this slogan to mount the usual anti-Russian campaign. This time the object of the attack proved to be the trade agreement of 1832, which had led to an especially active development of commercial ties between Russia and the United States just at the beginning of the twentieth century. The average annual import of American goods into Russia in 1901–3 reached a volume of 46,000,000 rubles. The Russian export to the United States, amounting to 4,600,000 rubles, was considerably more modest.[50] The United States occupied a prominent place in imports to Russia—in 1910 fourth place, while in 1911 it had moved to third place.[51] During these years treaty relations continued to expand. In 1904 an agreement was reached according to which the rights of the corporations of one country were recognized in the courts of the other. This served to consolidate the achievements of the Americans in Russia, for Russian corporations were practically absent in the United States. In 1911 another agreement appeared, concerning the protection of seals in the Bering Sea area, bringing the number of Russian-American treaties to thirteen.

How can one explain, then, the campaign mounted in the United States for the denunciation of the treaty of 1832, culminating at the end of 1911 with its liquidation? If we go according to the propaganda slogans of the day, the denunciation must be regarded as an action dictated by the devotion of the ruling circles of the United States to humane principles. The principal arguments of the proponents of abrogation of the treaty of 1832 were czarist despotism in general and discrimination against Jewish immigrants from Russia, who had returned to the empire on commercial business, in particular.

Jacob Schiff, the George Kennan newspaper *Svobodnaya Rossiya* financed by him, and all the groups who took part in the campaign for denunciation, asserted that the czarist government prohibited American Jews in large numbers from entering Russia. In 1911 Secretary of State Philander Knox refuted these statements, pointing out that during the past five years the State Department had established only four cases of refusal on religious grounds of visas to American citizens applying for admission to Russia.[52] The czarist government did put obstacles in the way of the entrance of those of its former subjects who had left Russia illegally, without having fulfilled their military obligation before leaving.[53] To the extent that some of them had prospered in the United States and found themselves among the financial and commercial elite or close to it, such refusals became the object of official governmental attention. When Sergei Witte arrived in the United States on the unenviable mission of concluding peace after the war that Russia had lost, Theodore Roosevelt, at the demand of the "crusaders," suggested that the czarist government should "consider the question of granting passports to reputable American citizens of Jewish faith."[54]

At the beginning of the twentieth century the Jewish community in the United States already represented an impressive force, having become one of the most important centers of world Zionism. Following the logic that whatever is good for Jewry must also be good for the country of their sojourn, the Zionists, seeking to strengthen their positions in the United States and in Europe, mounted a campaign against Russian-American trade. Superficially this gave the appearance of a struggle against czarist despotism, to which it was easy to attract broad segments of the population. To the extent that the Jewish community was influential in itself, and also taking into account that the interests of its leaders coincided with the policy of the American expansionists who had run up against Russian opposition, the ruling classes of the United States saw in this a mighty combination of forces with which it was necessary and advantageous to reckon. In his own way, Thomas Bailey was right when he noted that in the campaign for denunciation of the agreement of 1832, "Our people were crusading for American and not Jewish principles,"[55] which should be read as follows: it was of advantage to the expansionists to enlist the Jewish community in the imperialist struggle against Russia. The Soviet historian M. Pavlovich is absolutely correct when he explains that "the question of passports for the 'honorable American citizens' of the Jewish faith could in itself be only one of the elements that led to the exacerbation of Russian-American relations but certainly not the fundamental reason for the conflict and the breaking off of the Russian-American trade agreement of 1832."[56]

We cannot take seriously the assurances of the participants in this campaign and of individual United States historians that the 1832 agreement was torpedoed in the name of humanism and human liberties, which were said to be a component part of the "evangelian mood"[57] of the Progressive Era, for example. The evangelian mood had a broad field in which to operate in the United States. To battle for humanism one did not even need to go to Alabama and Mississippi—one could remain in Washington and New York. The issue was the use of humanistic slogans in the imperialist struggle, in which the Zionists took an active part with great profit to themselves, thereby making the first major contribution to the deterioration of Russian-American relations.

It was especially easy for Jacob Schiff to run the campaign for denunciation of the treaty for he was not only a Zionist leader but also an expansionist trying unsuccessfully to obtain concessions in Russia, and an ardent proponent of pro-German orientation, which was a matter of no small importance with the world war looming imminently. American political figures not involved in the interests of the Jewish community took part in this campaign in part because it was a way to combat Russian influence in the Far East. The campaign also enlisted the efforts of those to whom it had a domestic political value, for preelection political considerations, in spite of the fact that denunciation of the agreement and exacerbation of relations with Russia by no means necessarily served to strengthen the international position of the United States. And what is more, this obviously led to a strengthening of the economic position of Germany in Russia to the detriment of the United States, and to a weakening of the American position in the Far East owing to improved relations between Russia and Japan.

The considerations of political intrigue won out, due in large measure to the Democratic leaders running for election in 1912. The vast majority in Congress voted for abrogation of the treaty. President Taft was not an advocate of sharp confrontation with Russia and did not want to give the denunciation of the agreement the form of an emphatically anti-Russian demonstration, for which the "crusaders" were striving hard. The chief executive was afraid that this would damage the interests of the United States, would strengthen the already apparent Russian-Japanese rapprochement, and would lend it an anti-American character. It was therefore politely conveyed to St. Petersburg in December 1911 that the government of the United States considered the 1832 agreement no longer in force beginning 1 January 1913. In light of this, we can in no way agree with the view of Max Laserson that for Russia the denunciation was "a diplomatic lesson in human rights," a blow greater than any military defeat of the Russian state.[58]

The abrogation of the 1832 trade agreement put a damper on expanding Russian-American trade, but not for long. Within the circles of the Russian monopolist bourgeoisie and high officialdom an influential pro-American party was being formed to favor rapprochement with the United States. The brothers Guchkov emerged as its leaders. In 1912 Lenin even referred to A. I. Guchkov as "the American Guchkov."[59] In 1913 this group created the Russian-American Chamber of Commerce, which was especially active during the war years. American industrialists and financiers also watched the Russian market with close attention, realizing that the exacerbation of Russian relations with Germany and the involvement of England and France in the imminent conflict in Europe were opening alluring prospects for them in Russia.

At the beginning of the twentieth century contacts between Russia and the United States in the sphere of culture and learning were developing more actively. In our country, those giants of American literature, Mark Twain and Jack London, were well known. The works and activity of Henry George, in which Tolstoy took a great interest, made a great impression on the Russian public. The progressive Russian public was familiar with the works of the American utopians. On the other hand, Tolstoy and other outstanding Russian writers (Chekhov and Maxim Gorky) came to be better and better known to the American reader. Beginning at the end of the nineteenth century, the music of Tchaikovsky began its triumphant progress across the country, and Tchaikovsky visited the United States on tour. Evidence of the growing connections in the sphere of learning is the fact that the outstanding Russian historians M. M. Kovalevsky and P. N. Milyukov gave lectures in the United States. These were arranged by the University of Chicago,[60] which played an important part in organizing Russian studies in the United States.

Revolutionary Social-Democratic Russia also paid close attention to life in the United States, not for ideological inspiration, but because it placed a high value on the technological and economic achievements of that country, and on the traditional struggle of the American working class for its rights. In 1906 Maxim Gorky visited the United States with the intention of mobilizing the democratic American public in support of the first Russian revolution. Not much came of this. The great proletarian writer was not very well pleased with America. He was amazed at the heartlessness and spiritual oppression he found there. "The light of inner freedom, the freedom of the spirit, does not shine in people's eyes," he wrote of the people of New York. "I have never seen such a monstrous city, and never have people seemed so insignificant to me, so enslaved."[61]

Nevertheless it should be noted that the revolutionary faction of the American workers hailed the first Russian revolution and tried to assist it as much as possible. The Industrial Workers of the World organization, in response to an appeal from the International Socialist Bureau on 22 January 1906, held mass meetings in many American cities to express support for the Russian workers and to raise funds to assist them. In a number of cities these meetings were organized jointly with the Socialists. Leaders of the IWW hailed the Russian Revolution as "the greatest struggle for human liberty ever witnessed in the annals of history."[62]

Lenin wrote a number of works about the United States. He was the first to debunk the theory that America was exceptional, showing in his analysis of premonopolistic and monopolistic capitalism in the United States that its development had followed the general laws brought to light by Marxist political economics. He also wrote articles on the development of agriculture in the United States, and about American bourgeois reformism during the Progressive Era. He exposed the class nature of progressism, emphasizing that bourgeois reformism is a means of struggle against socialism.

The First World War opened wider opportunities for American

capital in Russia. The removal of German capital and the undermining of French and British economic opportunities forced the weakening czarist regime to turn for help to the United States. President
Woodrow Wilson, one of the active participants in the campaign for
denunciation of the 1832 trade agreement with the despotic czarist
government, now saw the conclusion of a new trade agreement that
would ensure the predominance of United States interests in the
Russian Empire as a most important aspect of relations between the
two countries. Wilson assigned this as a first-priority task to Missouri
businessman David R. Francis when he appointed him ambassador to
St. Petersburg in 1916.[63] Having arrived in Russia, Francis set to work
with enthusiasm to accomplish what had proved beyond the powers of
his predecessor. He informed Washington of the boundless opportunities for American capital in Russia. However, he, too, was unsuccessful in concluding the trade agreement.

But even without the trade agreement, American imports to Russia
were growing at an astonishing rate: from $31,000,000 in 1914 to
$555,000,000 in 1916.[64] Military orders occupied first place in the
economic connections between the two sides. John White, who had
been a secretary in the embassy in 1915, later recalled: "American
businessmen were coming in to St. Petersburg all the time that I was
there, and getting good war contracts."[65] Taking advantage of the
difficulties that beset the czarist government, the American monopolies imposed disadvantageous conditions on their Russian cus-
tomers. However, the necessities of war drew the Russia of Nicholas II
and the America of Wilson ever closer together.

In 1916 the American-Russian Chamber of Commerce was formed
in the United States with the purpose of broadening economic expansion in Russia. For the first time in the history of Russian-American
relations the bankers of the United States began to subsidize the czar's
government, lending him $150,000,000 over the period of the war
years.[66] Thus the House of Morgan confidently intruded into Russia.
Czarism, which for decades had opposed American penetration into
the Russian economy, no longer had the strength to defend itself
against the penetration of Yankee capital. The czarist regime was
prepared to squander the natural resources of the country and to
satisfy the demands of the American expansionists which only very
recently had been considered the fantastic pretensions of wealthy

provincials. This was one of the signs and portents of the approaching collapse of the Russian autocracy.

The United States and the Provisional Government in Russia

The sixth and last chapter in the pre-Soviet history of Russian-American relations proved to be the shortest—from February to October 1917. But during this short interval of time the relations were very active—on the part of the Americans even feverishly active.

American literature gives a one-sided presentation of the allegedly enthusiastic reaction of the ruling classes of the United States to the February Revolution in Russia. Actually the reaction was conflicting, and as the revolutionary process deepened it became increasingly hostile. On the one hand, the government and the expansionists saw great opportunities in Russia under the provisional government. The February Revolution gave Woodrow Wilson a political winning trump for his declaration of war against Germany. "To make the world safe for democracy," that democratic cloak for the imperialist goals of the United States in the First World War, looked more respectable in the light of the fact that America had entered the war as an ally not of czarist, but of a new, bourgeois-democratic Russia. The expansionists regarded the course of events in Russia even more optimistically inasmuch as the provisional government from the outset was oriented first and foremost toward the United States.

However, there were also some very weighty reasons for the cooling of American enthusiasm for Russia as she appeared in 1917. Even with all the ballyhoo about the alliance of the "two democracies," the ruling circles in the United States could see no less than two big drawbacks in Russian events. One of them—the danger that the Revolution might take Russia out of the war—was even discussed openly. There was less talk of the other—the threat that the Revolution held for the entire bourgeois world. In the memoirs of David Francis, published in 1921, the February Revolution is referred to as a "remarkable uprising."[67] But it must be kept in mind that it earned this flattering title only after the "unpleasant uprising" of 7 November 1917 had taken place.

In the light of this, the goals of Washington's policy toward Russia were as follows: to strengthen the economic and ideological and political position of the American bourgeoisie in revolutionary-democratic Russia, to make full use of the Russian potential in the war against Germany, and to prevent the Revolution from developing into a socialist one.

Thanks to the energetic efforts of Ambassador Francis, the United States was the first country to recognize the provisional government. Francis did everything possible to make the official announcement of recognition on 22 March, four hours before similar actions were taken by the British and the French. In his telegram to Secretary of State Robert Lansing on 19 April, the ambassador reported that the embassy was continuing to receive letters expressing gratitude for the recognition, which came at "a most critical time" in the existence of the new government.[68] The liberal bourgeoisie, which had been brought to power by the February Revolution, came forward to express Russia's gratitude. The United States embassy did everything possible to encourage the pro-American mood among the bourgeois circles of Russia. On its initiative a semiofficial organ of rapprochement with America—the Russian-American Committee—was created.[69]

It was the United States that played the more active role in Russian-American relations in 1917, the activity manifesting itself even in the economic sphere, mainly through official government channels. Within a short period of time three missions were sent to Russia—the Root mission, the Stevens mission, and the Red Cross mission—which all had one single goal: to strengthen American influence and support the counterrevolution in every direction. Most important of these was the Root mission,[70] which arrived in Vladivostok on 3 June 1917. Its composition was selected with great care. Included were officials (Elihu Root), businessmen (Samuel Bertron and Cyrus McCormick), the military (Chief of Staff General Hugh Scott and Admiral James H. Glennon), the Russian expert Charles R. Crane, the clergyman John R. Mott, and, finally, two delegates from among the "workers"—James Duncan, vice-president of the AFL, and the "socialist" Charles E. Russell. All of the goals of American policy in Russia mentioned above may be clearly discerned in the activity of the Root mission.

The mission made it clear to the provisional government that it would recommend to Woodrow Wilson that he render financial and other assistance to Russia, but only on the condition of stability, that is, counterrevolution on the part of the regime and continuation of the war. Elihu Root and his colleagues failed completely in trying to reeducate revolutionary Russia in the spirit of bourgeois America. The "workers" delegates behaved shamefully. The prestige of the AFL among the revolutionary workers was low, and the precepts of Samuel Gompers made no impression. As late as 2 April 1917, Gompers sent a telegram to the St. Petersburg soviet, which Ambassador Francis delivered to P. N. Milyukov to be used at his own discretion. In it the president of the AFL admonished the Russian proletariat that "freedom" is a "product of evolution," and warned against widening the Revolution. "Even in the Republic of the United States of America, the highest ideals of freedom are incomplete, but we have the will and the opportunity."[71] The Russian workers did not perceive AFL vice-president James Duncan as a person of their own class. The potential of Charles Russell was seriously undermined by the fact that by the time of his voyage he had already been expelled from the Socialist party of the United States, a fact that was widely publicized in the Russian revolutionary press. As a result, the Root mission did not make contact with revolutionary Russia. Instead the ties of the United States with the counterrevolution were strengthened, reinforced by the promise of loans.

On 12 June 1917 the Stevens mission arrived in St. Petersburg, having as its goal to appropriate the main railroad routes of Russia and put the great Siberian main line in order, placing the transport facilities at the service of the imperialist war and the counterrevolution. John F. Stevens was appointed advisor to the Russian Ministry of Transportation, and thereupon played an important role in the struggle against the Revolution.

The mission of the American Red Cross, which arrived in Petrograd on 7 August 1917, was also charged with important political tasks. R. S. Ganelin in his study writes: "There can be no doubt that the propaganda campaign of the Red Cross had not only military but also political goals. Directed against the Bolshevik party, it was by no means confined within the framework of the question of war and peace."[72]

The ruling circles of the United States set out to allocate loans to the provisional government. Altogether, $450,000,000 was appropriated, but actually much less was received.[73] We must say that private business in the United States did not manifest as much enthusiasm for investment in Russia as the Russian bourgeoisie and its provisional government had expected. The latter sent an extraordinary and very impressive embassy to the United States, headed by Professor B. A. Bakhmet'ev, assistant to the minister of trade and industry, inasmuch as the czarist ambassador, Yu. Bakhmet'ev (bearing the same surname as the new ambassador), had refused on 17 April 1917 to recognize the authority established by the February Revolution.[74] Bakhmet'ev explained to his government that American business had reservations regarding investment in Russia because of the "anarchy" in the Russian state.[75] He proposed winning the confidence of the business world of the United States and turning more boldly toward Washington, strengthening ties with American capital. In August 1917 Admiral A. V. Kolchak set out to visit Washington as a guest of the United States government,[76] and soon became the main hope of Woodrow Wilson in the struggle for the "Russian democracy."

In July 1917 the counterrevolution in Russia scored a temporary victory. An end was put to dual rule. From this point on American interference in Russian affairs increased sharply, coming completely into the open. Ambassador Francis demanded that the provisional government arrest Lenin, but it displayed what he regarded as "decided weakness."[77] In August 1917 a national conference was called, summoned to consolidate all the forces of the counterrevolution. Woodrow Wilson addressed a homiletic telegram to this forum, in which he expressed "confidence in the ultimate triumph of ideals of democracy and self-government against all enemies within and without."[78]

When things began to go very badly for the counterrevolution, the American embassy unleashed a storm of activity in two directions: it demanded the establishment of "discipline" in the army and the transfer of power to General Lavr Kornilov. Francis informed Washington more than once that he had demanded that Kerensky raise the level of discipline in the army. The ambassador placed his reliance on Kornilov, praising him in every possible way as a "good soldier, patriot," an educated person who knew seventeen languages.[79] Francis' support of Kornilov was opposed by the leaders of the Red Cross mission, William Thompson and Raymond Robins, who favored the other "patriot," Kerensky.[80]

The failure of the Kornilov faction was a disappointment to Francis and the ruling circles of the United States as a whole. The counterrevolution in Russia quickly lost its force. With the ground cut out from under him, Francis proposed organizing an armed intervention—even before the October Revolution. On 6 November 1917, in a panic, he inquired of Robert Lansing: ''What would you think of our sending two or more army divisions via Vladivostok or Sweden to her [Russia's] aid if I could get the consent of Russian Government therefor or even induce Government to make such a request?''[81]

But the following day the Socialist Revolution took place in Russia. Russian capitalism had come to an end.

2

The First Years of Soviet Power

Emergence of Soviet Foreign Policy

The Great October Socialist Revolution inaugurated the stage of contemporary history in the development of mankind. This phase is a period of general crisis for capitalism; of socialist revolutions and the successful socialist transformation of the world; of the crisis and collapse of the colonial structure of imperialism. As long ago as 1916, Lenin, in a work on imperialism, showed that monopolistic capitalism marks the eve of socialist revolution. During the years of the First World War capitalism entered a state of general crisis, which became the determining feature in the history of the bourgeois world after the October Revolution. The general crisis of capitalism is not the cyclical crisis of overproduction, but a crisis in all of the foundations of the society based on the principles of private property. The decisive factor in the general crisis of capitalism was that in the largest country on earth the bourgeois system was destroyed and successful socialist construction was begun.

Capitalism does not make way passively and automatically for the history of the new social system. The entire purport of the social activity of the bourgeoisie as a class in recent times is directed toward opposition to socialism. This takes an infinite number of methods and forms. The capitalist states stepped out into contemporary history carrying the banners of armed intervention against the first socialist state. Subsequently armed "expeditions" against socialism were used more than once in all parts of the world except Antarctica and Australia. In addition, every hour and every minute there was and there is now being conducted an ideological-political struggle by the bourgeoisie against the world of socialism.

It must be emphasized especially that both objectively and sub-jectively, through conscious activities of the bourgeoisie and its institutions, capitalism is striving in the most recent period to adapt somehow to the principles of socialization. Naturally, historically the most effective form of realizing the objectively developing process of abandoning private property is the establishment of socialism, which is exactly what the general and fundamental sense of social revolu-tions, in all their various forms, consists of. But capitalism, making use of all of its resources and institutions, acting under the leadership of the state, through which the collective interests of capitalism are expressed, strives to direct the development of the principles of socialization along unnatural, abnormal lines. For a relatively long time capitalism has succeeded in adapting to the objective process of socialization and directing it to state-monopolistic channels. At the same time the bourgeoisie makes use of socialist achievements, especially in such areas as control of the economy, social security, and education.

Most important in state-monopolistic development has been bour-geois adaption to the processes of socialization. The fact that the bourgeoisie has turned to using the category of socialization for the purpose of preserving the decaying foundations of private property contains within it inner contradictions of colossal force. The adaptation of private-property relations to the objective process of socialization with respect to both property itself and also to the solution of socioeconomic problems is the root explanation for the relative viability of capitalism in the twentieth century, although the doom of this system was proved with scientific authenticity by Karl Marx as early as the middle of the nineteenth century and has been demon-strated convincingly in recent times.

But there is also another completely different side to the application of state-monopolistic methods to preserve the bourgeois system. Al-though the ruling class achieves temporary success in specific critical situations in setting out along the bourgeois-collectivist path as a way out of the general crisis of capitalism, at the same time it inevitably undermines the foundation of private property. The development of state-monopolistic capitalism, reflecting the decay of the foundations of private property, creates objective preconditions for the establish-ment of a socialist method of production. It was for this reason that Lenin felt that "state-monopoly capitalism is a complete *material* preparation for socialism.''[1] Gradually the meaning of what has happened in contemporary history has crystallized more clearly. In a general, schematic framework, it comes down to the following dilemma: socialism or state-monopolistic capitalism—which system affords the greatest scope for the development of productive forces, the social progress of mankind, the true emancipation of the personality; which of them creates the practical conditions for the achievement of the age-long dream of mankind—to put an end to war? Contemporary history measures about six decades. In the course of this historically brief period the answer to the questions that have been posed has already been given: the superiority of socialist principles over state-monopolistic ones, in spite of all the shortcomings and difficulties of socialist construction, is obvious.

Having overthrown the power of the bourgeoisie and the landowners and converted the means of production into public property, the Soviet socialist state took a new line in principle in foreign policy, as well. The fundamental foreign-policy problem of the Soviet state came to be to ensure external conditions that would favor the consolidation of the victory of the Socialist Revolution and successful socialist construction. Accordingly, the foreign-policy course taken by the new nation was indisputably revolutionary. But this has nothing to do with the assertions of those historians who consider that the Soviet state saw as its chief foreign-policy goal stirring up ''world revolution'' and ''inciting'' the workers in capitalist countries to strikes, mutinies, and insurrections. By the way, apropos of ''world revolution,'' the Bolshevik party never advanced the slogan of ''world revolution'' as a policy for undermining the existing regimes in other countries, or as an idea for a worldwide march against capitalism. If, during the years of military intervention, slogans were advanced against the governments of countries engaged in the intervention, this was a legitimate form of response made necessary by the struggle against governments which, on their own initiative, without any provocation on our part, had started a war to destroy the socialist system and to seize the territories of a sovereign people. The communist conception of revolution itself starts out from the premise that Socialist revolution is the result of the inner contradictions of capitalism, and not that it is something introduced from outside.

On the other hand, the Soviet state always regarded itself as the bulwark of the international Communist movement in the sense that through the successful building of socialism it promotes the worldwide historical process of turning capitalism into socialism by revolution. From the first day of its existence, it declared that it would help peoples struggling against colonial oppression and racial-national discrimination. In other words, the Soviet state never engaged in the export of revolution, bearing in mind that revolution, unlike the Bourbon family, cannot be brought in a carriage from abroad; but at the same time it was always an important factor in the international revolutionary movement. It is important to emphasize this, for some historians to this day from time to time accuse the USSR either of inciting "world revolution" or of "departing" from this position and displaying national narrow-mindedness. The international and the national aims of the foreign policy of the socialist state have always been in complete harmony.

From its first years, the Soviet government tried to build its relations with capitalist countries—and these up until the end of the Second World War were the full-time concern of the foreign policy of our country—on principles which somewhat later came to be called the principles of peaceful coexistence among states that have different social systems. The theoretical grounds for these principles, laid down by Lenin, passed through three basic stages: before the Revolution, from 7 November 1917 to the end of the Civil War and the period of the armed intervention in 1920, and in 1921–22 mainly in connection with the Genoa conference.

The notion of the inevitability of peaceful coexistence flows out of Lenin's theory of the possibility that the Socialist Revolution would triumph initially in one country only. This was a new position in Marxist theory, formulated by Lenin during the years of the First World War. Even before the victory of the Revolution, the Bolsheviks took into account the inevitability of working out some forms of cooperation with the capitalist nations after the overthrow of the old system in Russia. Although no concrete politically programmed arrangements to this end had been worked out before 7 November 1917, the Bolsheviks came out against continuation of the imperialist war in the event that they succeeded in seizing power, which opened the possibilities of bringing into being the principles of peaceful coexistence.

In 1917–20, Lenin's principles of peaceful coexistence take on more definite expression in the political activities of the revolutionary government. They encountered tremendous difficulties in their path. The greatest of these was that the capitalist nations did not wish to coexist with Soviet Russia, having unleashed against her a war on a broad front: from the kaiser to Woodrow Wilson. The Soviet people had to defend their right to peaceful coexistence in a difficult armed struggle forced on them by world imperialism.

There were also domestic difficulties. The revolutionary forces in power found it difficult to work out at once the entire complex of methods of interrelations with the world of capitalism abroad that met them with hostility. This was complicated further by the fact that in the extraordinary conditions of those times slogans like "revolutionary war," "world revolution," and other petty bourgeois, adventurist formulas were popular among a significant faction of the party and the workers. One can only be astonished at how quickly and successfully the Revolution detached itself from this Trotskyist-Bucharinist adventurism. It chose at once, unerringly, the course of peace, solving all the remaining problems as it went along, gathering experience in foreign policy and instilling moderation in the hotheads.

The foreign-policy activities of the Soviet state began with the peace decree adopted 8 November 1917. It reflected with remarkable accuracy the essence of the initial stage of revolutionary foreign policy. It opened by addressing itself to the peoples of the world, and above all the workers of the capitalist countries, but did not stop here. It was also addressed to the bourgeois governments with the proposal to enter into peace negotiations. It was pointed out in the decree that the Soviets were prepared to discuss counterproposals. This was nothing but a manifestation of an objectively functioning conformity to law, the law of the inevitability of positive cooperation between states having different social systems.

During the first months of its existence, the main specific problem that the Soviet government had to solve was the question of getting out of the war. It must be said that it got out of the war with great difficulty. A separate peace was signed, but through no fault of Soviet Russia, which displayed patience and tact, permitting the members of the Entente (including the United States) to enter into the negotiations. In the process of concluding the Peace of Brest-Litovsk an important stage in the formation of the principles of Soviet foreign policy was passed. Lenin came out categorically against a mechanical interpretation of the interrelations between the national and the international aspects of the Revolution. When sharp disagreements emerged among the party leaders with respect to the conclusion of the Brest-Litovsk peace in January 1918, he showed that it would be an unforgivable mistake to formulate the course to be taken by counting on an immediate revolutionary outbreak in Europe. A true revolutionary, said Lenin, is one who strengthens the revolutionary power he has won in one country and in this way promotes the progress of socialism throughout the world, rather than nurturing illusions of a "European revolution" or giving way to despair when he sees that it is not making progress.

Inasmuch as proletarian revolution had not taken place in other countries, Soviet power in Russia, according to Lenin, must enter into contact with bourgeois governments, striving for peace and the creation of conditions for the strengthening of the Russian socialist bastion. He rejected the views of those who held that the Revolution has no right to maintain contact with these other governments, and said that in that case the socialist republic "could not exist at all, without flying to the moon."[2] The head of the Soviet government condemned resolutely the adventurist conception of instigating international revolution. Thus, we have before us three conceptions of world revolution: the bourgeois conception, used as a propaganda bugbear for purposes of counterrevolution; the opportunist, adventurist conception, that is essentially petty bourgeois; and the Leninist position, viewing the international revolution as an objective worldwide process of replacement of capitalism by socialism, demanding the support by the revolutionary forces of the world for revolution in one country, pointing out that the truest form of service to international revolution on the part of Soviet Russia had to be the consolidation of its own achievements and successful socialist construction.

The Brest-Litovsk peace, with all of its disadvantages for the Soviet state, laid one more stone in the edifice of the policy of peaceful coexistence. In the note of 18 September 1918, from Georgi V. Chicherin, the people's commissar for foreign affairs, to the German consul general in Moscow, Chicherin said: "The Worker-Peasant

Government resolutely wishes to maintain good-neighbor relations and *peaceful coexistence* [italics ours] with Germany, despite all of the differences in the systems of the two states, and it is convinced that the German Government also wishes to have peaceful coexistence with it ... the Peoples' Commissariat firmly believes that Russia and Germany will continue to move along the path of peaceful coexistence."[3]

It had no sooner liberated itself from the threat of German intervention, than Soviet Russia, in the spring and summer of 1918, was subjected to invasion by its former allies. Now the proposals for peace, for the cessation of the undeclared war against the Soviet state, were already addressed to the countries of the Entente. From August 1918 to December 1919 the government of the Russian Soviet Federated Socialist Republic (RSFSR) did this eleven times.[4] However, the outcome of the intervention was settled without resorting to direct or indirect negotiations—the interventionists were simply driven out or forced to clear off and return where they had come from.

The years of the intervention did not promote the spread of the principles of peaceful coexistence at all. Nonetheless, during this period the Soviet government developed this idea substantially. It tried not to exacerbate relations with the bourgeois countries and, being guided by socialist interests, did everything possible to establish normal diplomatic relations with them. Chicherin, in his report at the meeting of the Central Executive Committee of Soviets on 17 June 1920, when the imperialist intervention by way of Poland was at its height, said: "Our slogan has been and remains the same: peaceful coexistence with other governments, whatever they may be."[5]

The victorious conclusion of the Civil War and the expulsion of the foreign interventionists greatly improved the prospects of peaceful coexistence. The Soviet state was interested in adjusting its economic ties with the outside world. It strove to make fuller utilization of these economic opportunities for the building of socialism under the conditions of the New Economic Policy (NEP) announced at the tenth congress of the Russian Communist party in March 1921. The leading capitalist countries, in their turn, needed to reestablish their former ties with Russia, without which it was difficult to count on the normal functioning of the economic organism of the world. The capitalists also entertained the hope that they could achieve through economic pressure what they had not been able to achieve through arms—the liquidation of the socialist system in Russia. Bourgeois propaganda began to talk about the renunciation by the Bolsheviks of "world revolution," and even about the internal capitulation of Soviet power to Russian capital. In essence, this same position was asserted by the Trotskyist opposition as well. Neither the capitalists nor the Trotskyists understood, or they chose not to understand, the nature of the NEP. The NEP was intended for active socialist construction, for the building of socialism in the USSR. For this reason our state was most interested in constructive peace.

The foreign-policy activities of the Soviet government in preparation for the Genoa conference of 1922 and its conduct there played an exceptionally important role in forming the basis of the Leninist principles of peaceful coexistence. At this time an important step was made in working out a single foreign-policy course for all the Soviet republics, and thereby the formation of a united Soviet state. The delegation of the RSFSR spoke at Genoa on behalf of all the Soviet republics (Ukraine, Belorussia, and the others). It warded off all of the attacks of imperialist diplomacy and made it clear that the Soviets would not make any concessions in matters of principle. In addition, in the spirit of the principles of peaceful coexistence, which by this time had been clearly worked out, the Soviet government announced that it was ready to establish firm ties with the bourgeois countries based on equality, nonintervention, and reciprocity.

Of fundamental significance was the programmatic announcement of Chicherin at the opening of the conference: "While adhering to the principles of Communism, the Russian delegation recognizes that in the present historical epoch, which permits the parallel existence of the old system alongside the new socialist system that is arising, economic cooperation between nations representing these two systems of property is imperative for general economic reconstruction. The Russian government therefore places the greatest importance on the first point of the Cannes resolution concerning mutual recognition of the different systems of property and different political and economic forms that exist today in different countries. The Russian delegation came here not to propagandize for its own theoretical views but for the sake of entering into economic relations with the governments and commercial-industrial circles of all countries based on reciprocity, equality, and full recognition, without reservation."[6]

Monopoly of foreign trade is the cornerstone of Soviet foreign economic policy. This idea was expressed by Lenin as long ago as the first days of the Revolution, while in April 1918 he signed a decree on nationalization of foreign trade according to which no operations in foreign trade could be carried on except through the state body, the Peoples' Commissariat of Foreign Trade. With the lifting of the economic blockade of Soviet Russia in 1920, the imperialist nations mounted an attack on the monopoly of foreign trade which was intensified with the transition by the Soviets to the NEP. G. E. Zinov'ev, L. B. Kamenev, N. I. Bukharin, and others declaimed against monopoly or for its relaxation. But through the efforts of Lenin all attempts to weaken it were swept aside.

The matter of "concessions" occupied a certain place in the foreign-policy program of the Soviet government during its first years. It was held to be significant economically and politically. Economically, concessions were felt to be expedient to attract the more advanced technological methods of the bourgeois countries and their capital, for the Soviet republic had need of both. Politically, concessions might contribute to the "reeducation" of the more aggressive circles of the interventionist bourgeoisie, serving to cool their militaristic anti-Soviet ardor. However, the Soviet government did not exaggerate the importance of concessions. In general, as the experience of the 1920s showed, they did not take hold, although their number was not inconsiderable.

The year 1922 concludes an important phase in the history of Soviet foreign policy, the period of the formation of its main principles. The Soviet state found the optimal form of solving its national and international problems. The Bolshevik party, having emerged as the initiator in the creation of the Communist International, helped all the revolutionary forces of the bourgeois world to work out the correct programmatic and theoretical arrangements. In doing this, the Soviet government and the Bolshevik party did not engage in the instigation of revolutions, nor permit any interference in the affairs of other nations.

Peaceful coexistence is a special form of the class struggle. The

Soviet people have promoted the revolutionary process in the world through successful socialist construction. They have derived the benefits of a peaceful breathing space and of economic and diplomatic relations with the bourgeois countries. In entering into business ties with the land of the Soviets, the world bourgeoisie has also derived economic benefits, at the same time hoping to localize and overcome the "Russian contagion," to bring about the demise of socialism. History has made peaceful coexistence objectively inevitable for a protracted period of time. And the fact that international capital has gone along with this, having no other way out, and that one or another of its elements have rejected peaceful coexistence more than once and have turned back to the age-old formulas of interventionism, have made clear which of the two sides has regarded these principles with the lesser enthusiasm.

In the resolution of the All-Russian Central Executive Committee on 17 May 1922, on the activities of the Soviet delegation at the Genoa conference, it is noted that "the entire course of international relations during recent times gives evidence of the inevitability at this stage of historical development of the temporary existence simultaneously of the communist and bourgeois property systems, and forces even the most implacable enemies of Soviet Russia to seek paths of understanding with the communist property system, after their four-year endeavor to liquidate this system by force has ended in collapse."[7]

The Soviet state consolidated itself firmly in the international arena. It looked ahead to the future with confidence, threatening no one and feeling no fear of the old, capitalist world. The formation on 30 December 1922 of the Union of Soviet Socialist Republics gave the Soviet People new strength and created a mighty stronghold for peace and socialism.

Jumping ahead, we may now say that the principles of peaceful coexistence, originated in the Soviet foreign policy during the first years of Soviet power, were destined to have a great future, especially in the last two decades. They have been rooted firmly in the practice of international relations and in the code of international law. The Soviet Union has continued to be their major bearer and promoter. The Constitution of the USSR, adopted in 1977, has incorporated those principles in the Soviet fundamental law. Among the basic aims of the foreign policy of the USSR, according to the Constitution, is that of "consistently implementing the principle of the peaceful coexistence of states with different social systems" (Article 28).

The United States Faces the New Russia

The ruling circles of the United States received the October Revolution in principle in the same way as the bourgeoisies of the rest of the world. While there were certain special nuances, underneath everything there lay the usual features typical of the bourgeois outlook making no pretense at being exclusively American. In defining their relation to Soviet Russia the American bourgeoisie and its government took into account the following main considerations: (1) in having nationalized foreign holdings and canceled the debts incurred by prerevolutionary governments, the Russian Revolution had inflicted damage on the American bourgeoisie and its government; (2) when it declared its intention to conclude peace and shortly afterward succeeded in doing so, Soviet Russia ceased to be an ally in the war against the German bloc and thereby disturbed the calculations of the United States and the whole Entente to use the Russian armed forces for its own purposes; (3) with one stroke the Revolution canceled out those glowing prospects of insinuating American influence into Russia which appeared so promising when the provisional government was in power; (4) the Revolution was socialist in nature, had overthrown the power of the bourgeoisie in one sixth of the planet, and was exerting a revolutionary influence on the entire world, even on its most stable sector, the American one.

The first factor was not in itself of essential significance in the elaboration of the course of the United States with respect to Russia, for the material losses were not great, and furthermore, if the American government had wished, it could have entered into direct negotiations with the Soviet government and reduced the economic loss to a minimum. Nonetheless, American propaganda regarded this argument as being of value and put it into circulation, adding to it the thesis that the Soviet government had deliberately violated all sorts of agreements, and continued to make use of the argument for a very long time. The second consideration was at first more substantial, but very quickly lost all significance. However, it was in the two first directions that the United States government found propagandistic justification for its hostile policy toward the new Russia. But the real sources of the hostility, its actual moving forces, were rooted in the last two considerations, although official Washington preferred to remain silent about this for completely understandable reasons. Nothing at all was said about the third factor, while the fourth was used only in an absolutely perverted way—in the form of a hysterical clamor to the effect that Soviet Russia thought only of undermining and overthrowing foreign governments, including the government of the United States.

The bourgeois United States gave the October Socialist Revolution a hostile reception, in the strict sense of the term. The American armed intervention in Soviet Russia is a fact well known to the readers of both countries and it is unnecessary to set forth these events in detail. We will only point out that the reasons for the intervention and its goals are set forth inadequately in many American works.

It must be admitted that some Soviet works also suffered from certain errors. The book of M. Pavlovich, for example, which came out in 1922, when the Japanese invaders had not yet been expelled from within our borders, contains this kind of uncritical assertion: "We can only sympathize with the somewhat intensified American influence on Kamchatka and the entire littoral of the Okhotsk Sea."[8] In 1934, apparently carried away by the friendly atmosphere created by the establishment of diplomatic relations with the United States, another Soviet historian wrote: "When the October Revolution threw off Kerensky, the practical Americans attempted to achieve their main goal—restoration of the demolished eastern front—with the aid of the Bolsheviks."[9] In this account the main goal of the American intervention is, of course, presented in a distorted form. And many years later, A. E. Kunina gave way to another extreme, asserting that "the United States came forward as the initiator and active participant" in the intervention.[10] The participation of American imperialists in the intervention is undeniable, but after the Treaty of Brest-Litovsk, blame for initiating the intervention rested on the shoulders of Anglo-French and Japanese imperialism.

These erroneous, careless formulations, however, represent only a peripheral influence on Soviet historiography. Basically, Soviet authors always grasped correctly the counterrevolutionary essence of the

American intervention and the active participation of the imperialist circles of the United States in the "crusade" against bolshevism. In recent Soviet studies, the role and goals of the United States in the intervention are explored objectively and fully, drawing on diverse sources, among them Soviet and American archives.[11]

American historians have put forth a number of theories to explain the intervention: some say that American troops were sent to Russia to restore the eastern front in the war with Germany, to suppress German penetration to the east, and were therefore carrying out a mission against the kaiser; others, that the intervention was directed against Japan, which, taking advantage of the weakness of Soviet Russia, had decided to seize a part of the Russian territory; still others say that in sending soldiers to Russia Woodrow Wilson wanted to promote "self-determination," for which the "Russians" were fighting.

First to appear was the version that the intervention was conceived as a means for restoring the eastern front, as a way of saving Russia from kaiserism. The United States government announced that at the very least it hoped to insure the safety of the military supply depots in the Murmansk-Arkhangelsk region and to prevent the arming of German war prisoners in Siberia. At the same time it was not in the least interested in whether there was a threat to Soviet ports from the Germans. Democratic Senator Claude A. Swanson, in a speech on 7 January 1919, justifying the intervention without qualification and demonstrating the low level of his geographic knowledge and conversance with naval matters, said: "The port of Vladivostok and this port of Archangel are the two most important ports and were in considerable danger at the time of the Russian collapse. Germany was trying to get both."[12] Supported by this kind of thinking, the government zealously prepared the anti-German version for justifying the intrusion into Russia. For the sake of greater plausibility it gave out the propaganda that the Bolsheviks were "German agents." For a sizable sum it acquired "documents" that allegedly proved this. Edgar Sisson, an official representative of the United States, bought them in Petrograd, and they entered into history as the "Sisson documents," "proving" that bolshevism acts as an "arm of Berlin," not of Moscow. At the personal instruction of Woodrow Wilson they began to be published in September 1918.

The thesis of the American government and of subsequent historians that the intervention was directed against Germany is refuted by a whole series of arguments. In the first place, there was no threat to Arkhangelsk or Murmansk, and certainly not to Vladivostok from Germany and Austria-Hungary. In the second place, the assertion that the Americans were aiming to protect the Czechoslovak corps in Siberia against the German and Austrian prisoners of war, allegedly armed by the Soviets to fight against the Czechoslovaks, does not stand up under critical examination. It is a well-known fact that the head of the American Red Cross mission, Colonel Raymond Robins, a steadfast enemy of Germany, sent Captain William Webster (American) and Captain W. L. Hicks (British) to Siberia in the spring of 1918 to verify this assertion. They ascertained that the Siberian Soviets were not arming the German war prisoners. This was true later, as well. One would have thought that their report would have removed this item from the agenda. But as Frederick Shuman writes, ''This report might have been expected to put an end to wild stories, but it did not. No attempt was made to discredit the report or to challenge its accuracy. All evidence points to the validity of its conclusions. Allied and American officials, however, had long since ceased to be capable of objective observation of affairs in Russia.''[13] In the third place, if the United States government had been concerned first and foremost with making the eastern front more active, it should have agreed to the most reliable method of achieving this—to enter into contact with the Soviet government. This would have been all the more logical in view of the fact that the Soviet government had officially inquired of Washington whether it was ready to extend assistance to Russia if she were to refuse to ratify the Brest-Litovsk peace treaty or if she were to be subjected to an unprovoked attack by Germany, and if so, how. The United States government did not go along with this, whereupon Colonel Robins, naively figuring out that as far as Russia was concerned Wilson was mainly interested in the fate of the eastern front, saw that there was nothing more for him to do there.

Occasionally in the American literature one encounters a position that presents the anti-German interpretation in a way that makes it appear less primitive, more refined. Christopher Lasch, for example, writes that so far as the United States government was concerned, ''Bolshevism itself was merely an extension of kaiserism.''[14] This would seem to rescue the anti-German version from any vulnerability to attack. However, to continue our argument, as a fourth reason against the validity of this notion we may point out that the Siberian intervention began at a time when the days of kaiser's Germany were numbered, and it was expanded to its full extent after the world war had already come to an end. Its full swing came in 1919, when the counterrevolutionary, anti-Soviet purport of the expedition appeared in all its nakedness. The liberal weekly *Nation*, on 19 July 1919, reflected exactly this interpretation of the American intervention: ''It is now perfectly evident that, despite the fact that we are at peace with Germany and that Germany has ratified the treaty, the Allies are going to carry on their unauthorized and unhallowed wars against Hungary and Russia. America may now trade with Germany freely but not, the Government announced, with either Hungary or that portion of Russia occupied by the Bolsheviki.''[15] Finally, we may also point out, that the United States and its allies readily agreed to use the erstwhile troops of the kaiser to overthrow Soviet power in the Baltic area, that is, to spread the influence of kaiserism in that region.

Thus, it is impossible to take seriously the notion of a struggle against kaiserism as representing the true goals of the American intervention. In the clear class-oriented counterrevolutionary expressions of a memorandum composed by one of the government agencies in August 1918, there is not a word about the Bolsheviks being agents of the kaiser.[16] But just such a slogan was needed for propaganda purposes. It was customary at that time to label everything that was objectionable in the political scheme as ''pro-German and Bolshevist.'' [17] For anyone even moderately familiar with the history of domestic politics in the United States during that period, the true sense of the ''German'' terminology of the ruling circles should be clear. It was employed in the class struggle against revolution and against any radical tendency of that time. Even wide circles of liberals who had come out for recognition of Soviet Russia were made out to be ''Germans.''

The Bolsheviks were no greater ''advocates of kaiserism'' than Eugene V. Debs, who found himself in prison, or than any of the other opponents of the anti-Soviet intervention in the United States. Within the United States it was awkward to brand such wide segments of the population ''kaiserists,'' especially after 11 November 1918, but this description of bolshevism, first used on 7 November 1917, continued thereafter. In January 1919 the *Washington Post* came out against "a Germanized Russia." This was found necessary, as with other organizers of the intervention, to justify the counterrevolutionary campaign into Russia. The newspaper expressed itself quite frankly: "The extermination of the Bolsheviki is a necessity of life to free men and free nations."[18]

The second explanation, that the intervention was directed against Japan, had less vitality, even though it came far closer to objective reality as compared with the antikaiser fantasy.[19] It is right to say that one of the goals of the United States military expedition to Siberia was to contain the Japanese, or at any rate to control their excessively determined activity. But this was only one of the motives for the intervention. The United States government realized that it could find in the Soviet government a most reliable ally in opposing Japanese penetration of Siberia, but it made no approach to the Soviets. Up until the end of the Japanese intervention the United States still took no decisive step against Japan, choosing the lesser of two evils. It must also be remembered that American intervention did not confine itself to the Far East. It began even earlier in the European part of northern Russia, and the notion of containing Japan from there would have been just as implausible as the notion of striking at Germany from Vladivostok.

But some American historians do look objectively at the real reasons for the intervention. Among these we may point to the works of Frederick L. Schuman and William A. Williams, in which the idea of the counterrevolutionary, anti-Soviet nature of the American armed interference in Russia is brought out persuasively enough.

An analysis of the specific actions of the United States government during those years and a theoretical understanding of the entire course of its international policy in recent times show that the true practical goals of the intervention were the following: first, to overthrow the revolutionary power; second, to consolidate American positions in the "new" Russia. Under existing conditions, the second goal seemed attainable, for France and Britain were weakened, Germany routed, and Japan set itself against Russia through its plans and actions in Siberia. As for the first goal, there existed in the United States the conviction that Soviet power, precarious even without this, would fall as soon as the Russians saw that Woodrow Wilson "himself" was proposing to make Russia "safe for democracy." The expectation of the rapid fall of Soviet power prevailed in bourgeois public opinion in the United States. According to Walter Lippmann and Charles Merzer, between November 1917 and November 1919, the *New York Times* reported no less than ninety-one times that the collapse of the Soviets was inevitable.[20] The expansionist circles of the United States held the hope that Woodrow Wilson would inspire the Russian people to overthrow the Bolsheviks, and that in return, as a sign of their gratitude for having had their country made "safe for democracy," the Russians would throw their doors wide open to the Americans.

The American-Russian Chamber of Commerce, the center for the expansionists of this bent who were formulating Russian policy, pictured the immediate future in February 1918 as follows: "Without any question, Russia will present at the termination of the war, the largest and most favorable field for the extension of American business of any foreign country. Assuming a liberalized Germany, there undoubtedly will be close relationships between Russia and Germany, but the United States, if American interests maintain their interest in Russia, and are ready to grasp their opportunities, should be an extremely important factor in the Russian field."[21] In September 1918 the executive committee of the Chamber of Commerce, developing the principles of "an American policy for Russia" further, and declaring "hearty accord with the Administration" on the question of intervention, urged "to consolidate the work of this expedition" and to add a "civil-economic mission" to the army which would consolidate what had been achieved through military means.[22] The expansionists increased their distribution of *A Message to the American People*, by Catherine Breshkovsky, published in 1919, with a foreword by the ancient champion of "Russian freedom," George Kennan. In it, in plain terms, we find: "Americans, come to Russia! Do not hesitate to invest your capital, and right on the spot convert our raw materials into all kinds of products."[23] All of this, of course, was to be done after the overthrow of bolshevism.

Intervention and Its Opponents

The anti-Bolshevik campaign began with the first day of Soviet power. The United States government realized at once what had taken

place in Russia. On 10 November Francis was already telegraphing to
Lansing: "Of course we should make no loans to Russia at present."[24]
And on 24 November he inquired of his chief: "What do you think of
treating Russia as China was treated."[25] Without hestitation, the
American government intervened in the internal affairs of Soviet
Russia. On 19 November Francis even issued an appeal "to the
People of Russia," making it "on behalf of my Government and my
people." It was anti-Soviet in character, and urged them not to
submit to the new authority. He presumptuously proclaimed: "I have
not lost faith in the ability of the Russian people to solve their own
problems."[26] The Russian people paid no attention to this, nor to a
subsequent appeal to them by the American ambassador.[27] These
documents, along with a mass of others, some of which we will refer to
below, could have satisfied fully the inquiries of American political
figures and propagandists, striving so earnestly in the 1920s and 1930s
to find examples of the interference of the government of one country
in the affairs of another.

Interference in Russian affairs clearly was from the outset counterrevolutionary in nature. Woodrow Wilson had already condemned the
Bolsheviks in his speech at the annual meeting of the AFL on 12 November 1917.[28] The president's message to Congress of 4 December, in which he proposed declaring war against Austria-Hungary, is
worthy of analysis. In preparing the document in question, Secretary
Lansing composed a memorandum (2 December) in which he assessed
the nature of the Bolsheviks: "The one thing they are striving to bring
about is the 'Social Revolution,' which will sweep away national
boundaries, racial distinctions and modern political, religious, and
social institutions, and make the ignorant and incapable mass of
humanity dominant in the earth. They indeed plan to destroy civilization by mob violence."[29] It is doubtful whether Lansing and all of
official Washington conceived kaiserism in such terms! And yet it was
the similarity, in smaller measure, between kaiserism and bolshevism
that was used as grounds for the imminent intervention in Russia. On
4 December Lansing presented the president with the draft of a
declaration on the Russian question composed in such harsh terms that
Wilson, while he approved of the content, did not accept its form for
publication.

However, notwithstanding all the liberal phraseology, anti-Soviet motifs showed distinctly through the Russian part of the message. Wilson characterized the October Revolution as "the sad reverses" and did not let slip the opportunity to link the events in Russia with German influence: "The Russian people have been poisoned by the very same falsehoods that have kept the German people in the dark, and the poison has been administered by the very same hand. The only possible antidote is the truth."[30] It was in seeking to discover the "truth" that Wilson came upon the "Sisson documents." William A. Williams was right when he concluded that "intervention as a consciously anti-Bolshevik operation was decided upon by American leaders within five weeks" after 7 November 1917.[31]

American historiography concerning the intervention has been most successful in dealing with the question of showing the torment that Wilson experienced before deciding on the intrusion into Russia. For the Democratic president, an apostle of bourgeois liberalism who in April 1917 set out on a campaign to "make the world safe for democracy," it must indeed have been difficult to send troops into a revolutionary country which had made itself truly safe for democracy. It was much easier for the kaiser, Clemenceau, Lloyd George, and the emperor of Japan to make this decision. For six decades now American historiography has been tormenting itself, along with Wilson, trying to discover some moral or psychological justification for this unseemly act. Among present-day historians, George Kennan, bearing the same surname and being a distant relative of the "first American crusader for Russian freedom," maintains that the intervention only "coincided" with the Civil War and is indignant with "Soviet historiography," which dares to declare that the intrusion had as its goal the overthrow of the Bolshevik authority, when, in his opinion, it stemmed from "the necessities of the war with Germany.[32]

Kennan sees the tragedy of the intervention not in the fact that it mounted a counterrevolution, a civil war entailing massive destruction and slaughter, but in the fact that Wilson, by agonizing for such a long time and refusing to agree to demand urgently that the Allies intervene as soon as possible, sent his soldiers too late: "The American forces had scarcely arrived in Russia when history invalidated at a single stroke almost every reason Washington had conceived for their being there."[33] The end of the First World War was in sight. According to Kennan's tragic conception the intervention was a mistake, a belated measure. George Kennan cannot get around the problem of how the "tragic mistake" that he discovered in Wilsonian policy influenced future Soviet-American relations. Retrospectively, he consoles Wilson with the notion that even without the intervention relations with Soviet Russia would have turned out badly, inasmuch as nothing else could have been expected from the Bolsheviks: "All these traits of the Soviet official personality would have been present in any case to bedevil even the most faithful and enlightened of American efforts to moderate the differences and to reduce the gap."[34]

While Wilson did not decide to proceed with the military intervention at once, he did take an anti-Soviet position from the start. His fourteen points had a twofold anti-Bolshevik direction. First, his entire platform constituted a liberal-imperialist counterbalance to the Lenin revolutionary program of peace, an attempt to weaken the influence of the course of the Socialist Revolution. Second, the sixth point directly concerned Russia. It stipulated that German troops must evacuate Russian territory, but its wording showed that the "good will" promised by Wilson would be directed not to Soviet Russia but to Russia as she had been before 7 November 1917. The sixth point ended on a very solemn note: "The treatment accorded Russia by her sister nations in the months to come will be the acid test of their good will, of their comprehension of her needs as distinguished from their own interests, and of their intelligent and unselfish sympathy."[35] Events quickly showed that the "sister nations," among them the North American, did not pass this test.

The next important step in Washington's Russian policy was the appeal addressed by Wilson to the Second Congress of Soviets on 11 March 1918, which had the purpose of preventing ratification of the Treaty of Brest-Litovsk. "Although the Government of the United States," said the president, "is unhappily not now in a position to render the direct and effective aid it would wish to render, I beg to assure the people of Russia through the Congress that it will avail itself of every opportunity to secure for Russia once more complete sovereignty and independence in her own affairs and full restoration of her great role in the life of Europe and the modern world."[36] At first glance it may seem strange that Wilson, even if only for demagogic reasons, did not promise assistance to the Soviets in their struggle against Germany on condition that they refuse to ratify the Brest-

Litovsk treaty. But Wilson could not do this. He behaved like a man of
"principle." Any irresponsible promise, however hollow, might be
construed as some sort of recognition of Soviet power, which Washington did not want. He did not go beyond an appeal not to ratify the
peace treaty.

The telegram sent in response by the Soviet Congress showed
Wilson that he was dealing with a revolutionary-socialist sovereign
government. The president was finally convinced that the "Russian
people" must be "helped." But how? He racked his brain for some
means to justify Russia's enlightenment by force. Realizing this,
Francis telegraphed from Vologda on 2 May 1918 as follows: "In my
judgment time for allied intervention has arrived."[37] But for Wilson
that time had not quite yet arrived. He sought to combine the liberal
idea of the self-determination of peoples (with the purpose of strengthening American influence among the self-determined peoples), with
the idea of armed intervention. Unlike the president of the semi-
Fascist Poland of the 1930s, where the head of state, according to the
1935 constitution, was responsible only "to God and history,"[38]
Wilson, the "New Freedom" leader of bourgeois-democratic America, had to answer to a wider public.

The United States government found a solution to its problem in
the counterrevolutionary revolt of the Czechoslovak Corps, which began at the end of May 1918. This made everything much simpler for
Wilson. He ignored the opinion of his military advisers who, naively
believing that an anti-German operation was being planned, coun-
seled against it because of its apparent strategic futility, and made the
decision to go ahead on 6 July 1918.[39] On 17 July the secretary of
state sent the Allied ambassadors in Washington a memorandum
setting forth the American view of the intervention. The main part of
this document read as follows: "Military action is admissible in Russia,
as the Government of the United States sees the circumstances, only to
help the Czecho-Slovaks consolidate their forces and get into successful cooperation with their Slavic kinsmen and to steady any efforts
at self-government or self-defense in which the Russians themselves
may be willing to accept assistance. Whether from Vladivostok or from
Murmansk and Archangel, the only legitimate object for which American or Allied troops can be employed, it submits, is to guard military

stores which may subsequently be needed by Russian forces and to render such aid as may be acceptable to the Russians in the organization of their own self-defense.''[40]

The reference to safeguarding the military depots and defending the Czechoslovaks, that is, the entire anti-German part of the memorandum, must be regarded as propagandistic window dressing. The true problem was the plan to assist the Czechoslovaks and the ''Russians'' (in the American lexicon of the intervention period the term *Russian* did not include the Bolsheviks, the Soviets, and was synonymous with the term *anti-Soviet*) in ''self-defense'' against the Revolution, and ''self-determination'' on a counterrevolutionary basis. The anti-Japanese purport of the document must also be noted, especially when it says that the intervention must help the Czechoslovaks to cooperate ''only'' with their ''Slavic kinsmen.'' This was a hint to the Japanese, and to some extent also to the British and French, that the United States was opposed to dividing Russia into spheres of influence, that it was in favor of an open-door policy. However, in order not to dampen the interventionist, counterrevolutionary enthusiasm of their allies, the United States government also stipulated that it would not permit ''the least color of criticism'' of their behavior.[44]

The American interventionist army in Russia was not a very large force—about 5,500 in the North and as many as 12,000 in the Far East.[42] It did not engage in any major battles with the Red Army but did take part in individual skirmishes, counting 244 killed and 305 wounded in the North alone,[43] according to American casualty figures. The Americans contributed to the effort to overthrow Soviet rule by supplying, advising, and directing the White Army in Siberia, and guarding its lines of communications. General William S. Graves, the United States commander in Siberia, maintained with apparent sincerity that his soldiers were not fighting against the Reds, that they were not interventionists.[44] He argued that Congress had not declared war against Russia (at that time the Americans had not yet become accustomed to wars not sanctioned by Congress), and that there were almost no battles with the Red Army. However, the general himself acknowledged that thanks to the Americans, the railroads of Siberia were open only to the Whites, and that the Red Cross worked to help only the counterrevolutionaries.[45] Furthermore, at the very beginning of his memoirs, Graves writes: "Without the support of foreign troops, I doubt if Kolchak or his Government ever possessed sufficient strength to exercise sovereign powers."[46] The American railroad mission headed by John F. Stevens spared no effort in organizing transportation for the Kolchak "government," and took advantage of the opportunity to strengthen American influence in Siberia. To Stevens, the "value" of his Russian Railway Service Corps was in the help it gave to Kolchak.[47] Control of the railroad was equivalent to control of Siberia, so that the American efforts were not in vain.

The main contribution of the Wilsonian "measures," which had as their alleged goal to make Russia "safe for democracy" but actually served the investment banks of the United States, were not made through direct military action in our country but by giving every kind of aid possible to our homegrown Russian "champions of democracy." Kolchak was almost entirely dependent on the Americans. Denikin, Wrangel, the White Poles, and all of the anti-Soviet forces received every possible means of material support from across the ocean, as well as advice on military strategy. G. N. Tsvetkov writes that "there was not a single White Guard force which the American government would not have been willing to help militarily or financially in the struggle against the Soviet state," and that the general total of this assistance amounted to approximately four billion dollars.[48]

Together with its allies, the government of the United States also put in motion an active diplomatic effort against the Soviets. Through their combined efforts the Versailles conference became the headquarters of the interventionists and the White Guards. It was not by chance that Herbert Hoover characterized the Russian question as "among the worst problems before the Peace Conference."[49] On 22 January 1919 Wilson put forward a plan for summoning a conference of all the governments that had come into being on the territory of the former Russian Empire and were taking part in the Civil War to discuss conditions for a prompt cessation of hostilities. When the White Guards and their sponsors in the Entente defeated the plan, Wilson and Lloyd George sent the William Bullitt mission to Moscow with the task of sounding out Soviet conditions for peace. The American envoy was received by Lenin himself, and a draft Soviet-American peace proposal was agreed on very quickly.

When Bullitt returned to Paris, Wilson did not even want to speak to him, pretending that he knew nothing about the mission. Why did the president change his position so abruptly? Bullitt replied to this comprehensively at the meeting of the Senate Foreign Relations Committee investigating this diplomatic about-face in September 1919. When Senator Warren Harding asked "why the Soviet proposal was not given favorable consideration," Bullitt replied: "Kolchak made a 100-mile advance, and immediately the entire press of Paris was roaring and screaming on the subject, announcing that Kolchak would be in Moscow within two weeks; and therefore everyone in Paris, including, I regret to say members of the American commission, began to grow very lukewarm about peace in Russia, because they thought Kolchak would arrive in Moscow and wipe out the Soviet Government."[50]

Wilson felt that the fate of "Russian democracy" was most closely connected with Kolchak. Not only was he more dependent on the United States than the other White Guard leaders, but he also suited the Americans best. Kolchak's idea of a united and indivisible Russia played into the hands of the Americans first and foremost, and did not particularly suit the British and the Japanese. In the first days of Soviet power the ruling circles in the United States had not yet grasped the advantages of this idea for them, but before long they seized it tenaciously. They saw that the British and the French were firmly established in the outlying national areas of European Russia, while in the East, the division of Russia was a cherished dream of the Japanese as well as of the British. The Americans needed a united and indivisible Russia as the traditional counterweight against Japan and Britain. But this was by no means all, or even the main consideration, for the very active liberal-expansionist forces of Wilsonian America wanted to do more than merely check the ambitions of their allies. They hoped that in a united and indivisible Russia American capital and American bourgeois-democratic institutions would come to occupy a leading place. In December of 1920 in the "Statement of American Policy toward Russia," having emphatically condemned the idea of dis-membering the Russian state, and supported just as firmly the course of not recognizing the Soviets and expressed confidence in the speedy downfall of the Bolsheviks, the American-Russian Chamber of Commerce painted the ideal portrait of Russia as follows: "A strong, united Russia is of the utmost importance for the economic future of America. She will call on us for credit and for guidance in the development of her unmatched physical resources."[51] Of course, it was not so much a strong and united Russia that the expansionists of the United States needed, as a large and undivided Russia, so that it would not be subject to undue influence from Britain, France, and Germany, but at the same time would not be strong and independent enough to withstand American interference and choose the socialist path of socio-economic development.

The complete defeat of the White Guards and interventionists and the strengthening of Soviet power in almost the entire territory of the former Russian Empire meant the total collapse of Washington's Russian policy. Russia proved unsafe for Wilsonian bourgeois democracy. Wilsonian imperialist liberalism was bankrupt against the socialist democratism and patriotism of the Russian people. The great doctrinaire could not understand this, and decided that the Russians had simply not matured sufficiently to accept his "new freedom." This was both a political and a personal failure for Wilson. The collapse of Wilsonianism consisted first and foremost in the failure of America's counterrevolutionary, expansionist designs, and not in such historical trifles as the refusal of the Senate to ratify the Treaty of Versailles. "Thus," writes E. I. Popova, "it was more than the failure of intervention, more than the defeat of a military intrusion into another people's country—it was the complete failure of Wilsonian liberalism, its capitulation before a new idea and a new system."[52]

The defeat of Kolchak and Denikin taught the American government a lesson. It gave up continuing direct intervention, removing its troops from Russia in 1919–20. On 7 July 1920 the State Department announced the removal of restrictions on trade with Russia in nonmilitary goods. It was stipulated that this was not a "political recognition" of "any Russian authority" and that individuals and corporations that entered into trade relations with Russia "will do so on their own responsibility and at their own risk."[53] This decision was influenced by the United States government's apprehension over the Anglo-Soviet negotiations that began in the spring of 1920; it did not wish to leave the Russian market entirely to Britain.

Faced with the inevitability of formulating a new Russian policy, the Democratic government proved incapable of advancing any constructive ideas. Secretary of State Bainbridge Colby's note to the Italian ambassador on 10 August 1920 only reemphasized the Russian policy of 1917-20 and charted the course the United States was to follow for the next thirteen years, up to the time when the next Democratic government came to power. Formulated when the Polish-Soviet war was at its height, the note was in reply to an inquiry from the Italian government about the American attitude to that conflict, and amounted to a diplomatic demarche against the Soviet state.

The Colby note[54] was the most expressive and fundamental document of the State Department during the entire period of nonrecognition of the land of the Soviets. Two principal themes stood out through the whole message—abuse of the Soviet government and the notion of the territorial integrity of the Russian state. In Colby's estimation, "the existing regime in Russia is based upon the negation of every principle of honor and good faith, and every usage and convention, underlying the whole structure of international law; the negation, in short, of every principle upon which it is possible to base harmonious and trustful relations, whether of nations or of individuals." He ascribed to the Bolsheviks the fantastic statement that the very existence of Soviet power in Russia was dependent on the overthrow of the governments "in all other great civilized nations, including the United States." "The diplomatic service of the Bolshevist Government," warned the secretary of state, "would become a channel for intrigues and the propaganda of revolt against the institutions and the laws of countries, with which it was at peace, which would be an abuse of friendship to which enlightened governments cannot subject themselves." Needless to say, the history of Soviet relations with the bourgeois states up to that time had made these conclusions groundless.

Along with justification for the nonrecognition policy, the idea of Russia's territorial integrity occupies an important place in the note. Secretary Colby was prepared to exclude Finland, Poland (territory having a Polish population), and, with certain reservations, Armenia (where he still hoped to establish American influence) from a united Russia. Washington did not want to see Russia divided further, openly disapproving of the program of the Supreme Council of the Allies favoring independence for the Baltic States and the Caucasus, and the activities of the Japanese, who held under their military control a part of the Russian Far East. According to Vera Dean, Wilson "had opposed recognition of the independence of Estonia, Latvia, and Lithuania and had privately expressed the opinion that these countries would eventually be reincorporated into Russian territory."[55] As we know, the United States recognized the above-mentioned states only in July 1922. Wilson's government was even more opposed to a change in the status quo in the Far East. Recognizing as permanent the historic boundaries in that area, it did not want the Japanese or any other power coming forward with the notion of cutting into Russian territory.

We have noted already why the United States adhered to the position of the territorial integrity of Russia. There is no doubt that this aroused some interest on the part of the Soviet government, which perceived a certain difference between the approach of the United States and of the other imperialist nations to the problem of our borders. But in Colby's note even this idea, which was to some extent positive, bore a distinctly anti-Soviet character. During the course of the intervention and the Civil War, those in the ruling circles of the United States became at least partially aware of the great concern of our people about safeguarding the territorial and political integrity of their country. Especially instructive to the Americans was the experience of the Russian Far East, where the population demonstrated that even being out of touch with the main centers and isolated amid the White Guards, when it found itself far distant from Moscow in the full sense of the word, it did not conceive of any existence except as part of the united family of the peoples of our country. The Americans saw that one of the reasons for the victory of the Bolsheviks was that the peoples of Russia found in them their most national party. Bainbridge Colby decided to "deprive" the Communists of this sort of popular support. "Thus only," he reasoned, "can the Bolshevist regime be deprived of its false, but effective, appeal to Russian nationalism and compelled to meet the inevitable challenge of reason and self-respect which the Russian people, secure from invasion and territorial violation, are sure to address to a social philosophy that degrades them and a tyranny that oppresses them."

While Colby's note was a malicious anti-Soviet libel, in the part that concerned territory it did give official America a certain basis for claiming in the future that during Russia's difficult years it stood for the integrity of the Russian state and held back those who wanted to enrich themselves at the expense of Russian land. This is exactly what Franklin Roosevelt did when he told M. M. Litvinov in November 1933 that the United States had "protected" the Russian Far East from Japanese seizure during the first years of Soviet rule. Colby's note finalized the active interventionist work of the United States government in Soviet Russia and began a new phase of American policy in which the ruling circles counted mainly on the belief that, without American recognition, the Bolshevik regime would collapse, or at the very least decline in strength.

In carrying out its anti-Soviet policy Wilson's government received encouragement and support from many of the bourgeoisie, whose counterrevolutionary and interventionist attitudes often went even farther than the official steps taken by the president. With few exceptions, the press was resolutely against the Soviets. A flood of calumny was directed against revolutionary Russia, including the assertion that women had become public property. Among the most active enemies of Soviet Russia was the National Civic Federation, including a wide spectrum of reactionaries and conservatives, from the biggest monopolists to trade-union bureaucrats. The Zionists, who had earlier been in favor of the "Russian democracy," also joined the anti-Soviet chorus. Louis Marshall, president of the American Jewish Committee, declared: "Everything that real Bolshevism stands for is to the Jew detestable."[56]

The expression of bellicose anti-Soviet views was in fashion in the Congress. Talk about "a state of war" between Russia and the United States was frequently heard on Capitol Hill, although the White House and the State Department tried their best to avoid such "harsh" words because they did not fit in with the liberal camouflage used to cover the armed intervention. On 14 January 1919 Senator Charles S. Thomas of Colorado asserted in a devastating speech that "Bolsheviki long ago declared war against us," that "Russia is the center from which all Governments are being attacked."[57] Senator Porter J. MacCumber of North Dakota went farthest in bellicose appeals, proposing on 14 February that the president increase the American army in Russia to 500,000 men in order to "liberate" the Russian people "from the assassins who now hold them in subjection."[58] On 3 March, when Kolchak was beginning his attack, he repeated his appeal, urging that the interventionist army be brought up to a strength of half a million.[59]

To be sure, other voices were also heard within the walls of the Capitol. Senator Hiram Johnson of California on 12 December 1918 introduced a resolution in which he pointed out that there existed a "state of war" between Russia and the United States without the sanction of Congress and demanded that the the secretary of state provide the Senate, "if not incompatible with the public interest," all of the information on the basis of which the American government had sent troops into Russia.[60] On 7 January 1919, another very prestigious senator, Robert M. LaFollette of Wisconsin, declared that "the Congress and the country ought to know why we are making war upon the Russian people."[61] And on 9 January Senator William Borah of Idaho warned the White House, "If we ever go into Russia to set up a government by force we will leave millions of our boys in nameless graves, bankrupt our Treasury, and in the end come out something as Napolean did." He spoke out in the spirit of peaceful coexistence: "I take the position that the Russian people have the same right to establish a socialistic state as we have to establish a Republic."[62]

Revolutionarily and progressively inclined Americans, together with some liberals and even a few conservatives, spoke out against intervention and for recognition of and friendly cooperation with Soviet Russia.[63] Naturally the revolutionary sections of the American working class and intelligentsia hailed the Socialist Revolution in Russia with special warmth. Most of the socialists spoke out in defense of our revolution and fought resolutely against the intervention. With the appearance of the Communist party in the United States in 1919 there arose the most steadfast center for the struggle for Soviet-American rapprochement, for friendship between our peoples. *Ten Days that Shook the World*, a book written by John Reed, the founder of the Communist party in the United States, played a leading role in exposing misinformation about Soviet Russia, and propagandizing for the great humanism of the Socialist Revolution. The eminent American publicist and writer, Lincoln Steffens, also did a lot to disseminate the truth about the Soviet state.

Still another staunch friend of Soviet Russia was Eugene V. Debs, who found himself in prison shortly after the Russian Revolution for having spoken out against the imperialist war. "Eugene Debs and

John Reed," writes a biographer of Debs, "found common cause in their belief in the Bolshevik Revolution."[64] In the election campaign of 1920 Debs told the Socialists: "I heartily support the Russian Revolution without reservation."[65] Although he did not agree in all matters with the Bolsheviks, he remained to the end on the side of the Revolution. In December 1922 he had this to say about the Bolsheviks: "For five years they have stood with more than Spartan courage against the foul assaults of the whole criminal capitalist world.... The Russian Republic stands triumphant, gloriously triumphant on its fifth anniversary, a beacon light of hope and promise to all mankind!"[66]

Refuting slanderous statements made about the revolution in Russia, Norman Thomas, the future leader of the American Socialists, wrote in a pacifist magazine, *The World Tomorrow*, in September 1918, "The truth is that Russia is now in the process of working out the most significant social experiment since the French Revolution. In the Soviet form of government she has made a unique contribution to the organization of the political state. But that is the smaller part of the story. Her great task is that she is striving to secure economic democracy as a basis for the development of mankind."[67]

The AFL supported Wilson's policy toward Russia unconditionally. In his memoirs Samuel Gompers expresses regret that "all our efforts to prevent the second Russian revolution failed."[68] The AFL leaders, speaking in favor of the intervention, at the same time joined the campaign against the "Reds" in the ranks of their own trade unions. Nonetheless, at the congresses of the federation, the question invariably came up of putting an end to the intervention and recognizing Soviet Russia. Within the labor union movement sympathy for the Soviet state was greatest among the clothing workers' and ladies' garment workers' unions. Sidney Hillman, president of the Amalgamated Clothing Workers of America, a Russian emigrant, paid a visit to his former homeland and returned to the United States "full of enthusiasm for the workers' republic."[69] In 1920 a trade-union alliance for the establishment of trade relations with Russia was organized.[70]

Colonel Raymond Robins carried on a very active propaganda campaign in opposition to the anti-Soviet intervention, and tried to bring to the American public an understanding of the true significance of what had happened in Russia. He often appeared before bourgeois audiences, trying to persuade the business world and American statesmen to look at the Russian situation sensibly and without bias. Robins emphasized the hopelessness of military intervention as a means of struggle against the Revolution, appealing for positive action as a counterbalance to revolutionary ideas and a guarantee of preserving bourgeois values. In a speech before a group of businessmen in June 1919 he urged: "Against idea there must be idea. Against millennial plan there must be millennial plan. Against self-sacrifice to a dream there must be self-sacrifice to a higher and nobler dream."[71]

In general, the movement to put an end to the intervention and to recognize Soviet Russia took a great many organizational and political forms in the United States. It proved one of the real factors in ending the intervention and the blockade.

First Contacts

In the struggle against world imperialism the Soviet government did not make any distinctions in principle between the behavior of the ruling circles of the United States and their accomplices in the counter-revolutionary campaign. Soviet officials often spoke of President Wilson in uncomplimentary but accurate terms. Among the people, the impression that the Americans were interventionists also took root. In 1919 the most popular revolutionary poet, Vladimir Mayakovsky, would address the president of the United States as follows:

> I shall come to him,
>   I shall say to him:
>   "Wilson, . . . well,
>   Woodrow,
> Do you want a pailful of my blood?"[72]

All the same, the Soviet government had grounds for expecting that the ruling circles of the United States would not take so hostile a position as Germany, England, France, and Japan. This expectation stemmed from the fact that the American capitalists had less to lose than the British, French, or Belgians, that the United States had no territorial claims in Russia, as Germany and Japan did. In some measure the Soviet government relied on the unselfishness of the

Americans, and even more on their practicality and keen business sense. It expected that the United States would try to get trade going with Russia, seeing that the positions of her competitors were weakened.

As we have noted earlier, during the critical days of the ratification of the Brest-Litovsk peace treaty, the Soviet government did not rule out the possibility of turning for assistance to the United States if German aggression were to continue. In May 1918 the Supreme Council of National Economy's Committee on Foreign Trade worked out a plan for economic relations between Soviet Russia and the United States, which Lenin gave to Colonel Robins to take back home for the information of interested parties. The plan noted that "today and in the immediate future, after the conclusion of a general peace, Germany will have to yield its first place as provider of industrial and consumer goods to Russia. Another country, highly developed in capital but not so ravaged by war, will take its place. In the immediate future that country can ony be America."[73]

In spite of the fact that the United States had participated in the intervention, Lenin consistently moved toward establishing business relations between the two countries. When an American correspondent asked, "What is the position of the Soviet government with respect to an economic understanding with America?" he replied, "We are decidely for an economic understanding with America—with all countries, but *especially* with America."[74] It was to the Americans that Lenin addressed the first words he ever spoke directly about the coexistence of the two systems. In September 1919, replying to the question about peace and concessions from *Christian Science Monitor* correspondent Isaac McBride, the head of the Soviet government, explained: "A durable peace would be such a relief to the toiling masses of Russia that these masses would undoubtedly agree to certain concessions being granted. The granting of concessions under reasonable terms is also desirable for us, as one of the means of attracting into Russia the technical help of the countries which are more advanced in this respect, during the coexistence side by side of Socialist and capitalist states." At the same time, Lenin added that this should not be taken to mean a lessening of faith in the worldwide victory of socialism, emphasizing that "Soviet power will win the whole world."[75]

In February 1920 he told another American journalist, "Apparently some American entrepreneurs are beginning to understand that it makes more sense for them to conduct profitable business with Russia than to wage war against Russia, and this is a good sign. . . . I see no reason why a socialist state such as ours cannot have unlimited business relations with the capitalist countries."[76]

The Soviet government most often approached Washington with proposals for peace and an end to intervention, believing that if there was any chance at all of achieving these things, it was most likely to be found there. On 24 December 1918, M. M. Litvinov, the Soviet representative in Stockholm, sent a special note to Wilson. In it he took the occasion to inform the president: "In addition to the proposal for a general peace transmitted recently by the Soviet Government to the Allies, today I formally notified the ambassadors of the United States and of the Allies in Stockholm that I am empowered to enter into negotiations for the peaceful resolution of all questions that constitute reasons for hostile actions against Russia. The principles proclaimed by you as a possible basis for solving European problems, your open declarations of your effort and resolve to arrive at a settlement that meets the requirements of justice and humanity prompts me to send you the present observations, inasmuch as most of the points in your peace program fit into the more far-reaching and broader program of the Russian workers and peasants who are today the masters of their land."[77]

On 12 January 1919 an equally complex question was put to Lansing by Peoples' Commissar Georgi V. Chicherin. He asked why American troops remained on Russian territory, since the war with Germany had already ended. The United States government had to face up to its spurious explanations for the intervention. Actually, there was nothing to say in reply to Chicherin's question. "My bewilderment about the reasons for the presence of American troops in Russia," he wrote, "was shared by the American officers and soldiers, and we sometimes had occasion to hear expressions of this bewilderment directly from the men themselves. We pointed out to these Americans that their presence amounted to an attempt to reimpose on the Russian people the yoke of oppression which they had thrown off, and the result of this disclosure was entirely favorable to the good relations between us."[78] The American position was saved only by the fact that the

United States did not recognize the Soviet government and was therefore not obliged to make any answer to these embarrassing questions.

The Soviet government took one more important initiative in its efforts to normalize relations with the United States. In 1919 it appointed L. Martens its official representative in the United States. His behavior in America was more dynamic than that of Francis Dana had been in eighteenth-century Russia. Martens did not interfere in the internal affairs of the United States, nor break any of its laws and customs. As instructed by his government, he followed the line of establishing economic ties with interested American firms and individuals, and furnished information about economic and business conditions in Russia. In a memorandum to the State Department on 19 March 1919 he proposed "ending the present policy of boycotting Soviet Russia and establishing a material and cultural exchange program."[79] Martens' mission, however, met with a different fate from Dana's. It was obstructed in every way possible, including raids of his office by the police. Under such conditions of course, official recognition was completely out of the question.

After the arrival of Colby's August note, Martens' sojourn in the United States became even more difficult. The Department of Labor demanded his expulsion from the country, and he finally left the United States on instructions from Moscow. Ordering him to return home in December 1920, Chicherin wrote Martens: "Convey to the American people, especially the workers, the assurance of our unalterable goodwill, our gratitude for their many manifestations of sympathy and cooperation, and also tell them of our willingness to renew our historic friendly relations with all of the American people."[80]

Colby's note was to some degree a surprise to Moscow. Only a month earlier the United States had removed the barriers to trade with Russia. The anti-Soviet demarche of August set United States policy back to the worst times of the intervention. There was now no chance of normalizing relations while Wilson's administration was in power.

On 10 September 1920, the Soviet government replied to Colby's note in a telegram circulated among all its representatives abroad—an important document in the history of Soviet foreign policy.[81] In it Chicherin, with his characteristic aptness of expression, struck to the ground Colby's anti-Soviet scheme, and instructed all the diplomats to make a complete revelation of this malicious attack by the United

States. The peoples' commissar explained to the neophyte Soviet diplomats that Colby's note "constitutes a political attack on the policy and on the very system of Soviet Russia that is completely unprecedented in diplomatic experience." The circular telegram dealt with the key question of the correlation between the revolutionary movement abroad and the domestic policy of the Soviet state:

> The Soviet Government recognizes clearly enough that the revolutionary movement of the working masses in each country is their own affair and constitutes their own problem; that it should adhere steadfastly to the view that the communist system cannot be foisted on another people by means of force; and that the struggle to achieve it must take place through the efforts of the working masses of each country. Inasmuch as in America and in many other countries the working masses have not seized power and have not even been convinced of the necessity to seize it, the Russian Soviet Government considers it essential to establish and to maintain unswervingly peaceful relations with the existing governments of these countries.

In parrying the thrusts of Washington, the Soviet government did not assume an isolationist posture. Chicherin encouraged his colleagues to believe in the possibility of normalizing relations with the United States:

> Mr. Colby is very mistaken in his belief that our countries can only have normal relations if a capitalist system prevails in Russia. We hold, on the contrary, that it is essential to the interests of both Russia and North America to establish between them even now, despite the fact that their social and political systems are antithetical, the completely proper, lawful, peaceful, and friendly relations necessary for the development of commerce between them and for the satisfaction of the economic needs of both countries. The Russian government is convinced that not only the working masses but also the more farsighted representatives of the business circles of North America will reject the shortsighted policy, deleterious to America itself, which is expressed in Colby's note, and that in the future normal relations will be established between Russia and North America, *just as between Russia and Britain*, despite the profound opposition between their systems.

The Soviet government did not expect that the Democrats would normalize relations with the RSFSR before leaving the White House, but they did pin certain hopes on the new Republican administration. Chicherin said at the meeting of the Communist party members of the Congress of Soviets that the Republicans, "influenced by business considerations important to the capitalist circles, will most probably enter into trade relations with us."[82] During this period American business interest in operating concessions in Russia gathered momentum. In the fall of 1920 Washington Vanderlip arrived in Moscow to negotiate for concessions having in his mind far-reaching expansionist plans. Lenin assessed his proposals as follows: "Here we have an unblushing imperialism, which does not even consider it necessary to veil itself in any way because it thinks it is magnificent just as it is."[83] A plan was advanced on our part: a contract for concessions would go into effect only when de facto normal relations had been established between Russia and the United States, which must take place before 1 July 1921. Since this condition was not met, the agreement did not materialize. But under pressure from interested business circles, the Treasury Department and the Federal Reserve System on 20 December 1920 removed the ban on the export of currency to Russia, although it was still not permitted to accept Soviet gold in payment.

When in March 1921 the Republicans moved into the White House, the Soviet government considered it a suitable time to approach the Congress and President Warren Harding with a proposal for normalizing relations. Washington did not delay in making its reply. On 25 March 1921 Secretary of State Charles Evans Hughes sent a telegram to Maxim Litvinov through the American consul in Revel, in which our modest proposal for trade was rejected on two counts: in the first place, Russia had nothing to trade with, and second, before having the audacity to talk about trade with America, the Soviets would have to make "fundamental changes" in their views concerning property.

Now the Republicans, too, had expressed themselves officially on the Russian question. In general they followed the course outlined by the Democrats: relations could be normalized only with the restoration of capitalism. This was a shortsighted policy even from the standpoint of the commercial economic interests of the United States. The businessmen who were interested in Russian trade did not regard Secretary of State Hughes as one of them. They brought pressure to bear on Secretary of Commerce Herbert Hoover, who was closer to commercial and industrial circles. Hoover protested officially to the State Department, pointing out that it was repeating its prewar error by allowing trade with Russia to be handled by Germany. He insisted on trade without German mediation, through direct American financial transactions, and fought for economic expansion in Russia, for the "installation of American technology in Russian industries."[84] But blind hatred of the Soviet system and lack of faith in the economic potential of the new Russia prevented him, also, from taking a sensible view of the prospects for American-Soviet relations.

The years 1921–22 are notable for increased American activity in Soviet Russia in connection with the drought and famine in the Volga region. The American people reacted with compassion to the misfortune that befell Russia, worn out by wars and foreign invasion. An extensive movement to help the starving population of our country got under way in the United States. Official agencies also took part in these activities. The undertaking had many aspects, all of which should be considered in evaluating it.

The chairman of the American Relief Administration (ARA), Herbert Hoover, and his associates, reflecting the point of view of those who earlier had organized the intervention, blockade, and boycott of revolutionary Russia, believed that the moment had come to exert real political pressure on the Soviets, to intervene in Russian affairs and achieve what they had been unable to accomplish through military means: to weaken Soviet authority, alienate the people from it, and restore the bourgeois order. But within the campaign for relief to Russia there were also many whose motivation was exactly the opposite: namely, to help the Soviet government. This was the position of the popular relief movement, which reached an impressive scope, and also unmasked the anti-Soviet intentions of Herbert Hoover. The "Friends of Soviet Russia" organization announced that its slogan was "famine relief without counterrevolutionary conditions," and that its principle was "to give without imposing imperialist and reactionary conditions as do Hoover and others."[85] The progressive forces of the country realized that Hoover's policy was not his personal policy but a reflection of the anti-Soviet intentions of the ruling circles. In the appeal of one of the leftist organizations it was emphasized that "The policy of Hoover is the policy of the American government."[86]

Along with the counterrevolutionary considerations at the top level, one other important point that is usually overlooked in the works of American authors is the economic interest American farmers had in sending Russia some of the reserves of their agricultural produce, which under conditions of crisis and depression might help to raise prices. Benjamin C. Marsh, one of the leaders of the National Farmers' Union, consistently expressed this point of view in his letters to Herbert Hoover and in public appearances, explaining that help to starving Russia would relieve "the tragic condition of our farmers."[87] He condemned Hoover for not being interested in the fate of American farmers. At the same time, Marsh noted that Hoover was trying, through the activities of the ARA, "to kill the Soviet government."[88] This observation is especially important inasmuch as it was made by an enemy of Soviet power who believed, as did Hoover himself, that American aid would help the Russians to "see the futility of the Soviet system of government."[89]

The Soviet government, although it found itself in exceptionally difficult circumstances, did not move in the direction of any concessions of a political nature. Knowing Herbert Hoover for what he was, it told the leaders of the ARA very plainly that in rendering relief to the starving they must refrain from any interference in the internal affairs of Russia. Under these conditions an agreement was concluded in Riga by Litvinov and Walter Lyman Brown, ARA director for Europe, on 20 August 1921. Occasionally conflicts arose between the ARA and the Soviet authorities. For example, when the active White Guard Arzamasov, one of the chief workers for the ARA in Tsaritsyn, was arrested, Colonel William N. Haskell, director of the ARA in Russia, sent a letter to the representative of the government of the RSFSR which showed the kind of language that was sometimes used by the relief organizers: "In view of all the above I have authorized Mr. Bowden, District Supervisor at Tzaritzin, to use his judgment as to what particular section of the Tzaritzin government shall receive relief supplies. I am not inclined to insist that he shall feed the city of Tzaritzin if in his judgment on the ground he has reason to believe that the local authorities are injecting political matters in the relief work there. There are so many people to be fed in Russia that I can find many places to use that part of our relief supplies which were originally intended to be distributed in the city of Tzaritzin."[90]

But threats of this sort were unusual. On the whole, the Americans realized that they were dealing with an established authority. James P. Goodrich, the former governor of Indiana, in April 1922 informed Herbert Hoover from Russia that "at this moment there is no hope of a counterrevolution or of any sudden change in the government."[91]

Although the dark political aspects of the activity of the ARA in Russia should not be disregarded, they are less important than the fact that assistance was rendered to the starving population of our country. The value of the goods sent to Russia through the ARA amounted to $62,000,000, including transportation costs. Of this sum, $14,000,000 was covered by the Soviet government. Furthermore, about $5,000,000 came to the ARA from other organizations acting separately. It must be noted that even the United States government, which did not recognize the RSFSR, appropriated $20,000,000 and turned this sum over to the ARA. When the activity of the American services working for famine relief in Russia was at its height (August 1922) as many as 10,000,000 people were involved.[92] The Soviet people and the Soviet government reacted to this assistance with gratitude. On 22 November 1922 Lenin received Haskell as his guest before the latter left for the United States and officially expressed the gratitude of the Soviet people and government to the American people. He was very interested to learn from Haskell of Herbert Hoover's intention to visit Russia and become acquainted at first hand with the conditions of her economy. On Lenin's instructions a letter was even sent to the secretary of commerce expressing positive reaction to Hoover's proposed visit. In accordance with a resolution of the Soviet of Peoples' Commissars of the USSR a letter was sent to Hoover on 10 July 1923, expressing gratitude for the assistance rendered the Soviet people.

In the early 1920s a campaign developed among American workers, farmers, and intelligentsia to extend technological and economic help to the USSR. A Society for Technical Aid for Soviet Russia was organized, and in 1921 it included 10,000 members. On 22 June 1921 the government of the RSFSR adopted a resolution "concerning American industrial emigration" which encouraged American technical assistance groups to come to Russia, but subject to certain conditions. The government feared that individual Americans, carried away by fleeting romantic enthusiasm, might recoil and be disillusioned when they encountered the practical difficulties in Russia. Chicherin was particularly skeptical about this kind of aid.[93] But Lenin enthusiastically supported the American initiative, stipulating, however, that all those coming in must understand in full measure beforehand the difficulties they would be facing.

The leaders of most of the American groups that arrived were Communists—William Haywood, S. Rutgers (a Dutchman), and others. An especially large undertaking in which American workers gave technological assistance to Soviet Russia was the organization and work of the "autonomous industrial colony of the Kuzbass," which functioned from 1921 to 1927.[94] Of course, the significance of all of these groups in the economic development of the Soviet state during the 1920s should not be exaggerated. The government of the USSR took a sensible view of their potential, did not encourage mass immigration, and repeatedly declared that it was desirable to have only a small number of well-organized bodies of production workers come to our country.

In the matter of concessions things developed somewhat differently, but the result was equally modest. The Soviets, for their part, were little concerned about the possible disappointment of American businessmen in the socialist system but took into account that a concessionaire would be active only under conditions that brought him profit. It tried to create a mutually beneficial situation. On 2 November 1921 the first concessional agreement was signed in Moscow between the Soviet government and the American United Medical and Pharmaceutical Company for the exploitation of asbestos deposits in the Urals. The first concessionaires were Armand Hammer and B. Mishel. Among the other American concessionaires, we should mention Averell Harriman, who engaged in exploitation of the Chiatura manganese mines in the Caucasus.

The Russian Far East, which from April 1920 till November 1922 saw the establishment of the Far Eastern Republic (FER), a buffer state friendly to the RSFSR, occupied a special place in Soviet-American relations during that period. The FER government included not only Bolsheviks but also representatives of petty bourgeois parties. American policy toward the Far Eastern Republic was fundamentally contradictory. Realizing that the Far Eastern Republic was not separated from the RSFSR by a Great Wall of China, the United States did not want to establish normal diplomatic relations with it. It persisted in the hope that the Socialist Revolutionary and Menshevik elements would gain the upper hand in Transbaikalia. If fundamental changes were to take place in Eastern Siberia, it would suit the United States completely, but only the Japanese were capable of "changing" the situation, and their presence promised nothing good for the Americans. This was the reason for the vacillation in American policy. The Americans recognized the Far Eastern Republic de facto; they sent to Chita, its capital, their consul, John K. Caldwell, and received in Washington the FER representative, B. E. Skvirsky, as well as a special trade delegation headed by A. A. Yazykov.

The ambivalence of American policy was evident at the time of the Washington conference of 1921-22. The United States did not permit either the RSFSR or the FER to attend the conference. The organizers of the conference took it upon themselves to be the "moral representatives" of the Russian people. The government of the RSFSR twice protested the discussion of Pacific problems without its participation and registered a special protest about consideration of the question of the Chinese Eastern Railway which concerned China and Russia exclusively.

But the United States government did not break relations with the FER, hoping to influence the course of events in Siberia. When the FER delegation arrived in Washington, it was received by the State Department. The contradictions in the United States position are obvious also if one analyzes the American attitude toward the Japanese occupation of the Russian Maritime Provinces. The Harding administration was opposed to any increase of Japanese influence there, but at the conference it restricted itself to simply including in the protocol an expression of its hostility to seizures of territory in Siberia.

The destinies of the Far East and Russia were decided by the Soviet people themselves, who by the end of 1922 had driven the last of the interventionists from within the boundaries of their country. The reliance of the Americans on a separate bourgeois Siberia as the prototype of the future united Russia, and the plans of the Japanese to seize the coastal region failed once and for all. By a resolution of the Peoples' Congress of the Far Eastern Republic on 14 November 1922, power was turned over to the Soviets, while the republic itself became part of the RSFSR. Skvirsky, who remained in Washington, became a representative of the interests of the RSFSR.

A notable chapter in Russian-American relations during the period in question were the negotiations about the possibility of sending to Moscow an American commission of inquiry following the failure of efforts to foist unacceptable economic conditions on us at the Genoa and Hague conferences. Although the United States did not take part in the conferences, it exerted considerable effort to see that they failed. Immediately after the end of the Hague conference an unofficial inquiry reached Moscow from the United States—under what conditions would it be possible to start negotiations on the reestablishment of business connections, and could the Americans depend on the reception in Russia of an American commission of experts?[95] This inquiry masked goals which were by this time familiar: to try to change the Russian situation by nonmilitary means, to secure a predominant position in the Russian economy, to squeeze out competitors, particularly the British and the Germans.

But the ruling circles in the United States had still not grasped that the Soviet side would cooperate only on an equal basis. The general principles of the reply to the United States government were set forth publicly by L. M. Karakhan, assistant to the peoples' commissar for foreign affairs, in an interview with a correspondent for the *New York Times* on 19 August 1922. He said, "Our government has no objections to individual American businessmen and business groups coming to Russia under general conditions for negotiations on economic matters. As for some special commission of experts or a commission of inquiry coming here, such a commission can be admitted only on condition that our representatives would be admitted to America on a mutual basis for an investigation of the American market. In general, we would welcome in every possible way the beginning of trade negotiations with the American government."[96] The Soviet government maintained this position also in the negotiations in Germany between the United States ambassador, Alanson B. Houghton, and Chicherin, who was undergoing medical treatment there. The Americans were offended at the proposal that the two sides negotiate as equals, and on 18 September 1922 broke off the negotiations on the basis of the alleged "Soviet refusal."[97] There was really nothing at which to be offended. The behavior of the Soviet government was irreproachably correct. "The Soviet government," read the answer from Moscow, "would be extremely receptive to any measure whatsoever based on mutuality that would permit each country to become acquainted with the economic situation of the other. But precisely because the Soviet government is striving to establish stable relations with America, it cannot regard a unilateral visit to Russia by an American commission of inquiry as a proper step. It is perfectly obvious that Russian public opinion would regard such a unilateral arrangement as incompatible with the principle of the equality of the two sides, and by this very fact attitudes would be created that would be harmful to the stability of future relations.''[98]

Some high government figures in Washington realized this also. James Goodrich, a member of the National Committee of the Republican Party, and a proponent of recognition of the RSFSR, proposed another version of mutual exchange of commissions which was acceptable to the Soviet side, and which posed no difficulties for the United States government inasmuch as it was based on the principle of equality. But the plan of the ex-governor of Indiana did not receive support in Washington.[99]

Such is a brief sketch of the complex and strained course of Soviet-American relations during the first five years following the Revolution. It is easy to see that they were rather active. The Soviet authorities were working out socialist principles of foreign policy, of peaceful co-existence between countries with different socioeconomic systems, and applying them in their relations with the United States.

The ruling circles of the United States were also active in their relations with Soviet Russia, so active that they did not refrain from the use of force. But this activity was fundamentally negative. And this accounts for the fact that the Americans did not achieve anything in Russia and spoiled their relations with our country for many years to come.

3

The Road to Recognition of the USSR

Political Relations

By the mid-1920s the Soviet people had restored the economy to its prewar level, and the Bolshevik party, implementing the New Economic Policy, brought to the fore the problem of socialist reconstruction. At the Fourteenth Congress of the Soviet Communist Party in December 1925 a program of socialist industrialization was adopted, the fulfillment of which ensured the reconstruction of the entire national economy along socialist lines and the building of a socialist society in the USSR. Two years later, in December 1927, at the Fifteenth Party Congress, a decision to begin the collectivization of agriculture was approved, and directives for drawing up the first Five-Year Plan were worked out.

The policy of building socialism encountered bitter opposition from the remnants of the classes that had been overthrown. Within the Bolshevik party itself there arose mixed opposition to the socialist policy, which eventually rallied around the ideological banner of Trotskyism. During the period of the Civil War and the intervention, the Trotskyists were redeemed by their revolutionary verbiage. Now, when the socialist reconstruction of the country became the order of the day, the counterrevolutionary nature of Trotskyism immediately rose to the surface. At the Fifteenth Congress Joseph Stalin made the accurate determination of what separated the Trotskyist opposition and the party; namely, the question of whether the victorious building of socialism in the USSR was possible.[1] The opposition—Trotsky, Zinoviev, Kamenev, and others—answered in the negative.

This was deleterious in two respects: the Trotskyist-Zinovievist bloc, which was still influential in the party, was sowing the seeds of capitulation and at the same time was giving foreign bourgeois propaganda grounds for accusing the USSR of unleashing "world revolution," for the idea of the opposition was built on the notion that socialism was impossible in our country without revolution in the West. It was not by chance that the enemies of socialism took Trotskyism under their wing, representing it as something "international," as opposed to the party's "national" policy of socialist construction.[2]

The Soviet peoples also regarded the construction of socialism as the paramount international revolutionary question, the solution of which would at the same time correspond to the basic aspirations of our own country. At one more turning point in history, the organic revolutionary unity of the national and international goals of the working class and of all workers was demonstrated once again.

To achieve all of this, peace was required. Having a profound interest in peace, the USSR was a major factor for peace. At the Fourteenth Party Congress, Stalin stated that in place of a period of war, "a certain period of 'peaceful coexistence'" had been established.[3] Beginning in 1924 the leading capitalist powers had started to recognize the USSR. Referring ironically to the United States, Stalin noted: "I think that America is the only one of the big countries that has not done so."[4] The USSR advanced a program of active commercial cooperation with the capitalist countries. Along with this, our country persistently sought to conclude nonaggression pacts with all of its neighbors and nearby nations. In the mid-1920s the USSR was already recognized as a leader in this campaign.

But peace in the 1920s was an unstable peace. Under these circumstances the government of the USSR sought in every way possible to secure recognition of the principles of nonaggression and peaceful coexistence. The idea of peaceful coexistence underwent further theoretical development and was put into practice in specific political ways. In a letter to the plenipotentiary in Rome, which is fundamental to the analysis of Soviet foreign policy during those years, Chicherin explained that "inasmuch as we have to maintain friendly relations with nations that differ from us socioeconomically and have different parties at the head of their governments, we base these friendly relations on practical interests, commercial or otherwise. This does not alter our social and political nature, nor the nature of the one with whom we are contracting. . . . This behavior on our part is in no way at variance with our program and our views. We merely remain within the limits of that practical, real area in which it is indispensable for us to be on good terms with the capitalist governments."[5]

At the International Economic Conference in Geneva the Soviet representative made the following announcement on 23 May 1927:

An important question has been put before the conference: the question of the establishment of the principle of peaceful coexistence of two unlike economic systems: the socialist system in the USSR, and the capitalist system in other countries. The Soviet delegation has enunciated this formula—an inescapable practical formula, stemming from the objective fact of the existence and interdependence of the world economic system. In enunciating this formula we were in no sense, even in part, repudiating any of the principles of our socialist system; it was not without purpose that we spoke of the existence of two different, two opposite economic systems. Has the conference taken any step toward the practical realization of the formula proposed by us? Yes, such a step has been taken, and this constitutes one of the achievements of the present conference. The step taken, like many others, is not decisive enough, but the resolution on this subject reflects this idea clearly.[6]

Through the efforts of the USSR, the idea of a peaceful coexistence thus took its place in the code of international law. Even under the aggravated international conditions of 1927, Joseph Stalin, in his report at the Fifteenth Party Congress, emphasized that "Our relations with the capitalist countries are based on the assumption that the coexistence of two opposite systems is possible. Practice has fully confirmed this."[7]

During the 1920s it was convincingly confirmed that peaceful coexistence is not an idyll in the interrelations between capitalism and socialism, but coexistence under circumstances of bitter class struggle in different forms. Two forms of stabilization—the socialist and capitalist—were the two directions that the class struggle had taken on the international scale, and the results in this stage of history were summed up toward the end of the decade.

Toward the United States, the policy of the Soviet state remained as it had been in the past. We were trying to attain recognition, and on this subject Maxim Litvinov said quite frankly on 10 December 1928 at the session of the Central Executive Committee of the USSR: "We have never concealed our regret at the absence of official relations between us and the trans-Atlantic republic with which we have no conflicts and foresee none."[8] During these years no one in the United States dreamed of anti-Soviet intervention. There were no essential conflicts between the two countries. At the 1927 Geneva conference the positions of the USSR and the United States on the matter of peaceful coexistence even proved to be very close. Commenting on the results of the conference, Professor Brynjolf J. Hovde of the University of Pittsburgh pointed with approval to the fact: "A strange spectacle was presented when the American delegates assisted the Soviet delegates to secure the adoption of a resolution admitting the possibility of a capitalistic and a communistic system existing side by side."[9]

Nonetheless, all efforts by the Soviet government to establish official relations were met with hostility on the part of the Americans. Wallowing in an orgy of prosperity, the American bourgeoisie came to believe that it was at the epicenter of world events, that all economic, social, political, and moral-ethical problems could be solved through the profitable functioning of the American system of rugged individualism. They hoped to correct the sinful "deviation" of the Russians from "normalcy" (and the slogan "back to normalcy" was the motto of the Republicans in the 1920 elections), from the habitual historical course, in a casual manner, having shown that Henry Ford had won a victory over Marx. And the specific array of conflicts among the imperalist powers during the twenties was such that the USSR did not represent a strong and necessary unit in the American conception of the balance of power.

Individual Soviet diplomats at first even got the impression that the United States was putting an end to its attacks on the USSR and might turn in our direction. It was not by chance that Litvinov in a letter on 13 January 1923 set Skvirsky straight: "Your information is very interesting, although unfortunately I cannot subscribe to your conclusion that a change will come in the immediate future in the relations of the government of the United States with the Soviet republic. Unwarranted optimism is just as harmful as undue pessimism."[10] There were no grounds, indeed, for optimism, inasmuch as Secretary of State Charles Evans Hughes had made some harsh anti-Soviet statements in March and July 1923.

The presidential succession in the United States is an important international event. The Soviet government listened attentively to hear what Calvin Coolidge would say about Russia, taking into account that he said very little in general, and trying not to let anything that he might say slip past them. In his first annual message to Congress on 6 December 1923, he expressed himself on the Russian question essentially in the same spirit as Secretary of State Hughes. He assured anti-Soviet circles that his government did not propose "to enter into relations with another regime which refuses to recognize the sanctity of international obligations. I do not propose to barter away for the privilege of trade any of the cherished rights of humanity. I do not propose to make merchandise of any American principle." All the same, the president raised the hopes, albeit in a moderate form, of both himself and of everyone else who in their assessment of Soviet affairs had already got into the habit of taking the wish for the reality: "Already encouraging evidences of returning to the ancient ways of society can be detected. But more are needed." When this has taken place "our country ought to be the first to go to the economic and moral rescue of Russia." Giving himself up to unwarranted optimism, the captain of the "rescue team" added that already "the time is near at hand when we can act."[11]

All the same, the Soviet government decided that in Coolidge's message there was some glimmer of a new approach to the USSR, a tendency to smooth over the excesses of Hughes' lexicon, and it addressed to the president on 16 December 1923 an expression of "its complete readiness to discuss jointly with your government all of the matters touched upon in your message, the foundation of these negotiations being the principle of mutual noninterference in the internal affairs of the other party." The government of the USSR offered to settle the question of monetary claims as well, "assuming, of course, that the settlement would be based on the principle of mutuality," that is, making it clear that there were claims we had against the United States.[12]

Hughes' reply followed, by way of the American consul in Revel on 18 December 1923. The proposals made by the USSR were rejected in an intolerably harsh form. Among the arguments adduced was that the Soviet government was repudiating the property rights of American citizens and refusing to compensate them, was not fulfilling its "obligations" to the United States, and, as the "most serious" argu-

ment, that it was conducting "propaganda to overthrow the institutions of this country."[13] According to Frederick Schuman, Hughes'
reply was "so curt and frank as to dispel completely all the illusory
hopes entertained in Moscow."[14] Hughes' slanderous attacks on
the USSR did not end with this. According to the testimony of a
high-ranking official in the East European division of the State
Department, that division "was largely occupied in supporting the
nonrecognition policy of Mr. Hughes."[15]

Hughes' anti-Soviet statement received a reasoned and harsh rebuff
from Chicherin, in *Izvestiya* on 26 September 1924.[16] The peoples'
commissar dwelled especially on unmasking the assertions that the
Soviet government was conducting subversive propaganda against the
United States through the Comintern. He pointed out, to begin
with, that the Communist party cannot be identified completely with
the Soviet government, and then emphasized that in the Comintern,
which is an international organization, "the Russian party is only one
of its many parts. Precisely for this reason any attempt to ascribe to
Soviet national bodies and their representatives abroad the role of
organs of the Comintern is a malicious, deliberate deception of the
uninformed public. Of course, the worker-peasant Soviet government
does express the will of the workers and of their party. In this lies its
radical difference from the right wing of the Republican Party and its
leader, Mr. Hughes, who express the will of the big bankers and trusts
of America. But from the fact that the Soviet government serves the
interests of the workers while Mr. Hughes and his government serve the
interests of capitalist magnates it does not follow that a compromise
between these governments is not possible. On the contrary, numerous facts give evidence that if they so desire, a compromise is entirely
possible."

The replacement of Hughes by Frank Kellogg in the position of
secretary of state in March 1925 was not regarded in the USSR as a sign
of change in American policy on the Soviet question, although the
departure of Hughes was viewed with relief. In the second half of the
1920s Moscow no longer addressed official proposals to Washington,
realizing clearly that this was hopeless. Secretary Kellogg continued
without change Hughes' anti-Soviet course, which Hughes in turn had
inherited from the Wilsonian Democrats. In January 1927 he accused
the USSR of efforts to establish a "Bolshevik hegemony" in Latin

America, using it as a base for subversive activity against the United States.[17] As should have been expected, this provoked sarcastic comments in Moscow. On 18 January 1927, Litvinov published a statement in which he said: "I will not be surprised if the enlightened statesmen of the great powers begin to attribute earthquakes in Japan and floods in America to 'intrigues' of the Bolsheviks. To refute these fantastic 'explanations' seriously would be to insult public opinion."[18] Like all earlier rebukes of American leaders with anti-Soviet leanings, this statement contained within it a constructive element, leaving the door constantly open for Soviet-American contacts.

A notable landmark in the Russian policy of the Republicans was a letter written by Kellogg on 23 February 1928 to Senator William M. Butler, the chairman of the National Committee of the Republican Party.[19] In reply to a proposal to analyze this policy over the past four years, Kellogg reiterated all the dogmas of those who were opposed to recognizing the USSR. He pointed out that it was impossible to establish ties with the Soviet government since it was controlled by "a group who hold it as their mission to bring about the overthrow of the existing political, economic and social order throughout the world and who regulate their conduct towards other nations accordingly."

The ruling circles of the United States armed themselves with a great number of doctrines hostile to the USSR, some of which came from the ideological and political package of the intervention period,[20] others arose later. Among the beliefs that went back to pre-Republican times the most important were that the Soviet regime maintained itself through force, did not keep its agreements, carried on subversive propaganda against the United States, had deprived American citizens of property unlawfully, and did not recognize debts incurred under the old regime. The Republican administration introduced two new assertions. At first the leading figures in the United States asserted that the USSR was an economic vacuum, but toward the end of the decade they declared that trade with the Soviet Union would develop more successfully without recognition than if it were recognized, for the Russians, stimulated by the expectation of recognition in the future, would supposedly strive toward it at any price and would thereby expand opportunities for American export.

Of all these, only two had any real validity: that of the confiscation of American property in Russia, and that of the liquidation of prerevolutionary debts. As history has taught us, revolutions are not accomplished with the permission of the authorities. Because of this historical law, Americans, of course, did lose some of their investments. But here some qualification is necessary. With the normalization of relations, the Soviet government was prepared to discuss claims to material losses under certain conditions. Russian counterclaims had to be taken into account—for there was a debt to be paid for intervention, also. However, the "economic legitimism" of Calvin Coolidge precluded the possibility of presenting any Soviet claims to the United States; moreover, the Republican "new Calvinism,"[21] in general, proceeded from the assumption that in the postwar economic, political, and moral world only the Americans could make demands while only others were obliged to respond. For the ruling circles, the intervention, in its material manifestation, took the form of a twofold loss: first they threw away four billion dollars for nothing, and then they had to answer the claims for damages of the government that had withstood their attacks. But this was a good lesson of history which, after all, is important to world civilization and is not to be had free of charge. As for trade without recognition, official Washington relied on the fact that the USSR was striving to attain recognition and improvement in trade conditions; its mistake was in raising this to an absolute assumption.

Beginning in the mid-1920s there were three main nonrecognition doctrines in the political arsenal—hostile Soviet propaganda on United States territory, confiscation of American property, and nonpayment of debts.[22] The first was obviously unfounded, and the other two could at any time have become subjects of constructive negotiations. But something more fundamental lay behind these empty doctrines: the "Calvinists" were swaggering; some felt that nonrecognition would hasten the reform of the Soviet system, while others attached no essential importance to the existence of any kind of Soviet Union, when there were more important and interesting things going on at the stock exchange.

The anti-Soviet emigrés contributed as much as they could to justifying the policy of hostility, sometimes coming up with added arguments as "people in the know," taking advantage of the fact that at that time there was only a handful of homegrown specialists in Sovietology. Prominent among the latter was University of Chicago professor Samuel Harper, who passed along an intricate route from supporting the authenticity of the "Sisson documents" to becoming a firm advocate of Soviet-American cooperation during the thirties and forties. Knowing of his connections with the State Department, which always consulted him, the emigrés tried their best to influence him in an anti-Soviet direction. In a letter of 18 January 1924, reviling the policy of Lloyd George on the Soviet question, the emigré G. Alex-eieef wrote: "Now if America began to trade in principles, we would have to recognize that not only Europe but America, as well, would rot through. So far, the statements of your Secretary of State convince us that your country, thank God, is in good health."[23]

The American propagandists developed their own peculiar clichés concerning the Russia of the NEP. Any shortcoming in Soviet life, whether real or imagined, was added to the collection of arguments about the inevitable collapse of Soviet power; all achievements—and gradually it became necessary to speak of these—were presented as justifications for the assertion that capitalism was reemerging in Soviet society, for socialism and achievements were still regarded as mutually exclusive phenomena. In this connection, the prophecy of collapse was connected with one opposition force (the Trotskyist), while the reemergence of capitalism was connected with another, the right-wing deviation of the party. "I am inclined to believe," wrote Alexeieef to Samuel Harper, "that the longer the NEP lasts and the larger the class of the new bourgeoisie becomes, the nearer is the end of the Bolsheviks. The process is clear, but it is absolutely impossible to reckon its length; it may be soon and it may not be for years."[24] Former ambassador B. A. Bakhmet'ev suggested to Harper in March 1925, that "a political NEP" is expected in the USSR, that is, a political regeneration.[25] Reflecting the opinion of the White emigrés and wider anti-Soviet circles, Bakhmet'ev was especially cheered at the news of the activization of the right wing, regarding it as "equivalent to a Thermidor." In a letter on 15 April 1929 he predicted that "with Stalin gone, outwardly bolshevism will continue, but it will be bolshevism without backbone. The forces of life will begin to assert themselves until a time when their advance may be translated into political change. As you see I attach a great importance to this Right slant."[26]

Since we have opened the subject of the Russian postrevolutionary emigration, we should say that the wave of emigration did not reach the United States at once. Those active in working against the Soviet government remained closer to the borders of the USSR; the more practical, so to speak, people who had not dreamed of intervention went to America. A sociological survey of Russian exiles conducted by a professor at a Los Angeles college in the late twenties showed that they were living in reduced circumstances, but tolerably enough so that in answer to the question, "What do you miss most in Amerca?" they answered only with the traditional Russian sigh, while the question, "What things do you like best in America?" they reacted with a mass of enthusiastic statements. Anna Kegeler, for example, along with her natural emotions about the parents and children she had left behind in her native land, also expressed her social feelings because of "money which I losted (*sic*) after the revolution in Russia."[27] Glafira Nasedkin, whose first husband had been a colonel in the czarist army, expressed herself perhaps most tellingly of all. With staggering feminine logic, her reply to the first of the above questions was "Servants!" and to the second, "Equality."[28]

In formulating their policy toward the USSR the Republicans of the twenties proved unable to look into the immediate future or even to make a sensible evaluation of the present. The 1929–33 depression, the effect of which was intensified by fundamental changes in the whole international situation, was still in the future. Proceeding as usual, they resorted to "reliable" old standbys like assertions about subversive Soviet propaganda against the United States. These and other anti-Soviet charges were frequently made in Congress, in the press, and in public political life as a whole. Senator Henry Cabot Lodge, for example, in an appearance on 21 February 1923, gave the following arguments against recognition: the Soviet government wants "to overthrow all capitalist governments," demonstrably does not honor its agreements, and violates the unalterable principle of private property.[29] Similar tirades were heard in Congress at the end of the decade, long after Lodge was dead.

There was also some agitation in favor of recognizing the USSR, but it was not very active. In its vanguard, as usual, were the Communists, the left-wing Socialists, the radical intelligentsia, the progressive trade unions. Certain political figures, clergymen, and representatives of the business world took part. The most prominent figure in the campaign for recognition was, of course, Senator William Borah. Between May

1922 and March 1933 he introduced in the Senate seven resolutions concering the establishment of diplomatic relations with the Soviet Union.[30] In response, the dyed-in-the-wool reactionaries three times accused him of being a paid agent of Moscow.[31] Official propaganda was unable to refute Borah's statement on 20 December 1923 that the Soviet government "either directly or indirectly" had *not* undertaken "any attempt to overthrow the American Government."[32]

Trade without Recognition

Such processes as the development of trade and the expansion of business and cultural connections between the two countries proved to be more productive along the road to recognition of the USSR. In the middle and during the second half of the 1920s Soviet-American commercial-economic relations were in the making.[33] The turning point became apparent in 1923–24, when a number of Soviet foreign-trade organizations were incorporated in the United States, in accordance with corporate law. The most important of these was Amtorg, created in 1924 in New York and active to the present day.

At the very beginning, Soviet-American trade consisted almost entirely of a limited volume of wheat, foodstuffs, and footwear exported by the United States. By 1924 cotton, metals, different kinds of industrial equipment, farm machinery, and automobiles were the predominant American products imported by the USSR. This reflected an evolution in the requirements of the Soviet economy during the restoration of the national economy and the transition to the building of socialist industry and collective farming. With increased industrialization there was an especially noticeable rise in imports of machines and equipment. The United States moved into second place (after Germany) as a supplier of machinery to our country. The USSR was fourth among the purchasers of American industrial equipment. The chief exports from the USSR to the United States were raw materials—furs, gut, bristle, flax, mushrooms, licorice, manganese ore.

The growth of Soviet-American trade was hampered by a number of major obstacles. One of these was that the USSR in those years did not have large reserves of currency. But taken by itself, this was still not a great obstacle, for the solvency of the Soviet foreign-trade organizations was unquestioned. The problem was that in the absence of official negotiating relations, American businessmen were unwilling to give Soviet contractors credit in the proper volume and under normal conditions. Furthermore, government agencies, which generally did not interfere very much in the growth of trade, sometimes put obstacles in its way; they banned the acceptance of Soviet gold in payment, asserted publicly that Soviet trade organs were engaged in anti-American propaganda, and so on. Business drew two conclusions from this: the opponents of trade shut themselves off more completely from the Soviet market, while those who did engage in trade demanded a higher interest rate in granting credit. Skvirsky mentioned this in his report to the Peoples' Commissariat for Foreign Affairs on 6 August 1925, at the same time pointing out as a "negative factor in all credit negotiations carried on by our responsible trade representative here" a "relative lack of coordination among our organizations, especially on the part of members of different organizations who come here from time to time."[34]

In the second half of the twenties there were noticeable changes for the better in Soviet-American trade. This was because American business saw in the Soviet trade organizations a permanent and dependable partner; because wider business circles at large became less receptive to rumors about "Soviet propaganda"; and because the government of the United States itself, toward the end of the decade, began in essence to encourage trade, even though it was afraid that it would be condemned for this by the most violent enemies of the USSR.

An important event was the reorganization of the American-Russian Chamber of Commerce, which took place in June 1926. The implacable enemies of the Soviet Union, who earlier constituted the majority of its members, were now gone. The head of the new chamber of commerce was Reeve Schley, vice-president of the Chase National Bank. While it did not come out for recognition of the USSR, it began to promote the development of Soviet-American trade. Having been convinced that the Soviets could be relied on to fulfill their agreements, in 1927 some banks (the Chase National, the Equitable Trust Company) started to expand their financing of Soviet purchases. Conditions were exceptionally advantageous for creditors: credit was granted for two to three years at a very high interest rate—as high as 7.5 percent. Prices of industrial equipment purchased from the United

States were fixed articifically higher for the Russians during these years—from 10 to 50 percent.

In 1927 the tenth anniversary of the USSR was observed in various public circles in the United States. The journal *Current History* conducted a symposium on the subject, "Ten Years of Bolshevism," held under the banner of rapprochement with the Soviet Union. Peoples' Commissar A. I. Mikoyan appeared at the symposium with an article on the foreign trade of the USSR.[36] He explained the principle of state monopoly of foreign trade and stressed the reliability of Soviet trade organizations as partners. Urging expansion of Soviet-American trade, Mikoyan pointed out: "Business collaboration between these two great countries can assist the future growth of their economy."

In October 1928 Amtorg concluded an important agreement with General Electric. The company opened an account in the amount of $26,000,000 for six years, on condition that the money be spent on the purchase of machines and equipment from it. The president of General Electric announced that with the fulfillment of the obligations of the contract by both parties, his company would consider as settled all its claims against the USSR for property that had been nationalized, estimated by the damaged party as amounting to $1,750,000.[37] This made a great impression on both business and government circles. It gave an example of how it was possible to settle all questions of mutual material claims.

In general, during the years 1923–29 Soviet-American trade developed rather successfully. Starting from zero in 1919–20, export to the United States grew from two million rubles in fiscal year 1922–23 to 149 million rubles in 1929, while import from the United States, correspondingly, grew from 15 million to 618 million rubles. In fiscal year 1924–25 imports from the United States reached 703 million rubles.[38]

While trade lies in the sphere of economic activity, it is not separated from politics by an impenetrable wall. Proponents of trade, as a rule, either agitated for recognition of the USSR or adopted a position of benevolent neutrality on this question. To be sure, in the second half of the twenties it was widely believed that trade and the establishment of diplomatic relations were unrelated phenomena, or in any case not dependent on one another. The opponents of recognition adhered to that view. But this was not the main line of resistance in the struggle against establishing relations, for everyone who was at all in favor of trade, sometimes even willy-nilly, promoted Soviet-American rapprochement.

Proponents of recognition, pointing to the growth of trade even without diplomatic relations, came to completely different conclusions. They stressed that with the establishment of official relations the prospects for economic cooperation would improve.

The Soviet government also tried to counteract the false notion that trade and diplomatic relations were unrelated. Indisputably, it regarded trade as a factor in the inevitable establishment of diplomatic relations. But it did not put trade to the purposes of political intrigue, seeing the important independent functions of trade with the United States. The Soviet point of view on the connection between trade and recognition and also on its independent role was expressed by Stalin in an interview with Thomas Campbell in 1929: "I realise that diplomatic recognition involves difficulties for the USA at the present moment. Soviet government representatives have been subjected to abuse by the American press so much and so often that an abrupt change is difficult. Personally I do not consider diplomatic recognition decisive at the moment. What is important is a development of trade connections on the basis of mutual advantage. Trade relations need to be normalised and if this matter is put on some legal footing it would be a first and very important step towards diplomatic recognition."[39]

The years 1927–28 saw the introduction of a new element into Soviet-American economic relations—agreements for technological cooperation in planning and constructing large industrial units in the USSR. Soon after, about 150 American firms sent their representatives to the Soviet Union. American technological experience was highly regarded in our country. Many were enthusiastic about combining Russian revolutionary scope with American efficiency. In Stalin's words: "We would like the scientific and technical people in America to be our teachers in the sphere of technique, and we their pupils."[40] In 1929 a Soviet delegation headed by the vice-president of the Supreme Council of National Economy, V. I. Mezhlauk, went to the United States to conclude an agreement for technical cooperation in the construction of an automobile plant in Gorky. The Gorky automobile plant and the hydroelectric Dneproges were the two largest Soviet projects in which the Americans took part. In 1930 more than forty of the largest American firms (Ford Motor Company, General Electric, Dupont Company, and others) had agreements with us for technical cooperation.[41] But in spite of this, Stalin's idea that the Americans might become the Russians' teachers in the realm of technology did not materialize: the Americans had no desire to assume such a lofty role, nor could they have laid claim to it.

If agreements for technical cooperation occupied a prominent place in Soviet-American economic relations for a short time, this cannot be said about concessions, which had been a matter to which the Soviet government had paid close attention from the time when it first came to power. In 1927 there were 110 foreign concessions in the USSR. The Germans held first place, the Americans second.[42] But the enterprises concerned were small and on the periphery of the Soviet economy. Foreign capital did not become established in the USSR. In 1928 investment by American firms in the Soviet Union amounted to 12.3 million rubles, which constituted 24 percent of all foreign investments.[43] Soon after, concessions dropped even farther into the background and were eventually curtailed by mutual consent.

Beginning in 1923 Americans in rather large numbers began to "discover" the USSR. Irving T. Bush, president of the New York Chamber of Commerce, was right when he told Litvinov on 6 June 1923 that one of the things that stood in the way of normal relations was the faulty and just plain false ideas about Soviet life prevalent in America.[44] It was a question first and foremost of deliberate misinformation, of which there was altogether too much in the United States, beginning as early as November 1917: the legends left behind by the "Sisson documents" and the testimony concerning the "nationalization of women" proved tenacious. Americans were presented with ideas, slogans, and representations of Soviet life that were a long way from the truth. Bourgeois propaganda painted every aspect of Soviet reality in an anti-Communist light. Even such a steadfast enemy of the Soviet Union as Pitirim A. Sorokin was to admit (in 1944, when his former homeland was busy saving the world from Hitlerism) that in the United States "some go so far as to find fault with Russia for *whatever* she does."[45] This bad habit developed in the United States from the first days of Soviet power, and as the French proverb has it, *Les mauvaises habitudes sont tenaces.* Let us take, for example, the question of the church in the USSR. The dominating cliché in the

United States was the notion that the church was persecuted by and dictated to by the authorities. However, those who had been in the USSR and seen for themselves that this was not so, but having got into the anti-Soviet mood, quickly formed another, no less false notion. They began to assert that the church, functioning "without serious interference from State authorities," was playing a more important role than ever in the life of the Russian people, that it was a form of secret protest against socialism.[46]

But even that part of American public opinion which was free of anti-Soviet excesses and standards knew little about life in the USSR, and this was an impediment to progress in broadening connections between the two countries. Nor were the leading statesmen of the United States distinguished for their knowledge of history and of the current condition of our country. The erudite Henry Cabot Lodge, who liked to show off by making excursions into history, in one of his speeches referred to Prince Rurik as the "tyrant or Duke of Moscow."[47] Even if this could be forgiven,[48] the condescension is inappropriate while reading the memoirs of Herbert Hoover when he writes about "Commissar of Foreign Affairs Kamenev."[49]

The Soviets were not well informed about the United States, either. In telling Chicherin of his meeting with Colonel Robins in Berlin, and transmitting his prognosis for the 1924 elections, the Soviet ambassador plenipotentiary in Germany wrote on 5 August 1923, that "the Democrats will run Borah as their candidate."[50]

The first large group to visit the USSR was a delegation of congressmen. Informing Skvirsky of the government's consent to this visit on 27 March 1923, Litvinov wrote: "It goes without saying that they will all have to pay for their own transportation and maintenance in Russia. Under the New Economic Policy the government does not invite guests at its expense. This will give the guests more freedom to form their own opinions and will save us from criticism and accusations of having staged some sort of 'ideal Russia.' "[51] According to their own assessment, the congressmen saw the Soviet Union in its true colors, just as it was. The results of the visit had a favorable effect on the cause of the Soviet-American rapprochement.

Visits by American trade-union delegations played a big role in overcoming false impressions about the USSR. The first trade-union delegation, headed by James H. Maurer, president of the Pennsylvania

Federation of Labor, visited the Soviet Union in 1927. It had extensive opportunities to become acquainted with Soviet reality. It was received by Stalin, the head of the Soviet state M. I. Kalinin, Chicherin, and other Soviet leaders. In the same year the delegation published a report on its visit, which gave an honest evaluation of the situation of the USSR and recommended recognition by the United States.[52]

This delegation was accompanied by a group of experts which included Stuart Chase, Paul Douglas, Jerome Davis, and Rexford G. Tugwell. The group came out in 1928 with a report of its own.[53] It contained much that was critical of the USSR, but not the slander that was found so often in American publications. We should note that the authors drew practically all of their critical materials from Soviet documents. It was easy to find in the report many positive reactions to the new Russia as well. The authors gave an especially high rating to educational achievements in the USSR. Although this book made no appeal for recognition of the Soviet Union, its contents as a whole strengthened the position of those who favored such a step.

In 1927, the celebration of the tenth anniversary of Soviet power was attended by an American delegation of rank-and-file workers who spoke out most positively in favor of friendship with the Soviet Union.[54] That same year a group of American students, representing forty universities, visited our country for the first time.[55]

Positive improvements in commercial-economic relations have already been noted above. Meno Lovenstein writes, "From 1921 to 1929, the opinion of the business and financial magazines shifted to a more dispassionate appraisal of Russia."[56] At the beginning of 1928 the American-Russian Chamber of Commerce sponsored an exhibition in New York devoted to Soviet industry, science, and education. On 21 May 1929, Skvirsky informed Moscow that a delegation of business-men was preparing to visit us, "the first more or less organized effort by members of American business circles to acquaint themselves with the economic situation of the USSR and with the prospects for Soviet-American trade."[57] A delegation of ninety entrepreneurs, accom-panied by a group of correspondents from leading newspapers, spent a month—from 15 July to 15 August 1929—visiting different regions of the country. On their return, many members of the group spoke out for expansion of economic ties with the Soviet Union.

The participation of Soviet people in the rescue of Umberto Nobile's

North Pole expedition in 1928 helped to dissipate hostile rumors about the USSR. As Skvirsky commented, "The entire American press was for the first time forced to come out with heartfelt praise of the USSR, without a single hostile word."[58] The successful flight of the airplane *Strana Sovetov* (Land of the Soviets) from Moscow to New York by way of the Far East in August-November 1929 aroused great interest in the United States. At the end of the decade the Americans also had evidence that the Russians were not all that rancorous, when the Soviet authorities cooperated in searching for the bodies of American soldiers who had taken part in the intervention, and transporting them to the United States.

The 1920s also saw the formation of Soviet-American scientific and cultural ties.[59] Writers and journalists with revolutionary tendencies had already visited the USSR at the time of the Civil War. Americans were very familiar with the historic statement made by Lincoln Steffens after his visit to Soviet Russia in 1919: "I have seen the future and it works."[60] Beginning in 1922-23, cultural and scientific contacts increased, became more regular, more bilateral; an exchange of books was arranged.

Among the first Soviet writers to visit the United States was Sergei Esenin, who came in the early 1920s. He found his sojourn in America irksome, as we can judge from his sketch, *Zheleznyy Mirgorod*, published in 1923. What is more, his visit came about by chance: it was a by-product of his love affair with Isadora Duncan. Like every Soviet visitor of that time, Esenin was astonished at the technological progress of the United States. Even he, a stranger to rationalism, was forced to admit that it might not be a bad idea to do a little borrowing in this area. But the rhythm of American life and its basic ideas were not to the taste of a man who came from the floodlands of the Oka. Unaccustomed to restraint, loving freedom, truth, and kindness, he expressed his dislike of the "crowds of venal and unprincipled journalists."[61]

More sensational and fruitful for the creative world was the visit to the United States of another great Soviet poet, Vladimir Mayakovsky, in 1925. Like Esenin, he was captivated by the technological genius of the Americans. He was especially struck with their ability as builders: "Americans build as though they were acting out for the thousandth time a most interesting play that they have been rehearsing. It is

impossible to tear oneself away from this spectacle of dexterity and
acuity." But in his appraisal of American reality he manifested more
social and class awareness than Esenin, embodying it in lines of
inimitable expressiveness. This is how he spoke of the American
nation: "Of it, more than of any other, we can say, in the words of
one of the first revolutionary placards: 'There are different kinds of
Americans, some proletarian, some bourgeois.' "[62] Mayakovsky said
that when he started out across the ocean he was striving to move
forward, but when he arrived he found he had moved backward, into
the world of the past—the world of capitalism, which he was dedi-
cated to fighting. He even reproved his predecessor in the discovery of
America a little for having acted too hastily:

> You are a blockhead, Columbus—
>   I'll tell you, honestly,
> that so far as I am concerned,
>   I,
>   personally,
> I would have closed America for a while
>   cleaned it up a bit,
> and then
>   discovered it again,
>   for a second time.[63]

His poems about America were filled with a spirit of competition, of
confidence in the superiority of the socialist system. In September
1929, in his poem "Amerikantsy udivlyayutsya" (The Americans are
amazed), he wrote:

> You bourgeois,
>   go ahead and marvel
>   at the communist shore—
> we
>   will not only overtake
>   but will surpass
>   your
>   fleet-footed
>   celebrated America
>   at work,
>   in the air,
>   in the railway coach.[64]

In the twenties, America became acquainted with Soviet theater and cinema. The guest appearances of the Moscow Art Theatre, under the direction of K. S. Stanislavsky, were very successful. The film *The Battleship Potemkin* demonstrated the high level of Soviet cinematography. During the second half of the decade about twenty Soviet exhibitions were organized in the United States.

Scientific ties were more modest, but even in this area certain changes for the better were clearly apparent. Nobel Prize winner Ivan P. Pavlov visited the United States, where he gave lectures. "The reception has been most friendly," he wrote from New York on 1 July 1923.[65]

The American intelligentsia took a lively interest in the "Soviet experiment." Scores of its prominent members came to visit the new Russia. Many were captivated by what they saw in the USSR. D. Mohrenschildt, who during the first years of the cold war wrote an article about the enthusiasm of American intellectuals for the Russia of the NEP, decided to "rehabilitate" them, pointing out that this had been a temporary, uncritical attitude, which had been corrected as information about the USSR was expanded.[66] But reform was necessary only in the case of those who had created for themselves a false impression of socialist construction, those who viewed Soviet Russia from a petty-bourgeois, anarchist, or Trotskyist point of view. The international adventurist, Emma Goldman, was already "disillusioned" in 1924, having left the USSR a sworn enemy of socialism.[67] The same fate overtook Max Eastman, Eugene Lyons, and other worshippers of Trotsky who, with the rout of Trotskyism, became hawkers of anti-soviet slander. Another group that was "reformed" was the Zionists, who at first had encouraged reemigration of Jews to the USSR, but beginning in 1928 discouraged this, having become convinced that socialist Russia was not a suitable place for the realization of their goals.[68] The majority of Americans who were kindly disposed toward us did not change their attitudes. Their conduct withstood all tests.

We would like to speak particularly about the visits to the USSR of two great Americans, W. E. B. DuBois and Theodore Dreiser. The first was, of course, most attracted by the equality of races, nations, and nationalities in socialist society. After his visit, he said: "If what I have seen with my own eyes and heard with my ears in Russia is

Bolshevism, I am a Bolshevik.''[69] Dreiser came to the USSR rather reluctantly, warning Moscow that no one should interfere with him, as an ''incorrigible individualist,'' in forming and expressing his opinion. And no one did. After spending eleven weeks in the USSR he wrote an interesting book. While the astute writer did notice some defects, he declared that, on the whole, the Soviet system was suitable for adoption by the entire world.[70]

Both Dubois and Dreiser became Communists toward the end of their lives. We do not write this to give the impression that after a visit to the USSR every American who has formed a favorable impression is sure to join the Communist ranks. To many American businessmen, journalists, political figures, union members, scholars, leaders in literature and art, clergymen, the Soviet Union appeared an object worthy of long-term and positive cooperation, even though they remained steadfast enemies of socialism. In sum, they understood the simple but very important truth, having realized and become convinced that what had taken place in Russia was not the affected swagger of a small group of extremists, but something deeper, more natural, more necessary, at least to the Russian people; something that could not be brushed aside; something that had to be taken into account and adapted to constructively, but with the greatest advantage to oneself.

Grasping this proved beyond the capacities of the Republican leaders. They were leading the Russian policy of the United States up its usual blind alley. The failure of this policy assumed a bipartisan character. Having begun as Wilson's ''tragedy,'' it ended as Hoover's ''tragedy.'' But neither the messianic dogmatism of Wilson nor the ''rugged individualism'' of Hoover were able to keep the ruling circles of the United States from eventually having to recognize the inevitability of peaceful coexistence with the socialist state, the necessity and usefulness of positive interrelations with it. Certain events and processes that occurred simultaneously in both the USSR and the United States at the end of the twenties and the beginning of the thirties played an important educative role in bringing this about.

In this period the fundamental difference between the capitalist and socialist forms of stabilization was made apparent by the course of events. On the one hand, the capitalist system suffered an unprecedented economic and sociopolitical shock. At the same time, the success of socialist construction in the Five-Year Plan laid a solid foundation for a socialist economy in our country. In the shortest possible time a powerful industry and large-scale collective agriculture came into being. During the years of the Five-Year Plan the cultural revolution was growing at a rapid rate. The USSR was becoming a land of universal literacy, and this created conditions for accelerated scientific and technological progress. A new culture was emerging in our country, national in form and socialist in content.

The Five-Year Plan in the USSR and the Great Depression in the United States

The 1929–33 depression, a watershed stage in the most recent history of capitalism, had tremendous consequences for the fortunes of the capitalist world. The evils of the capitalist method of production were brought to light as never before. All of the bourgeois countries began to experience accelerated developments of state-monopolistic capitalism in various forms. The depression radically changed the political countenance of many countries. Fascism raised its head, and militarism gained momentum, abruptly crushing the pacifism of the 1920s. Imperialism as a system became tangled in contradictions which grew for several years, finally resulting in the Second World War.

The Soviet nation always worked for peace, but it was only in the 1930s that the bourgeois countries came to an adequate realization of the strength of the USSR as a factor in the stabilization of international relations. To be sure, they realized it in different ways: the warmongers saw the Soviet Union as their chief enemy; the opponents of aggressive wars, as a partner in possible antiwar alliances. Both realized that they would have to include the USSR in their calculations. Looking ahead, we must say that the opponents of war in the ruling circles of the West became prisoners of their own machinations and did not make proper use of Soviet potential during the 1930s, while the aggressors were unable to resist the temptation of testing the strength of the USSR in practice.

The fulfillment of the Five-Year Plan heightened the interest of the Soviet Union in developing economic ties with the capitalist countries. The latter, under the conditions of the depression, were no less interested in trade with us. However, as before, they were reluctant to extend credit, without which the USSR was unable to constantly increase its imports. This compelled the Soviet Union to speed up exports, which aroused hostility in a number of the bourgeois nations. As a result, the volume of foreign trade of the USSR during 1930–33 declined by more than half: from 7,302 to 2,941 million rubles.[71]

The increased number of interimperalist conflicts and the intensification of attacks on the USSR undermined the possibilities for peaceful coexistence. Litvinov, who replaced the ailing Chicherin as commissar for foreign affairs in 1930, said at the meeting of the World Economic Conference on 14 June 1933: "Although the International Economic Conference of 1927 recognized the principle of peaceful coexistence at the present moment in the history of the capitalist and socialist systems, this principle has so far not been put into practice by all nations."[72]

Litvinov was not referring to the Fascist countries alone. There can be no doubt that he was also reproaching the United States for its continued refusal to recognize the USSR. It must also be kept in mind that the early 1930s saw the unleashing of a malicious and widespread anti-Soviet campaign in the United States which took a variety of forms. Propaganda and specific government measures against Soviet exports to the United States occupied a prominent place in this campaign. This time the "crusaders for Russian freedom" came out against "forced labor" in the USSR and against the practice of "dumping." At their demand, antidumping duties were introduced on matches, anthracite, asbestos, and other goods imported from the USSR. Along with this "liberal" measure went legislation banning the importation of goods produced by "forced labor." These measures were zealously implemented although the groundlessness of the above-mentioned anti-Soviet fantasies was obvious. Investigations carried out by agencies of the federal government did not confirm the false assertions of either "dumping" or "forced labor."[73]

What, then, is the explanation for this slanderous campaign against Soviet exports? Of course, there were certain business circles in the United States that produced goods with which Soviet imports were in competition. Under the conditions of the depression they reacted to this state of affairs more pathologically than usual. However, the danger of Soviet competition was incredibly exaggerated, and all of these matters that belonged to the economic sphere were carried over into the realm of the political struggle against socialism. Reactionary journalists approached this problem as "fighting the Red trade menace."[74]

Their propaganda pointed to the fact that Soviet exports had increased to some extent with the beginning of the Five-Year Plan. It is true that Soviet exports in general and to the United States in particular reached their highest level for the period between the wars in the years 1929 and 1930. The reason for this was twofold—the expansion of Soviet export opportunities and the fact that the Soviets were forced to turn possibility into reality because of the refusal by the bourgeoisie to extend the necessary credit to cover the cost of imports. The reactionaries drew their own conclusions from this. They got the notion that the Five-Year Plan would fail without imports from the United States, and that the Soviet economy would break down if they put pressure on it.

In the United States in the early 1930s there were a great many false assessments of the Soviet economy and of the prospects of the Five-Year Plan.[75] For example, we analyzed the articles in *Current History* on this subject. In January 1931 Henry D. Baker, the former American commercial attaché in Russia, wrote about the "inherent unsoundness" of the Five-Year Plan, predicting that the USSR can at best hope for a "Pyrrhic victory."[76] Professor Edgar S. Furniss wrote in issue after issue, monotonously and tediously, although without using strong language, of the "failures" of the Soviet planned economy.[77]

Attacks on Soviet export policies and on the Five-Year Plan merged into one. American propaganda and American policy found themselves once again, though not for the last time, caught up in the illusion that without American "aid" the Soviet Union would be unable to cope with its economic problems. These illusions were in part offensive, in part defensive designs of the American bourgeoisie. As far as the offensive aspect was concerned, some people still hoped that through a combination of nonrecognition and economic boycott they might turn the Soviet state from its socialist course. But obviously they did not have the strength to do this. The American bourgeoisie and its ideologists also had to consider another matter: how to prevent the achievements of Soviet socialism from having an influence in the United States. Though this influence should not be exaggerated, it must nevertheless be admitted that it did exist. The idea of a planned economy was attractive to many members of the intelligentsia. Unemployed workers discovered for themselves the truth about the possibility of permanent and full employment. The accelerated shift to state-monopolistic formulas as a solution to economic problems, and the trend to liberal social reform, were influenced significantly by the principles of socialism, especially with respect to economic planning and government responsibility for the social welfare of citizens.

In 1930 anti-Communist hysteria revived in the United States, with Congressman Hamilton Fish as its standard-bearer. Fish and his associates blamed all of America's misfortunes—and in the early 1930s there were many of them—on the subversive influence and activities of the Soviet Union and the American Communists, an explanation primitive in its simplicity. Appearing before Congress on 28 February 1930 he castigated the "liberals and progressives" for their sympathy with the "Soviet dictatorship" and was applauded by the members of the House of Representatives when he proposed an investigation of the activities of American Communists.[78] And two months later Grover Whalen, police commissioner of New York, following the tradition of the "Sisson documents," published falsified evidence purporting to show that Amtorg and the Soviet Information Bureau in Washington were nothing but emissaries from the Comintern to the Communist Party of the United States, and that the latter was preparing to overthrow the lawful government. In May 1930 the House of Representatives decided to create a committee headed by Fish to investigate Communist activity in the United States. But shortly afterward Whalen's false documents were unmasked as counterfeit, which even Fish's committee had to acknowledge.

In the campaign against "Communist propaganda," as in all of the other anti-Soviet ventures of the early 1930s, the factor of the Five-Year Plan is clearly discernible. Even the fight for "freedom of worship" in the USSR, led by Edmund Walsh, the former papal nuncio in Russia, took the form, in the main, of attacks on the Five-Year Plan, so dangerous for the reactionary "crusaders."[79] Hamilton Fish prophesied for the Soviet Five-Year Plan "near-collapse for want of capital," and assigned the United States a definite role in promoting this "collapse": "Unless American capitalists provide funds and extend loans and credit the famous 5-year program will come to a sudden and startling end."[80]

The Soviet government had to waste a great deal of effort warding off political attacks by the ruling circles of the United States. In December 1929 it rebuffed attempts to interfere in the Soviet-Chinese conflict unleashed by the antinational militarist circles of China under imperialist instigation. American interference became especially active just when Soviet-Chinese negotiations were nearing a successful conclusion. On 3 December 1929 Moscow issued a protest, which ended with the caustic passage: "In conclusion, the government of the Soviet Union cannot but express its amazement that the government of the United States of America, which by its own choice has no official relations with the government of the Soviet Union, can find it possible to address it with counsel and 'instructions.'"[81]

Nor could the Soviet Union remain silent about the campaign of discrimination against Soviet exports. In July 1930 P. A. Bogdanov, president of Amtorg, spoke out against the false charge that American manufacturers were threatened by Soviet competition. He cited irrefutable figures showing that the campaign against our exports were based on political and not purely economic motives. Bogdanov warned the organizers of the campaign: "There is no doubt that curtailing the importation of Soviet goods into the United States of America will have an effect on our purchases in this country."[82] Following this, Skvirsky proposed to the Peoples' Commissariat for Foreign Affairs that drastic retaliatory measures be taken, knowing that this would be certain to have a sobering effect on a certain part of the American business community. "Events have shown," he telegraphed on 13 August 1930,

> that in times of crisis the Americans have been aware of the importance of the Soviet market. When threatened with losing it, they reacted in a way that was to our benefit. This strengthened our position, and we must take that into account. At the next serious confrontation we ought to take a more decisive stand, and announce that we are taking our trade elsewhere, unless we get a trade agreement that would guarantee us elementary rights. This will surely force the business people concerned to put pressure on Hoover on our behalf. Without such pressure, Hoover himself will not undertake anything. Once we have taken a decisive stand, we must be prepared to carry it into effect. At present our position is weakened by the fact that at the same time that we issue a warning, we are placing an order [for goods] in the amount of $40,000,000. Here there are

many, including some in the government departments, who are convinced that we will not leave the market, for we cannot as yet afford to do so. The threat to our exports has lessened, but has not disappeared.[83]

On 20 October 1930 the Council of Peoples' Commissars of the USSR adopted a resolution providing that the Peoples' Commissariat of Foreign and Domestic Trade could take retaliatory measures against countries in which Soviet export goods were subject to discrimination. In his report to the Sixth Congress of Soviets on 8 March 1931, V. M. Molotov, chairman of the Council of Peoples' Commissars, warned that inasmuch as "the anti-Soviet activity of Fish and Company amounts to a virtual ban on the export of Soviet goods to America, the United States must reckon with the fact that this will inevitably and immediately have an effect on our imports from America, also."[84] A letter—"K voprosu o nashikh vzaimootnosheniyakh s Amerikoy" (Concerning the matter of our interrelations with America)[85]— addressed to the Politburo of the Central Committee of the Soviet Communist Party on 18 September 1931 by N. N. Krestinsky, assistant commissar of the Peoples' Commissariat for Foreign Affairs, is of great significance in showing the mood in the leading circles of the USSR with respect to discrimination against Soviet exports in the United States, and the anti-Soviet campaign as a whole. Its proposal to strictly curtail purchases from the United States as a retaliatory, defensive measure was put into effect.

This decision of the Soviet government resulted in appreciable damage to a certain sector of American business. It should be borne in mind that in 1931 approximately 40 percent of all machinery and various equipment exported by the United States was sold in the USSR, along with 66 percent of all exported metal-cutting lathes, 75 percent of all forge machinery, and 96 percent of all locomotives.[86] Because of the anti-Soviet crusaders, Soviet-American trade was suddenly and drastically reduced. In 1931 we imported goods in the amount of 801 million rubles; in 1932, 110 million rubles; and in 1933, only 58 million rubles.[87] In other words, exports to the USSR during the period of a most severe economic depression in the United States decreased almost eightfold within one year and almost fourteenfold within two years. This forced many people to think twice about

the consequences of the anti-Soviet spree, and undermined the doctrine that trade and recognition, or that trade and normal political
relations, were not related.

At the same time, the USSR remained prepared to enter into
friendly relations with the United States. Fifteen hundred American
specialists continued to work successfully in our country, among them
the prominent builder Hugh Cooper.[88] Actually, they all worked well.
They were treated with respect and goodwill, and many were awarded
Soviet decorations. Stalin, who did not often take notice of foreign
correspondents, visitors, or even accredited diplomats, met rather
often with the Americans. The general secretary of the Central Committee of the Communist Party was a very popular personality in the
pages of the American press. He could not stand sensation lovers in
the world of journalism. On 3 April 1932, in reply to a letter from
Richardson, a representative of the Associated Press wire service, he
expressed his opinion of rumors about his health in the style of the
well-known words of Mark Twain: "This is not the first time that false
rumors that I am ill are circulating in the bourgeois press. Obviously,
there are people to whose interest it is that I should fall ill seriously
and for a long time, if not worse. Perhaps it is not very tactful of me,
but unfortunately I have no data capable of gratifying these gentlemen."[89]

It was not only for economic reasons that the Soviet Union showed
an interest in normalizing relations with the United States. On the
whole, the curtailment of trade with the Americans in no way affected
the fulfillment of the Five-Year Plan, which did not depend on help
from the United States. In the early 1930s the first signs of the
approaching war began to loom on the horizon. At first the threat
appeared most obvious in the Far East, but beginning in 1933 it
appeared in Central Europe as well. Aggression touched both our
countries. History equalized the "chances" of the USSR and the
United States—the Germans attacked us without declaring war in
June 1941, and less than half a year later the Japanese did the same to
the Americans. The Soviet government proceeded from the assumption that Japanese militarism was a threat to both the USSR and the
United States. Therefore it formed its policy counting on the real
interest of the Americans in the Soviet Union as a factor in stabilizing
the situation in the Far East.

From the very first days of the Japanese aggression in Manchuria (1931) the United States government was forced to regard the USSR in a new light. This was noticed very quickly by Skvirsky, who reported to Moscow that the attitude toward him was changing for the better. "Even [Robert F.] Kelly," he wired on 21 April 1932, referring to the chief of the State Department's Eastern European division, "declared in a chat with me that the existence of normal relations between the United States of America and the USSR would have a favorable influence on the Far East."[90] Many, if not most people at the top level of government in the United States realized this. But the Hoover administration delayed making a positive decision on recognition of the USSR that was demanded by events. A further obstacle was that the leaders of both parties were counting on America being able to make the Japanese threat a problem for the USSR alone. The policy of encouraging aggression was already taking its first steps.

Be that as it may, under the Hoover administration and, to an even greater degree, in the New Deal atmosphere, which was quickly spreading during the election campaign of 1932, people were taking a closer look at the USSR as a factor in holding Japanese aspirations in check. Franklin Roosevelt met with Alkan Hirsch, an American citizen who was working as chief consultant for the Soviet chemical industry, and questioned him extensively about the state of affairs in the USSR. Reporting on the conversation to V. I. Mezhlauk, president of the State Planning Committee of the USSR on 12 September 1932, Hirsch mentioned that the presidential candidate was interested, among other things, in the Far East.[91]

In the 1932 election campaign both candidates preferred not to touch publicly on the painful Russian question, concentrating on urgent domestic problems. But recognition of the USSR was being widely debated around the country, and it was brought into the foreground of the preelection skirmishes. The positions of the proponents and opponents of recognition were clearly defined. By this time the arguments of both sides had been summarized and expounded more than once by specialists in international relations. This was done most completely in the survey "The United States and the Soviet Union," published on 1 November 1933 by the Committee on Russian-American Relations of the American Foundation. Members of the committee included Hugh Cooper, Thomas Lamont, Roscoe

Pound, and other well-known proponents of recognition of the USSR, but the report was made in an emphatically impartial style, without making any recommendations whatever.

The authors presented readers with twelve arguments against recognition.[92] The first argument began with the thesis: "The communistic and capitalistic systems are entirely incompatible." Among the other propositions was the assertion that the absence of recognition did not stand in the way of trade. The tenth point said that the establishment of diplomatic relations would not promote universal peace inasmuch as the USSR, devoted to the idea of world revolution, had no interest in peace. The report contained an equal number of arguments—twelve—in favor of recognition.[93] The eighth point deserves special attention: "To withhold recognition is, in effect, to deny that capitalistic and communistic systems can coexist in the same world. And that, in effect, is a challenge to war." The advocates of recognition used both economic and political arguments. They stressed the stability of the political system of the USSR, repudiated fantasies about "subversive propaganda," and saw in recognition opportunities for an expansion of exports and for consolidation of American positions in the world. Point 12 said: "If the U.S. genuinely desires to check imperialism in the Far East, it must cooperate with Russia. It can do so adequately only if there are normal diplomatic relations between the two countries." The calculation that recognition would prove to be "the best means of lessening or weakening Communism" was also cited as an argument in favor of recognition. This once again corroborated the fact that peaceful coexistence—and here we are speaking of the arguments advanced by people who held exactly this point of view—is a form of the class struggle.

Historians and public affairs analysts have repeatedly asked what the deciding factor was in the final American decision to recognize the Soviet Union in 1933. Statements of views on this matter add up to a dilemma: was Washington counting on the fact that trade would be expanded, or was it concerned with consolidating its position against Japan and Germany (sometimes there is disagreement as to whether it was against Japan or Germany)?

Before replying to this question, we must point out that any serious analysis of the reasons for recognition must begin elsewhere. Recognition became inevitable, first of all, because the USSR, as a result of successful socialist construction, had become a strong nation, the main support of peace in the world. Continued refusal to recognize the powerful socialist state was completely absurd. The "tragedy" of Wilson and Hoover was approaching its denouement. The fact that helped the ruling circles of the United States to recognize the futility of their policy on the Russian question was that just when American capitalism found itself in a state of the deepest decline, the USSR was successfully completing its Five-Year Plan. Even such people as Hoover and Hughes could no longer afford to slight the Soviet economic system. The depression was not only a social shock and an unparalleled economic collapse; it also gave rise to a psychological trauma that was difficult to cure, and delivered a colossal moral blow to the creators of the "most effective" system in the world, which during the thirties was so mercilessly humiliated by history in the face of the new social system. Hopes for the "collapse," or even the "regeneration" of socialism in the USSR, could now persist only in the minds of the most incorrigible dreamers. Peoples' Commissar Litvinov, analyzing the reasons for the prolonged and unsuccessful disregard of the USSR by the republic across the ocean, said at the plenary session of the Central Executive Committee on 29 December 1933:

> It lasted, not because the United States had greater quarrels with us than other countries did, or that it had suffered more than the others as a result of the revolutionary legislation. No, in essence it continued the struggle proclaimed by the entire capitalist world after the October Revolution against the new system of the Soviet state, which had set for itself the goal of creating a socialist society. This was a struggle against peaceful coexistence of the two systems. As it watched its companions-in-arms in this struggle, the other capitalist nations, abandon the front, one by one, it was as though America was saying to them: I understand you, you are weak, you are shattered, but I am sufficiently strong so that I can continue the struggle for all of you. It maintained its position staunchly for fifteen years, but has now finally given up the struggle.[94]

Now we will consider the role of those other factors affecting recognition mentioned earlier. Trade was, of course, one of the important stimuli, and its effect was further intensified by the depressed state of the American economy. But it was not the trade that was the deciding argument for recognition, even though probably more was said about it in public debates than about any other consideration. Joan Wilson writes that the government of Franklin Roosevelt "used the shibboleth of economic recovery effectively in 1933 to insure acceptance of Russian recognition."[95]

It was profitable to emphasize the trade factor in recognition both because of its practical effect and also for special political reasons. It provided a more or less safe refuge against the attacks of the dyed-in-the-wool reactionaries, who were accusing the advocates of recognition of being soft toward Communism: who in the world would accuse the big monopolists of Communist sympathies? But no less important was something else—the ruling circles who were conceding to the establishment of diplomatic relations with the Soviet Union did not wish to make it appear that the United States had enemies in the world. They were not prepared to admit this either to their enemies or to the USSR, for public recognition of this fact would have necessitated taking positive steps against such enemies and movement in the direction of collective resistance to the aggressor, jointly with the Russians.

With very rare exceptions, American historians have analyzed prewar international relations from an anti-Soviet point of view, later justifying the policy of encouraging aggression. They did not want to "exaggerate" Japanese-American conflicts and to show that the USSR and the United States had a common objective in taking joint action. This position did not appeal to them because of the United States' postwar relations with both the USSR and Japan. The same applies also to the German aspect of the problem. Finally, thrusting trade to the fore, the postwar analysts showed that hopes for a major expansion of trade proved to have been unjustified, and asked (some directly, others by intimation) whether there had been any sense in recognizing the USSR. Had this measure justified itself; had the game been worth the candle? Hoover, for example, answered frankly that it had not, that the liberals and Communists had betrayed Roosevelt, and that he had made a bad bargain, having opened the doors to "Communist infiltration" and "the attempt to collectivize the United States, particularly through the labor unions."[96]

Many American historians do not consider trade as the main stimulus toward recognition of the USSR, ascribing this role to political factors—the consolidation of American security in the Far East and in other parts of the world. But just as the proponents of the trade thesis complain that the expected trade expansion did not materialize, so those who emphasize the political factor allege that recognition did not lead to collective security because the Soviet Union violated the 1933 understanding, and proved an untrustworthy partner in the eyes of the Americans.

Recognition

The defeat of the Republicans in the 1932 elections removed the chief domestic obstacle on the road to recognition of the Soviet state. During its formative phase and its first months in office, the Roosevelt administration weighed all the arguments for and against with emphatic deliberateness, clearly inclining toward recognition. This was promoted in no small degree by the antimonopolist, democratic movement that had got under way during the years of the depression, directed against reaction, fascism, and war. Its demands invariably included establishment of diplomatic relations with the USSR. In 1933 the National Committee for Recognition of the Soviet Union was formed, coordinating the activities of a great number of organizations. The forces opposed to the normalization of relations remained active to the end. The American Legion, the National Civic Federation, the reactionaries in the AFL, the superannuated Daughters of American Revolution, and individual politicians and clergymen "of principle" would not surrender. Recognition took place in spite of them.

The ice jam began to move after Roosevelt, on 16 May 1933, addressed a message to the heads of the fifty-three nations taking part in the World Economic Conference. Among the addressees was the head of the Soviet state, M. I. Kalinin, who replied to the American president on 19 May 1933 in a very friendly tone. On the threshold of the inevitable negotiations, the State Department went into full swing. Among the great number of documents prepared in its offices, the 21 September 1933 memorandum to the president from Cordell Hull occupies a special place.[97] The secretary of state tried hard to persuade Roosevelt to take a harsh stand in the forthcoming negotiations with the Russians. He enumerated a large number of claims against the USSR, asserting that only the Russians would gain by the establishment of official relations. He proposed taking advantage of ''two powerful weapons'' against their partner in the negotiations: the fact that the Soviet Union was interested in obtaining credit, and the danger on its Far Eastern borders—and use them to win conditions favorable to the United States.

In his memoirs, Hull laments that the president did not heed his chief advice—to force the USSR from the beginning to meet the American conditions, and only after this to utter the word *recognition*.[98] Roosevelt realized that Hull's method was unlikely to lead to an agreement with the Soviet government, and decided to conduct the negotiations himself, sending the secretary of state off to a Pan-American conference in Montevideo.[99] Between 10 and 17 October 1933 there was a historic exchange of letters between Roosevelt and Kalinin, and a short time after that a Soviet delegation, headed by Peoples' Commissar M. M. Litvinov, started out for the United States.

The State Department and the specialists on Russian affairs, who had emerged by this time, prepared for the arrival of the Reds as if for the coming of the autumn hurricanes on the eastern coast of the United States, which are given women's names by the Americans to emphasize the impossibility of rationally predicting their behavior. But as a matter of fact, it was not difficult to predict the Soviet point of view. The Russian peoples' commissar was bringing a proposal to turn away from the inglorious past, as quickly as possible, under mutually acceptable conditions; to establish diplomatic relations and in the future to strengthen them in the interests of the Soviet and American people; to turn them into a strong link of collective security against Fascist aggression; to make them a mighty factor in promoting universal peace. Litvinov arrived in New York on 7 November 1933, on the sixteenth anniversary of the Great October Socialist Revolution.

The thought runs through Hull's memoirs, and even more through American historical analyses dealing with the recognition of the Soviet Union,[100] that Roosevelt did not handle this generally necessary step properly, and therefore recognition did not have satisfactory economic and political results. They start from the false premise that the Russians were striving for recognition at any price, while the Americans were (or should have been) in the position of a calculating salesman offering scarce merchandise. In retrospect, Roosevelt is reproached for softness, lack of foresight, and even negligence in the negotiations.

Robert Browder expresses this especially clearly in his analysis of the
agreement on debts, which he calls "a mistake." He writes:

> It was a particularly unfortunate move in the light of the circum-
> stances surrounding recognition. Russia was unusually anxious for
> diplomatic relations, and it is not at all improbable that if enough
> pressure had been exerted she would have made a definite settle-
> ment then and there. The Soviet Government and Maxim Litvinov
> would have suffered an immeasurable loss of prestige both at home
> and abroad if the negotiations had failed. If Litvinov had been
> given the alternatives of signing an agreement in detail or relin-
> quishing the prospect of recognition, he would very likely have
> complied with the demands of the United States.[101]

Comments like this at best corresponded to the mentality of the
Washington "maximalists" of 1933. But thinking in terms of practical politics, the president and his advisers, even if they had wanted to
indulge in a hyperaggressive course, could see that there was a more or
less definite point beyond which they could not go in putting pressure
on the Soviet government. They were also aware of their own personal
interest in the establishment of relations and their responsibility in
case of a possible breakdown in the negotiations, to say nothing of
prestige—this was as necessary to Washington in 1933 as air to
breathe. And, of course, if Litvinov's mission were to fail, it would not
mean much for Moscow. Soviet historians, therefore, have never
thought of the 1933 negotiations and their successful conclusion as a
gift from God to American capitalism.

Washington had to show that it had at least obtained some "concessions" from the Russians. Roosevelt was not the last American
president who had need of "concessions" from the USSR for domestic
consumption, who turned spur-of-the-moment diplomatic "victories" over the Russians into a weapon in the struggle against his
political opponents at home. In doing this, American leaders count
not only on the generosity of the Kremlin, but also on the difference
between the political processes in the United States and the USSR.
They believe that the Soviet system permits the Kremlin leaders to
evaluate circumstances simply objectively, while the American system
requires the additional freight of triumphal propaganda. As a matter

of fact, that is how things actually are, except only for the fact that the degree of sensitivity of Soviet public opinion to what takes place in Soviet-American relations is underestimated in the United States. But this does not give American propagandists and historians the right to transmute American mentality, conditioned by its peculiar political features, into objective reality.

The November 1933 negotiations dragged on longer and progressed with more difficulty than Moscow had expected. The reason for this was the behavior of the ruling circles in the United States. It was complicated also by their own prejudices, and even more by the prejudices of those whose opinion they had to take into account. Roosevelt, whose enemies would have thought he had sold out to communism even without these negotiations, had to convince the diehard reactionaries that in his talks with the Red delegation he was being tough and was driving them into a corner. Besides this, he had to prove that sixteen years of nonrecognition had been in some measure logical, just as the repudiation of this earlier course—which could occur only after the Soviet side had appeared before the eyes of the world cleansed of its sins—was also logical. To Roosevelt, Wilson was a teacher, while Hoover was a colleague from whom he had taken over power. Finally, America, shattered to pieces at home, and looked down on by the dictatorships abroad as a decayed democracy, had to show evidence of its strength.

All of this determined American tactics at the negotiations. Litvinov was prepared for the immediate conclusion of an agreement on establishing diplomatic relations, along lines which the Soviets had had in mind for a long time: first the two countries would enter into official relations, and then they would settle all their specific problems. Such a simple approach did not suit the Americans. Knowing that the USSR would offer the United States the same conditions that it would offer to other countries in similar situations, they wished to appear to have won these conditions with great difficulty, so that later, they could present it in this light to the general public. And on the other hand, though they knew that the USSR would not give way to extortionate claims of a material and political order, the Americans went ahead and made excessive demands in order to prove that the Soviet Union was intractable and thus justify the sixteen years of nonrecognition. Here a way was being prepared for the immediate future as well. Washington had no intention of opening the history of American-Soviet relations with a page telling of close political cooperation, in full view of potential aggressors. It was therefore important to represent the socialist state as a difficult partner.

In certain instances during these talks the Americans were forcing their way through an open door. This was especially true of the negotiations about the religious question and the legal status of Americans in the USSR. Hull showed what appeared to be an unaccountably moving concern about the state of religion in the USSR, which, in the light of what has been stated earlier, is entirely understandable. Litvinov politely pointed out to him that he was touching on the internal affairs of the USSR. "After a long argument on this subject," the peoples' commissar reported to Moscow on 8 November, "Hull stepped down from his position and declared that he expected, at the very least, a guarantee of religious freedom for Americans in the Soviet Union, without which the restoration of relations would be impossible. I replied that the position of the Americans with respect to religion would be the same as that of our own citizens and of other foreigners. If he should ask me what that position is, I shall answer that it ensures freedom of religion to everyone."[102] Thus, on the religious question one can see the intolerable meddling of the United States in the affairs of the USSR, and the fact that the problem itself was contrived. The problem was really very simple for the Soviet Union, if Hull's real concern was that the moral appearance of the American ambassador and of the entire staff of the embassy might be damaged on the territory of the godless socialist nation. "In reply to my question," wired Litvinov to the Peoples' Commissariat for Foreign Affairs on 18 November, when the negotiations had already been concluded, "why Roosevelt had been so insistent on the question of religion, Bullitt said frankly here it was exclusively domestic policy that played a role, and that the agreements concerning religion would give Roosevelt fifty votes in the Congress that he needed badly to carry out some economic reforms."[103] But, naturally, the Soviet Union could permit the American leaders, even Roosevelt, to win a "victory" over them only within the limits of decency.

The matter of the legal status of American citizens in the USSR looked exactly the same. By this time hundreds and even thousands of Americans had had the experience of a prolonged stay under the conditions of Soviet reality. Although they did not live in paradise, the atmosphere around them was quite pleasant, and they experienced no discrimination for either racial or religious reasons. If indeed there were any shortcomings in our treatment of foreigners, they were more likely to stem from the excessively deferential treatment accorded them. Nonetheless Hull and his assistants undertook the solution of this "problem." And again, joking aside, the desire for exclusiveness and privilege were distinctly apparent. "I referred once more to the equality before the law of our own and of alien citizens and to the inadmissibility of privileges," reported Litvinov to his government.[104]

Two other subjects that were discussed had more substance. These were the question of mutual noninterference in internal affairs, and the settlement of mutual financial claims. It must be said at once that the question of subversive propaganda and of interference in internal affairs were in a sphere where it was the Americans and not the Russians who were at fault, although the Americans, both at the negotiations and in subsequent historial accounts, took the completely opposite approach to the matter. As is known, the United States intervened in Soviet affairs with fire and sword, and with appeals by official figures for the overthrow of the lawful Soviet authority, not to mention the antics of more irresponsible groups—the propaganda agencies. On 17 November 1933, Litvinov told the members of the press in Washington that over the course of sixteen long years many in the United States "had amused themselves spreading wild cock-and-bull stories about the Soviet Union,"[105] and no one could ward off his well-aimed stabs.

The American side acted as though it were unaware of any hostile action against the Soviet Union originating in the United States, and at the same time demanded the impossible of Litvinov—the commitment to put an end to the struggle of the Comintern against capitalism. The Soviet peoples' commissar replied to Hull's demands that he should assume "responsibility for the Comintern" with a "decisive refusal."[106] Donald Bishop is right when he writes that the absence of the clause about the Comintern in the final agreement was "not an oversight."[107] But there is no justification for his assertion that this document contains an implied renunciation by the Communist International of anticapitalist propaganda.

The gravest problem in the Washington negotiations concerned the debt claims. The State Department estimated the total Soviet debt owed Americans to be an astronomical $771,000,000.[108] The Soviet position on the question of the prerevolutionary debt had been clearly formulated for some time. It included a repudiation of reciprocal claims, and the solution of unsolved material problems after the establishment of diplomatic relations, with the condition that loans would be granted (some payments might be allowed in the form of higher interest rates). So far as the USSR was concerned, the total amount of the real debt to the United States that it could recognize was small by comparison with its former debts to France, Germany, and Britain. It appeared to be at least seven to eight times less than the figure computed by the Americans. But the USSR could not give the Americans preferential treatment without reopening the whole question of indebtedness with the other countries with whom it had long since arrived at a settlement.

We must suppose that the American diplomats realized this, and, having seized upon this question, which for the "richest country in the world" was at bottom a trivial one, decided to show once again the "difficulty" of having normal relations with the Russians. As has already been pointed out, all of this made much sense from the standpoint of the American idea of refusing to cooperate actively with the Soviet Union against the rising aggressors.

After prolonged negotiations in Washington, clear mutual agreement was reached on three of the four above-mentioned problems. The agreement was spelled out in a public exchange of letters between Roosevelt and Litvinov. The declaration on religious freedom[109] was the only unilateral commitment of the Soviet government, which was not overly concerned about the religious practices of its diplomats and citizens in the United States. Two others—a commitment to abandon hostile propaganda and one on the rights of citizens—were reciprocal.

The question of financial claims, unlike all the others, was settled by a gentlemen's agreement and the initialing of a secret document. Litvinov notified Hull on the first day that the discussion concerning debts would be meaningless without taking into account counterclaims by the USSR. "If an immediate solution of the problem is desirable," said the peoples' commissar, "it is possible only if both sides give up all claims, after the example of Rapallo."[110] The United States government did not give up its claims, although it would have been quite easy for them to do so and would have shown the whole world straightaway that the two great nations were ready to meet each other halfway in order to cope with an impending threat. The Soviet side, of course, could not agree to meet the American claims, both because they were excessive and because this would have immediately complicated the relations between the USSR and many European powers.

But, realizing the importance of establishing friendly relations with the United States for the strengthening of universal peace, the Soviet delegation announced that after the establishment of official ties the USSR would be prepared to consider the question of satisfying a certain number of the American material claims, provided it were done in such a way as not to reopen discussion of the previously settled claims of the other powers. It was a result of this that the accord of 15 November 1933 was only a gentlemen's agreement, in the sense that the two sides, especially the Soviet side, could move on to final and official talks only after further consultation.[111] In its content, though, the document was logical and clear. It stated that after revised estimates were submitted by both sides, the United States could receive a sum of between $75,000,000 and $150,000,000 (the most likely figure being $100,000,000), subject only to one important condition. This was the extension of a *loan* to the USSR with a high rate of interest, which would reimburse Americans who had claims against the Soviet government.

The American literature contains assertions that Roosevelt and his advisers were "negligent" and showed poor judgment in negotiating the debt settlement. Negligence may be seen in the fact that the president promised the Russians the loan without having considered how the Congress would react to this, and also confused the idea of "loan" and "credit." It is hard to put much stock in this interpretation, for it is supported by neither the facts nor convincing arguments. The lexicon of finance among Americans is polished to the point of perfection. In the United States even a preschool child understands the difference between a loan and commercial credit, so that American historians, in trying to cast aspersions on the agreements of November 1933, are underestimating the capabilities of the statesmen and diplomats of the New Deal period. For the most part, these men were lawyers and specialists in corporate law. The provision about a loan for

the USSR was included not as a result of negligence, for in its absence
the understanding would not have reached the level of even a gentlemen's agreement; without this condition, the Soviet side would not
have accepted the compromise that was reached. Moreover, with this
initialed agreement the United States government placed itself in an
advantageous position politically. Despite the secret nature of the
document, Washington could at once begin to claim that it had won
an advantage. Second, the government had before it two alterna-
tives—to bring the understanding to a conclusion, receiving the
$100,000,000 and strengthening its claim that the Russians had made
concessions; or, on the contrary, to refuse to accept the conditions of
the loan, laying the blame for the failure of the proposed debt
agreement on the USSR, and in this way making it seem impossible to
enter into friendship and alliance with the Russians. As the immediate
future was to show, the United States government chose the second
course, forgoing the $100,000,000 in order to prove the logic of their
policy of nonresistance to aggression and their repudiation of collective
security.

In anticipation of the forthcoming negotiations, while they were
going on, and immediately following their successful conclusion, there
was optimism in both countries about the possibility of a substantial
increase in Soviet-American trade. No one had any doubt that American credits were an indispensable condition for this, as is clear from
accounts in the American press of that period. On 18 November 1933,
the Washington correspondent for the *New York Times* reported that
Smith Brookhart, former senator from Iowa who was a special adviser
on agricultural affairs to the administration, talked of bringing Soviet
purchases up to $520,000,000 a year by extending credit. Francis Cole,
vice-president of the American Manufacturers Export Association, and
Carl W. Linscheid, president of the Export Managers' Club of New
York, said the same thing. This was the way the situation was assessed
by experts and specialists. They expected "a government guarantee of
credit" and announcements of "a credit policy" to follow the recognition of the USSR.[112] After the conclusion of the negotiations in
Washington, an editorial in the *New York Times* pointed out, "As a
factor in American industrial and commercial recovery Russian trade
will depend in no small degree on how much credit Moscow gets to
make purchases here."[113]

And so, when American historians write about the unwarranted hopes for a substantial increase in trade, they are unable to find reasons for the disappointment on both sides of the ocean. The root lies on the American continent, and this was clearly comprehended by the contemporaries who commented on the agreements of Roosevelt and Litvinov. The *New York Times* editorial mentioned above said that the United States was confronted with "an ultimate choice between a revision of our import regulations or a disappointment in Russian trade to those who now hail recognition as an introduction of an annual export business to Russia of $300,000,000 to $500,000,000."[114] The disappointment was a consequence of the policy of only one side—the ruling circles of the United States.

Incidentally, this demonstrates once more that trade considerations were not the deciding factor that made for the American initiative which culminated in recognition of the USSR. In a statement made in connection with the establishment of official relations, Colonel Hugh Cooper, president of the American-Russian Chamber of Commerce, who by virtue of his position had no personal interest in belittling the importance of the trade factor, stressed its "secondary importance" and pointed out as the prime moving force that led to recognition of the USSR its "greatest value to world peace."[115] Senator Robert Wagner, one of the main creators of the New Deal, also assessed the establishment of relations in this way. He called it "an effective contribution to efforts to bring about univeral peace."[116] The Americans did not lose sight of the paramount interest of the United States in normalizing political relations with a nation that was acquiring an ever-increasing importance as a positive force in its plans to contain the excessive activity of Japan and Germany.

The government of the United States was interested in the political value of establishing diplomatic relations with the Soviet Union, and was guided by the notion of the balance of power. It wanted its enemies in Europe and Asia, who were growing stronger, to know that America had ties with a great Eurasian power which was also threatened by them, and that these ties might lead to definite political collaboration. In his report on a conversation with Roosevelt, Litvinov wrote to Moscow on 8 November 1933: "Hull had probably told him about the remark made by me that morning about the presence of two sources of military peril, and Roosevelt, leading the conversation onto this subject, figured out for himself that I had meant Japan and Germany, which both have expansionist policies. He stressed that the Soviet Union stands between these two aggressors, but that together with America we would perhaps ward them off."[117]

At this stage of the pre-Second World War period, Roosevelt wished to keep the door open to cooperation with the Soviet Union, but was in no hurry to take any definite steps in that direction. He needed a strong counterforce to use against Germany and Japan, but only wanted to use it in case of necessity.

The United States did not wish to begin its relations with the USSR by establishing close political and economic cooperation. This restraint was reinforced by the traditional anti-Soviet elements in the United States, which were attacking the president's policy on the Russian question. Republican Senator Arthur Robinson (Indiana) called recognition of the USSR "a terrific mistake," a step "inimical to America's best interests."[118] Herbert Hoover had the wisdom to refrain from public comment, but as everyone knew, he took the same position as Senator Robinson. The ruling circles of the United States began at once to contrive conditions for restraint in Soviet-American relations. The White House and the State Department deemed it unnecessary to tie their hands by active cooperation with the Soviet Union, but rather chose to remain uncommitted. Then if some crisis were to erupt, it might be possible to profit from it, not checking the aggressor, leaving this task to their newly acquired partner, the USSR.

Despite all of the negative aspects of the Roosevelt-Hull Russian policy, the course taken by the Democratic administration in establishing diplomatic relations, realized in the 1933 agreement, was fundamentally of tremendous positive significance. This act was a great service to the cause of peace and antifascism. This was its essential importance. Diplomatic relations were arranged at a time of crisis preceding a storm. When the final test came, both sides had already developed a tradition of mutual trust which had its origins in November 1933.

In the Soviet Union the resumption of relations with the United States was greeted with gratification and even enthusiasm. This strengthened the traditional goodwill of our people toward the Americans and opened up good prospects for cooperation. Litvinov announced to members of the press in Washington on 17 November

1933: ''Yesterday's exchange of notes not only creates conditions indispensable to the rapid and successful settlement of the unsolved problems of the past, but, what is more important, opens a new chapter in the development of genuinely friendly relations and peaceful cooperation between the two greatest republics.''[119] This same idea was expressed by Kalinin, head of the Soviet state, in his radio address to the American people on 20 November 1933. From the most authoritative Soviet tribune, that of the Congress of the Communist Party, Stalin observed that ''this act is of very great significance for the whole system of international relations,'' emphasizing that the establishment of Soviet-American relations ''improves the chances of preserving peace.''[120]

4

On the Eve of the Second World War

Major Foreign Policy Concepts

During the second half of the 1930s the USSR finished laying the foundations of socialism and set about carrying out far-reaching plans for perfecting the socialist society. With the successful conclusion of the second Five-Year Plan (1933–37), "all of the exploiting classes were liquidated once and for all, the causes giving rise to the exploitation of one man by another and the division of society into the exploiters and the exploited were completely destroyed."[1] The triumph of socialism in our country was reflected and consolidated in law in the new constitution, adopted 5 December 1936.

Great economic and sociopolitical tasks were set before the Soviet people by the third Five-Year Plan (1938–42), approved at the eighteenth Congress of the Communist Party in March 1939. The "fundamental economic task" laid down by the Congress for the third Five-Year Plan was the goal of overtaking and outdistancing the most developed capitalist countries, including the United States, in economic matters, that is, in per capita production.[2] "The fulfillment of the third Five-Year Plan," read the resolution, "will be the best evidence of the triumphant force of Communism in its historical competition with capitalism."[3] Here was reflected once again the Soviet, Leninist view of world revolution, which has nothing to do with instigating revolts or with "revolutionary interference" in the affairs of other peoples.

The Stalin personality cult, which was decisively condemned by the Twentieth Congress of the Communist Party of the Soviet Union in February 1956 and by a special resolution of the Party's Central Committee on 30 June 1956,[4] caused substantial damage to successful socialist construction, to the introduction of the principles of socialist democracy into all spheres of life, and to the international prestige of the USSR. The 1956 resolutions point out the objective and subjective reasons for the appearance of the Stalin personality cult. In 1937 Stalin began to propagate mistaken views about the aggravation of the class struggle as the Soviet Union advanced toward socialism. This was at a time when socialism had already triumphed in our country, while the exploiting classes and their economic base had been liquidated. In practice, this erroneous theoretical formulation served as the basis for the grossest violations of socialist law and for mass repressions.

All of this was used by bourgeois propaganda in the struggle against socialism and the Soviet system. Distorting the nature and essence of the personality cult, the enemies of socialism strenuously propagandized the false thesis that the personality cult is a natural outcome of the socialist system. However, the most important fact about Soviet society in the thirties was not the historically accidental phenomenon of the Stalin personality cult but the successful construction of socialism; the superiority of socialism over capitalism had been proven, and the peace-loving nature of the Soviet state, the bastion of social progress, antifascism, and peace, had been demonstrated.

During the thirties peaceful coexistence, the basis of Soviet foreign policy, underwent further development. The capitalist world was rapidly splitting into two hostile camps, one of which—the Fascist—was frankly aggressive and intent on redrawing the map of the world. Under these circumstances, the foreign-policy doctrine of the USSR was modified to take into account the obvious difference between the Fascist bloc and the mixed system of the bourgeois-democratic nations. The Soviet Union emerged as a determined opponent of the aggressive plans of world fascism and an advocate of cooperation with the non-Fascist countries.

In December 1933 the Central Committee of the Soviet Communist Party decided to launch a campaign for collective security. It envisaged the possibility of concluding pacts for joint resistance to aggression and the entry of the USSR into the League of Nations. Thus, the struggle of the Soviet Union against the imminent military threat followed two main courses. In the first place, the Soviet people were building a strong productive potential which increased both our defensive capacity and our moral-political unity. Second, the Soviet government, having advanced the concept of the interdependence of peoples, summoned all peace-loving, nonaggressive nations to create a system of collective security. Entering the League of Nations in 1934, after Japan and Germany had withdrawn, the USSR tried to use this forum for organizing collective resistance to the Fascist aggressors.

Beginning in the mid-1930s, the struggle against fascism and the military threat intensified in all parts of the world, involving people of various shades of opinion, from Communists to liberals and conservatives. The historic decision of the Seventh Congress of the Communist International, which took place in Moscow in the summer of 1935, played a large part in activating this struggle. Here the slogans of the Popular Front—against reaction, fascism, and war—were advanced. This helped to overcome factionalism in the Communist movement and strengthen the forces opposing reaction, fascism, and war, the true bearers of which were the most chauvinistic, militaristic, and terroristic elements among the monopolist bourgeoisie, the military cliques, and the official bureaucracy of many countries.

The Soviet government had some success in its struggle for collective security but not as much as it aimed for. In the ruling circles of Britain, France, and the United States, those at the top usually shut their eyes to aggression, rejecting collective action with the USSR against the Fascist warmongers. Moscow tried repeatedly to convince them of the ruinous consequences of such behavior. Litvinov spared no effort in propagandizing for the principles of collective security. Western statesmen and public opinion recognized him as the leader in the campaign to achieve it. But no real joint opposition to the aggressors resulted, and the chances for this lessened as the thirties wore on.

When the Nazis seized Austria, the Soviet government appealed for specific measures to oppose them, either through the League of Nations or outside of it, depending on the counterproposals of those on whom Moscow was depending.[5] Britain and France declined the Soviet proposals, and the American government did not even reply to them. The Munich agreement of 1938, in which Britain and France betrayed Czechoslovakia with the blessing of the United States, demonstrated convincingly that the ruling circles of the West not only were not seeking, together with the Soviet Union, to restrain the aggressors but, on the contrary, were pushing them to the East, closer to the boundaries of the USSR. After Munich, the Soviet Union found itself more and more noticeably in a state of diplomatic isolation, inasmuch as the bourgeois-democratic countries did not wish to conduct businesslike negotiations with it. The position of London and Paris—again, bolstered by Washington—at the Moscow talks of 1939, showed once and for all the unwillingness of the Munichites to go along with us, and their secret desire to bring the USSR into conflict with Germany in Europe and with Japan in Asia.

At the Eighteenth Congress of the Soviet Communist Party, Stalin stated: "The new imperialist war became a fact."[6] A resolution of the congress also named the chief perpetrator of the war—fascism: "The posture of capitalism takes its tone from the Fascist countries, with their internal bloody terror and their foreign imperialist aggression, which has already led to the second imperialist war, with the participation of a number of countries in Europe and Asia, and threatening to spread farther."[7] The congress also severely condemned the policy of the bourgeois-democratic governments, which had connived with the aggressors. Stalin warned that "the big and dangerous political game started by the supporters of the policy of nonintervention may end in a serious fiasco for them."[8]

As Fascist aggression moved closer and closer to the boundaries of the USSR, Moscow found no dependable partners and allies, but instead met with hostile treatment from the French and British, who encouraged Germany and Japan to attack the Soviet Union. Under these circumstances, the Soviet government had to rely in much greater measure on its own strength alone, and to conduct its foreign policy with this in mind. In May 1939 V. M. Molotov himself assumed the position of peoples' commissar for foreign affairs. This meant not that the USSR was moving toward isolationism but rather that this peoples' commissariat was elevated in importance because the country was forced to recognize the failure of all previous efforts to organize collective security, and to depend to a greater degree than before on its own resources. The paramount task before the peoples' commissar-premier was to try to reach an agreement with Britain and France for joint action against aggression.

Today the whole world knows that the Anglo-French-Soviet conference in Moscow failed because the Western participants were hardened Munichites, for whom the trip to the eastern capital was a by-product of their secret desire to encourage Hitler toward a policy of eastward expansion. To stop the plans of the aggressors and of those who were conniving with them, Moscow agreed to the proposal of the German government to conclude a nonaggression pact, which was signed on 23 August 1939. This wrecked both the immediate plans of the Axis powers and the anti-Soviet calculations of the Munichites. This is precisely why the Munichites and like-minded historians ever since have tried so hard to make this action of the Soviet government appear as a betrayal.

As we have mentioned already, the economic depression of 1929–33 was an extremely important landmark in recent capitalist history. The capitalists sought various ways out of this critical situation. Some countries adopted fascism, either wholly or in part. Others took the path of a more flexible socioeconomic policy, moving the liberals, who were boldly breaking with the traditions of bourgeois individualism, to the fore. In still others, the changes took a radical-progressive form, in some places even bordering on revolution. In spite of all the political diversity and even the obvious antagonism between these methods, they were unified to some degree by one thing they had in common—an accelerated development of state-monopolistic capitalism.

The New Deal of Franklin Roosevelt in the United States, which fits into the second of the above-mentioned patterns, was most peculiarly characterized by two features: the speeding up of state-monopolistic development, and liberal social reform aimed at silencing popular protest and preventing any revolutionary solution to the crisis of capitalism. The depression dealt a shattering blow to the myths of American "exclusiveness," so popular during the prosperous period of the twenties. Within a short time everyone saw that the United States was the same kind of "European" country as Britain, France, or Germany; that they were all developing according to the general laws of capitalism and suffered from exactly the same evils. In the United States the idea of rugged individualism was deeper rooted than in Europe. Thus, here the repudiation of laissez-faire and the conversion to "European," that is, state-monopolistic measures, recommended in the theory of John Maynard Keynes, was especially traumatic.

The adoption by the American individualist bourgeoisie of a more collectivist point of view reflected the hopelessness of their position; it was a response to the demands of the working masses that the capitalists as a class be forced to assume responsibility for the social consequences of the depression. Recognition of the positive value of statist collectivist methods was also influenced by the achievements of socialist construction in the USSR. The idea of planning, and the notion that the state was responsible for the fate of each person, acquired widespread popularity in the United States. The conditions necessary for the statement of the tasks of a revolutionary-socialist reconstruction of society did not exist in the United States, but the bourgeoisie had worked itself into such a state of fear that many of its members did not rule out the coming of a revolution. One cannot say that a revolutionary situation existed in the United States in the thirties. On the other hand, here, in contrast with Germany, tremendous resources were available which, with proper mobilization by the state, might be used to overcome the consequences of the depression and modify in a historically positive way anachronistic bourgeois institutions that had taken shape as long ago as the end of the nineteenth century.

That is how the New Deal came into the world, giving rise to both unwarranted hopes and to unfounded accusations against the Roosevelt reformers. In the immense literature on the New Deal,[9] the question of how it ended is usually posed as well. In our opinion, the New Deal as a policy of liberal social reforms had been exhausted by the end of 1938 and came to an end on the eve of the Second World War. But the state-monopoly side of the New Deal did not disappear. On the contrary, it gathered even more momentum during the war years and in the postwar period. This demonstrates the inevitability and objectivity of the state-monopolist development of present-day capitalism, which finally leads to the complete negation of the system of private property.

The foreign policy of the United States during the period of the New Deal was very contradictory. The Roosevelt administration, of course, saw that the Axis powers were a danger to the national interests of the United States. But it would not take a leading role in the struggle against the aggressors, preferring to leave that to others. Among these others, it counted most of all on the USSR, and because of this made far-reaching plans to weaken both the Fascist nations and the socialist state. Nonresistance to aggression was being dictated by still another result of the 1929–33 depression: the American economy could not seem to recover its former effectiveness, in spite of the fact that the most experienced political figures stood at the national helm. Aggravation of the international situation might bring important stimuli and at last force the rusty economic machinery to function actively. And that is what did actually happen.

The Practice of Soviet-American Relations, 1933-39

To a considerable extent though, the establishment of Soviet-American relations in 1933 did become a factor for the prevention of war. Both countries had a stake in containing the aggressors, who had to take this into account. But it must be admitted that Soviet-American relations did not play as great a role as they might have in staving off the Second World War.

In December 1933 the first American ambassador, William Bullitt, arrived in Moscow, and in the following month, A. A. Troyanovsky, the first Soviet ambassador to the United States, also took up his duties. Bullitt was well received in Moscow. Even before his talk with Stalin on 20 December 1933, the American ambassador told Molotov, chairman of the Council of Peoples' Commissars, on 15 December: "I must emphasize the quite exceptional warmth with which I am surrounded here and which is beyond any praise."[10] In both capitals there was much talk of peace and friendship at that time. In the speech he made when he delivered his credentials to President Roosevelt, Troyanovsky used the word *peace* seven times in one passage.[11]

But Bullitt's mission to Moscow was not calculated to establish effective cooperation in the name of peace, and not because Bullitt, a noted liberal and "sovietophile" married to Louise Bryant, the widow of John Reed, who had founded the Communist Party of the United States, tried (as often happens in similar situations) to atone for his "sins" through a "tough" position toward the USSR. Rather, when the liberal Bullitt, who was inimically disposed toward the Soviet Union, was replaced in his position in Moscow by the conservative Joseph Davies, who was friendly toward us, the situation did not change for the better on the important questions: Soviet-American political cooperation against the aggressors did not ensue. This was made impossible by the fundamental principles of America's prewar foreign policy.

Bullitt was very active from the time of his arrival in Moscow, and was helped by the fact that, unlike other ambassadors, the doors of the highest Soviet officials were open to him. In a conversation with *New York Times* correspondent Walter Duranty on 25 December 1933, Stalin said: "Bullitt made a good impression on me and my comrades. I had never met him before but had heard much about him from Lenin, who also liked him. What I like about him is that he does not talk like the ordinary diplomat—he is a straightforward man and says what he thinks. In general, he produced a very good impression here."[12] In this interview, Stalin was guided by an elementary rule of diplomacy: not necessarily to say what is the case, but to be sure to say what is necessary. However, possibly due to some kind of subtle calculation, he neither said what was the case, nor, what is more important, what was necessary in order to praise an ambassador. It is doubtful whether Bullitt was a straightforward man and told the Soviet leaders what he was thinking. And there can be absolutely no doubt that even if a high-ranking diplomat is indeed such a man, one should try to single out some other qualities of his praise.

At first the Soviet leaders actually did like the American ambassador, associating him with the 1919 mission and with the establishment of diplomatic relations, in which he played a prominent role. Probably this put Bullitt even more on his guard, bearing in mind that even without this, influential anti-Soviet and anti-Communist circles of the United States regarded him as a pink; that even his own uncle, the clergyman James Bullitt, condemned recognition of the USSR in the most disparaging terms: the United States had "disgraced itself by establishing relations with a country which is beyond the pale—a pariah among nations."[13] He did not want to damage his image even further, and, realizing that Washington had no intention of using Soviet-American relations as a means to collective security, decided to distinguish himself in Moscow, but not in the way in which those who had at first been impressed by him had expected.

William Bullitt began his ambassadorial work with blackmailing hints that since Japan was always a threat to the Soviet Union, the Soviets should be compliant toward the United States. The ambassador having taken the initiative, the Americans without delay found an area in which the USSR should yield to them. Reopening the negotiations about debts, the American government repudiated the main principle fixed in the Roosevelt-Litvinov understanding, namely, the granting of loans to the Soviet Union. The Americans who took part in the negotiations, and historians of this episode, tried to justify the repudiation of the loan by the confusion between the terms *loan* and *credit*. They pointed out that in 1934 Congress had prohibited extension of loans to any government that had not paid off its debts to the United States. This thesis was unsound even if only because the USSR was not a debtor of the United States in the strict sense of the word, but also because the Johnson Act need not have been applied to the Soviet Union, even judging by the wording of law itself.

But there are more substantial objections as well. Americans often say that foreigners, and among them Russians, do not understand all the complexities involved in the working out of foreign-policy decisions by the United States, especially the sensitivity of the president's position, which is bound by certain limitations. This argument has been applied to the relation between the gentlemen's agreement on debts and the Johnson Act. A similar point is made about the present situation in Soviet-American relations. It goes without saying that the functioning of the internal political machinery of the United States in adopting a decision on the Soviet question is a complex matter, and probably the foreign observer does not always see all of the fine points of this process. But the Americans did not choose to understand what is a more important and obvious truth: people in the Soviet Union, as in any other country about which the United States makes decisions, are not in the least obliged to admire the "democratic" method by which the final point of view is worked out. After all, the Congress, the courts, and the administration constitute a unified national system, in the name of which the president appears in his official relations with other countries. It is no concern of the Soviet Union, strictly speaking, how the Soviet policy of the United States is formed; what it wants is to enter into negotiations and agreements with plenipotentiary representatives of the United States, to conduct business responsibly, proceeding on the assumption that the other side's representative is also empowered to negotiate and is serious about doing so. In the debt negotiations which took place after the establishment of diplomatic relations, the Americans tried, in the international forum, to use as an argument the imperfections (if they were imperfections) of their own foreign policy-making apparatus—the excuse was that the Congress had failed to back up the president's commitment and the commitments were erroneously made. This was a very peculiar defense, which claimed an exceptional place for the United States in international law.

The negotiations went on for a long time, more than a year. The Americans, for their part, violated the main condition of the gentlemen's agreement, thereby repudiating the Anglo-Saxon tradition, highly revered in Western literature, that a gentleman keeps his word. The Russian Communists proved to be more gentlemanly than the American squires. As if that were not enough, William Bullitt began to blackmail Moscow; according to him, the refusal to make the concessions demanded would worsen the condition of Soviet trade and the position of the USSR in the Far East. On 10 April 1934 Litvinov wrote to Troyanovsky: "We must overcome Bullitt's inclination to blackmail, and we can do this only through self-control and composure. We must show that cutting off trade with America does not make the impression on us that Bullitt expected, that it is a blow not against us, but only against those Americans who are interested in trade."[14]

On 31 January 1935 Cordell Hull announced that there had been a failure to reach agreement on the debt question, groundlessly laying the blame for this on the USSR. Litvinov immediately refuted this assertion in a statement published on 3 February 1935 in *Pravda*. He pointed out that the Americans had violated the main condition of the 1933 understanding—that they had refused the loan. "In its proposals, the Soviet side kept strictly within the limits of this agreement," said the peoples' commissar, "bringing its concessions to a point beyond which we could not go without a reconsideration of the entire Washington agreement. We refused to enter upon this course, which might have led to a complete annulment of the results achieved in Washington and to the necessity for new negotiations on all the basic questions previously resolved."[15] In the same statement, Litvinov emphasized that the unsuccessful outcome of the negotiations need not stand in the way of the development of trade or hamper efforts to preserve peace.

American diplomacy was mistaken in calculating that the USSR would try at any price to win the favor of the United States in the difficult international situation. But it did achieve a certain negative result by leaving a troublesome knot in Soviet-American relations which was used as an excuse whenever Americans found it necessary to explain why they did not join with the Soviet Union to oppose aggression.

As is apparent from the logic of his actions and from the written record, William Bullitt wanted to show that Litvinov did not understand the importance of Soviet-American rapprochement, and even entertained the hope that he might achieve Litvinov's dismissal. He thought that the Japanese-German peril was so great that Stalin and the higher military chiefs (whom he had started teaching how to play polo, and generally courted in every possible way) would demand that Litvinov yield to the Americans in the matter of the debts.[16] The ambassador hoped to gain the favor of "those leaders in the Soviet hierarchy who desire close collaboration with the United States." "I propose," he continued in a telegram to Hull on 30 June 1934, "to take the general attitude that we are most anxious to cooperate with the Soviet Union but that Litvinov is indifferent to the establishment of such collaboration."[17]

In order to put pressure on the Soviet government and to sow discord within the leading circles of the USSR, on 6 February 1935 the State Department announced the recall of its naval attaché, the closing of the consulate general, and a reduction in the embassy staff. The correspondence between Chargé d'Affaires John C. Wiley and Hull during this period shows that Washington was hoping for the downfall of Litvinov as a result of American pressure, and was very disappointed when it saw that this did not happen.[18] At the same time it gives evidence that the Americans were concerned lest Moscow make public the gentlemen's agreement and demonstrate to the whole world who it was that had violated it. On 19 February Hull even forbade Wiley to hold a press conference, warning him of the danger of saying too much.[19] The stunt of putting pressure on Moscow to oust Litvinov burst like a soap bubble. All that remained was a barrier that now stood in the way of the development of Soviet-American political cooperation.

In the summer of 1935 another such barrier was erected. By this time the government and broad sectors of the American public could see with their own eyes that the USSR was not merely a peace-loving nation but was firmly disposed to take joint action with other nations in the name of peace. One proof of this was the decision of the Harris Foundation at the University of Chicago in the fall of 1934 to devote the next annual summer symposium to the theme, "The Soviet Union and World Problems." The seminar was held 24–29 June 1935. Ambassador Troyanovsky took part in it, giving a report on basic principles of Soviet foreign policy. In opening the seminar, Professor Samuel Harper stressed the appropriateness and timeliness of the Fund's decision, inasmuch as "the Soviet Union has been one of the most active forces, at times the initiating force, in the efforts of the last year to further the cause of peace through programs of collective security."[21]

The growth of this kind of sentiment put the United States government on its guard, for it was not ready to participate in a program of collective security jointly with the Soviet Union. It was necessary to counteract the atmosphere that prevailed in forums such as the seminar in Chicago. The State Department was constantly looking for convincing arguments to show that the USSR would not be a suitable ally.

While negotiations about debts were still in progress, Bullitt began to consider the possibility of raising the question of Comintern activities and accusing the Soviet Union of violating its agreement to give up subversive propaganda. It was impossible to find even one instance of interference by official Soviet figures in the internal affairs of the United States. Nor was there any anti-American propaganda being carried on in the USSR. In the United States, however, hostile activities and statements with respect to the Soviet Union were the order of the day, and not only for Russian emigrés and the Hearst press, but also for people with some official status and authority. For example, in June 1935 Admiral Sterling Yates Jr., issued a statement that got worldwide publicity, calling for a joint campaign with Hitler against the USSR.[22] Franklin Roosevelt, as supreme commander-in-chief, was obliged to curb this sorry fire-eater, but did not even reprimand him publicly. In reply to the protest by Ambassador Troyanovsky, the State Department informed him that the Department of the Navy had told the admiral that what he had said was out of line.

Impervious to the beam in its own eye, American diplomacy began to look closely to see whether there were not any motes in that of the Soviet Union. As there proved to be no evidence of Soviet violations of the 1933 agreement, a spurious attack was planned. The Seventh Congress of the Comintern was considered a convenient opportunity. The State Department and the embassy in Moscow prepared for the congress in their own way, planning a propaganda attack beforehand.[23] Bullitt did not restrict himself to the subject of the so-called Soviet violations, but criticized the decisions of the congress in substance as well. He expressed deep concern about the slogan of the Popular Front and advised the president to make a declaration which "might have a powerful influence in stripping the mask from the united front movement, not only in America, but also in Europe."[24]

Spurred by reactionary propaganda, the United States government protested to the Soviet government for convoking and conducting the congress of the Communist International in Moscow, regarding this as a violation of the Roosevelt-Litvinov understanding. As might have been expected, the Soviet side rejected the protest. In a statement by Tass on 28 August 1935 the reasons for the rejection were explained— "The government of the USSR cannot accept and has not accepted any responsibility for the Communist International." And Moscow reaffirmed the "immutable aspiration of the USSR to the further development of friendly cooperation between the USSR and the United States, which would serve the interests of the peoples of both countries and would have a great significance for the cause of universal peace."[25] The note cited, from the Peoples' Commissariat for Foreign Affairs to the American embassy, does not touch on the substance of the decisions of the seventh congress. Since it was dealing with the official representative of the United States president in the USSR, the peoples' commissariat behaved rightly in not engaging in debates on the Comintern position but simply pointed out that according to the 1933 agreement the Soviet government assumed no responsibility for the activities of the International.

But historians have a right to depart from this strictly legal position, especially as American officials as well as the press had delved into the nature of the Comintern's business. The resolutions of the congress were leveled against fascism and war, which one would have thought would please the United States government. The Comintern proposed a program that left a broad sphere of action for both liberals and even for conservatives who wished to oppose Hitler. It was precisely this that troubled those of the United States who did not wish to be associated with the Communists, whether against war or fascism. The reasons for their criticism of Comintern policy varied. Furniss, for example, lamented the alleged repudiation by the Communists of revolution, of the struggle against capitalism; he grieved over the fact that the seventh congress had worked out a "reformist" platform.[26] The bourgeois ideologists would not have been frightened by the Communist party slipping into reformism. They were alarmed at the exact opposite—the strong aspects of the new Comintern line, and its close adherence to the historical tasks of the prewar period.

While the bourgeoisie and the petty bourgeois ideologists were attacking the seventh congress for "reformism" and "subterfuge," American officials sought to accuse the USSR of interfering in their national affairs. In his talk with Roy W. Howard on 1 March 1936, Stalin showed once again that American protests to the USSR were groundless and unreasonable, observing in passing that the United States government did not suppress the activities of anti-Soviet terrorists on its own soil. "We can coexist in peace, if we will refrain from caviling at each other over every trifle," concluded Stalin stoically.[27]

The American literature, on the whole, tends to take a sensible, skeptical attitude toward this strident but inglorious chapter in the history of the diplomacy of the 1930s. Samuel Harper has called the Hull-Bullitt demarche "a bit premature, and certainly immature."[28] Pauline Tompkins points out that "even conservatives failed to share Secretary Hull's alarm."[29]

The episode with the seventh congress of the Comintern cannot be understood properly except in the context of the general course of American foreign policy in that period. In the summer of 1935 the serious aggression of the Italian Fascists against Ethiopia was gathering force, which once again and even more clearly posed the question: what were the great non-Axis powers about; why did they do nothing to restrain Mussolini's aggression? Putting even greater pressure on the strain in Soviet-American relations, Washington was preparing an alibi for itself ahead of time. It was as though it were saying to the world: it is impossible to cooperate with a malicious defaulter on debts which is conducting subversive activities despite its solemn commitments. And this was exactly what the Fascists wanted. "Yet at the hour of Signor Mussolini's adventure in Africa," Williams observed, "the United States concluded that a major issue was raised by the

Comintern meetings of 1935 in Moscow. One can but conclude that the Roosevelt administration determined, despite Soviet leadership in the organization of resistance to Hitler, Mussolini, and Japan, to press a highly legalistic issue to the point of serious aggravation.''[30]

The establishment of diplomatic relations served to promote an expansion of Soviet-American trade by comparison with 1932–33, even though the anti-Soviet forces in the United States did everything they could to ensure the realization of their prophecy that recognition would not lead to an increase in the volume of trade. In 1935 the first trade agreement was concluded. In the course of the negotiations the Soviet side raised the question of normalizing trade conditions by a mutual grant of most-favored-nation treatment. The United States government decided that this would be of no advantage to them. In a telegram of instructions to Chargé d'Affaires Wiley on 27 March 1935, Hull explained: ''An offer on the part of the Soviet Government to extend most-favored-nation treatment to American imports or not to discriminate against American goods would, in view of the Government monopoly of foreign trade, be valueless, and consequently completely unacceptable.''[31] In short, it considered that the USSR should have granted the most-favored-nation treatment to the United States automatically following the establishment of diplomatic relations. The Soviets, on the other hand, faced the prospect of working to obtain most-favored-nation treatment from the United States, where there was no monopoly of foreign trade, and where the government was in a position to bargain to get something of equivalent value from the contractor in return. From this it became apparent that the Americans were, after all, just as interested in the growth of trade as the Russians. The United States agreed to grant the Soviet Union certain tariff advantages, and asked us to commit ourselves to purchase annually goods in an amount not below a minimum sum that was fixed in the agreement. The Soviet side refused to agree to any minimum volume of imports from the United States fixed by the agreement, so as not to tie its own hands, but agreed to declare its intention (not an obligatory term) to purchase goods in the amount of $30,000,000 annually. The agreement of 13 July 1935 did contain these two fundamental conditions: the Soviet declaration of their stated intention and certain customs-tariff privileges for our exports to the United States.

On 4 August 1937 a new trade agreement was signed. The discussions involved in drafting it centered on two questions: whether the declaration of most-favored-nation treatment should be unilateral (only on the part of the United States) or bilateral, and what the volume of Soviet purchases from the United States should be. As before, the Americans refused to accept most-favored-nation treatment from the Soviet side. They felt that they must try to get a real concession, and not this symbolic declaration, inasmuch as the USSR supposedly could engage in trade only on the basis of most-favored-nation treatment with any nation that it recognized. Hull specifically instructed Ambassador Davies to take this position, feeling that Davies lacked an adequate understanding of the matter, and was ready to accept from the Russians a supposedly unreal concession.[32]

The picture that emerged from this was a strange one. The Soviets absolutely refused to accept most-favored-nation status from the Americans unilaterally. The Americans rejected a bilateral declaration of this principle—that is, they were turning their backs on the advantage we were offering. Hull felt that, by accepting such a concession (he put *concession* in quotes), the United States would weaken its position in wringing from the Russians the promise to bring their purchases up to $40,000,000 annually. He also had a certain political calculation in mind. He did not want the world to get the impression that there was some sort of Soviet-American "entente."

In this respect the agreement turned out to be complex, more complex legally than it is usually presented in American and Soviet literature. The United States did in fact grant, and the USSR did accept, the status of most-favored-nation for Soviet goods. But the Americans accepted this principle from the USSR for American products only in part. This was set down in the so-called exportation clause from the United States.[33] This article specified that goods exported from the United States would fall in the most-favored-nation category, but said nothing about how these goods would be treated in the USSR. We can judge that the most-favored-nation principle was not to be applied absolutely also from the Tass report on 8 August 1937. It explained that the agreement provided for the unconditional and unrestricted application of most-favored-nation status to the import of Soviet goods into the United States and for conditions for the export of American goods to the USSR.[34] In this agreement the USSR did not bind itself by promising to bring purchases from the United

States to a specified minimum volume, but in a special note the Soviet government declared its intention to raise the volume to $40,000,000 during the year that the agreement was to be in effect.[35]

The creation of a relatively favorable contractual framework improved Soviet-American trade conditions. The volume of trade began to rise steadily, as the following figures, given in thousands of rubles, show:[36]

Year	Export to the United States	Import from the United States
1933	48,669	57,783
1934	49,756	62,296
1935	92,508	102,755
1936	103,513	166,321
1937	101,443	185,600
1938	67,126	308,376
1939	64,727	228,980

As a result of the progress made in the socialist reconstruction of industry, the structure of Soviet imports from the United States underwent a noticeable change. The import of agricultural machinery, automobiles, and metallurgical equipment was sharply curtailed; the purchase of textiles was practically discontinued. But the import of the latest technological wares, modern machine tools, and electrical equipment increased substantially. The main articles of Soviet export to the United States before the war were furs, manganese ore, coal, timber, and linen fabric.

In the American literature one often finds statements to the effect that as the USSR made progress in creating its own industry, it lost its former interest in the American market, which is what explains the modesty of the above figures by comparison with 1927–30. Authors who are more hostile to the USSR add that the Russians had nothing with which to buy, for they had exhausted their resources in the struggle for industrialization. Neither version is accurate. Both are acknowledged to be efforts to justify the position of the opponents of recognition of the USSR, to corroborate their "clairvoyance."

One should not go to extremes in assessing Soviet-American trade during the second half of the thirties. It must be kept in mind that during this period world trade in general was not flourishing. Act-ually, the Soviet Union was not obliged to buy from the United States goods which it produced itself at home. But purchases from the United States increased sharply by comparison with 1933, in 1938 exceeding that level fivefold. What interfered with a greater increase in Soviet-American trade was not the condition of the Soviet economy, but American commercial and economic policy toward the USSR. Imports from the United States were held back by unsatisfactory credit and financial conditions. Even after 1933, the United States remained the only large country that refused to give credit for trade with the Soviet Union. On the whole, though, trade relations were developing satisfactorily.

After the establishment of diplomatic relations, Soviet-American contacts increased in a number of areas, and important progress was made in the direction of rapprochement between the Soviet and American peoples. Close cultural ties were established. During the thirties translations of the works of Maxim Gorky, Mikhail Sholokhov, Leonid Leonov, Aleksandr Fadeev, Aleksei Tolstoy, and other Soviet writers began to appear in the United States. The literature of Socialist realism, and Socialist ideas themselves gained considerable popularity among Americans at that time. In the Soviet Union, the names of Dreiser, Sinclair, Hemingway, Steinbeck, and many other American literary figures were reaching a wide circle of readers.

Americans became interested in the study of the Russian language. At the University of Moscow, the Anglo-American Institute began to operate successfully, offering courses in Russian language, history, and literature. The heroic flights of Soviet pilots over the North Pole to America in 1937 gave rise to both a feeling of respect for the Soviet people and an awareness of the geographic proximity of the two countries. Representatives of the USSR were generally welcomed cordially in America. A. I. Mikoyan, who visited the United States in 1936 (when he was a member of the Politburo and peoples' commissar for the Food Industry), wrote in 1971: "We traveled across America from east to west and back, and nowhere did either the American police or the authorities create any difficulties for us. We visited factories wherever we wished, never once being refused anywhere. The attitude of all the ordinary people, workers, employees, directors of companies, and everyone with whom we had contact was most courteous and obliging. The atmosphere at that time was cordial, the attitude toward Soviet people could not have been better, not what it is today, thirty-five years later."[37]

After 1933 Americans in the Soviet Union were regarded with even greater interest and respect than earlier. This mutually friendly atmosphere, although it did not lead to political cooperation on the key problems of the prewar period, proved in the end to be not a hollow abstraction. This was confirmed by the events of 1941, a tragic year for both countries.

Lost Political Opportunities

Before that, though, the cordial relations that developed in many areas between Russians and Americans did not find a corresponding political expression. The United States government did not cooperate with the Soviet Union within the framework of collective security. It is hard to agree with the assessment of the state of our political relations given by Peoples' Commissar Litvinov in a letter to V. P. Potemkin, the ambassador to Italy, on 27 June 1934, at the height of the renewed negotiations about the debts: "Political relations leave nothing to be desired. A degree of cooling is noticeable as a result of Johnson's bill cutting off trade between us and the United States."[38]

It was precisely political relations that left very much to be desired between 1933 and 1941. The USSR was necessary to American political strategists as a force to resist the enemies of the United States in Asia and Europe. But this need was not important enough to make them enter into an alliance with the Soviet Union to suppress aggression. Such an alliance did not figure in Washington's plans. The government of the United States was carried away with the concept of "balance of power."

Guided by this principle, the Roosevelt administration always had at hand at least two arguments to explain its refusal to cooperate politically with the Soviet Union. One it created for itself, in the form of unsettled questions about debts and propaganda. The other was provided by American reactionaries, who up to 1941 had still not got used to even the elementary fact of recognition of the USSR, considering it a temporary skid to the Left by the "Communist" Roosevelt government. We are not yet speaking here of the isolationists;

isolationism did not consist entirely of connivance with aggression. The United States could have taken part in the political struggle against the Axis powers without violating the traditional principle of avoiding military alliances. Moreover, as events following the Second World War showed convincingly, when the ruling circles of the United States found it necessary, they set about energetically to "reeducate" the people and were able to reorient the country without much difficulty from isolationism to aggressive "collective security."

Congress remained the source of a variety of anti-Soviet influences. When the Americans led the negotiations about debts up a blind alley, drafts of a resolution to break diplomatic relations appeared on Capitol Hill. At the height of the excitement about the seventh congress of the Comintern, Republican Senator Arthur Vandenberg proposed reprinting a hysterical article from the *New York Times* of July 1935 disclosing the penetration of the Reds into the United States. Introducing this article into the Congressional Record Vandenberg demanded that the State Department take cognizance of this situation. He added that if the Russians had violated the 1933 agreement, "the agreement for recognition should be withdrawn."[39] The reactionaries in Congress regarded the mere recognition of the USSR as an effort on the part of Roosevelt "to Russianize and socialize America."[40] A lonely voice on the Hill was that of Congressman William B. Oliver, who answered the hostile statements of Hamilton Fish about recognition of the USSR. He pointed out to the reactionaries and isolationists that "the great underlying purpose behind the recognition of Russia was world peace, and it has had that effect, whether you agree with me or not."[41]

As has been mentioned above, the first American ambassador readily took his cue from the anti-Soviet circles, painstakingly removing the pink stains of the past from his diplomatic dress coat. He made it his business to disrupt peaceful coexistence between the USSR and the United States. Encouraging his government's fear of the Comintern, he wrote: "The problem of relations with the Government of the Soviet Union is, therefore, a subordinate part of the problem presented by communism as a militant faith determined to produce world revolution and the 'liquidation' (that is to say, murder) of all nonbelievers." This passage alone shows that Bullitt's way of thinking did not exactly make him a suitable ambassador to Moscow.

The report quoted above also contains such lines as the following: "There is no doubt whatsoever that all orthodox communist parties in all countries, including the United States, believe in mass murder."[42]

This forced Roosevelt and Hull to consider replacing Bullitt in Moscow, of transferring him to a more appropriate post. The ambassador himself realized that there was nothing for him to do in the USSR. He had lost touch with the leading Soviet circles, and along with this the capacity to make sensible judgments about what was going on in the country of his sojourn. And Roosevelt needed accurate information about the USSR, not as an immediate ally, but as a counterbalance against Japan and Germany, on which he wished to rely in carrying out his foreign-policy plans.

The new ambassador, Joseph Davies, had three main tasks before him: to conclude a new trade agreement which would provide for an expansion of Soviet purchases; to make a precise determination of the military-economic and political potential of the USSR and to correctly assess its importance as a factor in the power balance; and to delimit the extent to which the Soviet government would tolerate the appeasement of aggressors by the Western countries and trust their empty words, that is, to provide Washington with a reliable key to understanding at which point Moscow might abandon hope of an alliance with the nonfascist West and enter into possible negotiations with Germany and/or Japan to avert armed conflicts.

American bourgeois historians have often used harsh language to revile Davies, and this is understandable. During the years of the cold war it was necessary to condemn anything that had even the slightest trace of a decent attitude toward the USSR. Prejudice against Davies has been so great that his detractors[43] have ignored the elementary fact that he handled the tasks that he had been set brilliantly.

A trade agreement was concluded to the advantage of both sides. In a telegram to the embassy on 1 August 1937, Hull deemed it necessary "to commend the excellent work of the Embassy in reaching an agreement on so satisfactory a basis."[44]

Davies, unlike Bullit, in his reports to the president and the secretary of state presented the facts first, and not conjectures. He did not let himself be carried away with propagandist assertions about the breakdown of the Soviet economy, or political instability and the weakening of Soviet defensive capacity as a result of political repression. The ambassador assured his government that the Soviet Union was strong in every respect. Not everyone in Washington found this plausible, especially not those who were already convinced that the Soviet system could not endure. When everyone around him was reiterating that the Soviet government was "weak," he wrote to Hull (9 November 1937): "In any assessment of this government as a factor in the international situation it would, in my opinion, be a serious mistake to underestimate the strength of the government here."[45] In the summer of 1941 Davies was one of the few American political figures who correctly assessed the correlation of forces on the Soviet-German front, and predicted a victory for the USSR. He also told his chiefs that Soviet patience with appeasement would not last. Long before August 1939 he warned that if the Western countries were to enter into an agreement with Hitler at the expense of the USSR, the latter would also begin negotiations with Germany in order to protect its own interests. He also stressed that the policy of instigating Hitler against the USSR would force the Russians in greater or in full measure to depend on their own strength, and would destroy the bridge between East and West. In the light of this, the accusation that Moscow had "made a fool" of Davies, that he had not understood anything in Russia, looks ridiculous. On the contrary, he understood a great deal, judged the USSR more accurately than Bullitt, and thereby did the Roosevelt administration a great service. But even at that, Washington was interested in only one part of Davies' message: that the USSR was a real force. The other part, about Soviet readiness to join with the Western democracies in opposing Fascist aggression, was not very desirable even before the war. And after 1945, in the conditions of the cold war, this accurate assessment was completely rejected. From this stems the distorted political portrait of Davies as a diplomat.

He advocated active peaceful coexistence with the Soviet Union under the conditions of the imminent world war, but at the same time Davies pursued the course of ideological struggle against the socialist system. While his statement of the economic achievements of the USSR was correct, he explained them not by the superiority of social-ism, but by the fact that "the communistic principle here has in actual fact been abandoned."[46] In the spirit of peaceful coexistence, Davies, unlike the pathologically anti-Communist Bullitt, wrote that Russian communism was no threat to the United States. At the same time, he demonstrated bourgeois narrow-mindedness and ideological aggressiveness, representing the situation of the Soviet government in the summer of 1938 as follows: "To maintain its existence, this government has to apply capitalistic principles. Otherwise it will fail and be overthrown. That will not be permitted by the men presently in power, if they can avoid it. I expect to see this government, while professing devotion to Communism, move constantly more to the right, in practice, just as it has for the past eight years. If it maintains itself, it may evolve into a type of Fabian socialism, with large industry in the hand of the state, with, however, the agricultural and smaller businesses and traders working under capitalistic, property, and profit principles."[47]

On this point, Davies, like all of the other bourgeois prophets of the regeneration of Russian socialism, was mistaken. What misled him was the false presumption that socialism was incompatible with progress in the socioeconomic sphere and had no constructive potentialities. But Davies' critics prefer not to criticize him for this.

A more essential part of Davies' assessments of the position of the USSR at the threshold of the war than his false prophecies was his confidence in the possibility and necessity of the peaceful cooperation between our countries. In June of 1938, in his final report on his stay in the Soviet Union, he wrote "objectively, and without regard to ideological conflicts": "A common ground between the United States and the USSR, and one that will obtain for a long period of time, in my opinion, lies in the fact that both are sincere advocates of world peace."[48]

The United States government did not preclude the possibility of cooperation with the Soviet Union—but in the future, when the course of international events would have become completely clear. In the meantime it did not wish to take any positive step toward this end, using as an excuse the real and imaginary isolationism of the American people. American isolationism also became the redeeming argument for the postwar historians who had to find some explanation for America's failure to act against Fascist aggression, that is, for the American contribution to the outbreak of the war. This is a very weak argument. We will not go into the question of whether the American people were as isolationist in their attitudes as Roosevelt and Hull believed and postwar historians said they were, although there is reason to believe that the importance of this isolationism is greatly exaggerated, and the treatment of it is one-sided.[49] In any case, it appears indisputable that the United States government rejected the Soviet proposals for cooperation, realizing their value and seeing the consequences of its rejection. It did not explain to the people the danger of isolationism and the positive value of the Soviet proposal on collective security, nor did it advance such proposals on its own initiative. Here again we have a situation where the peculiar features of the American political process, among them the important role of domestic politics in the working out of foreign policy, claim the right to consideration under the code of international law.

The Soviet government was, of course, demanding too much of Washington in proposing joint measures against aggression within the framework of collective security. In the 1930s, probably for the last time in its history the United States could permit itself to behave in neutralist and isolationist fashion, although it was already considered a great world power at the turn of the century. America's ruling circles had not yet developed a sense of "world responsibility." The time for this had not yet come; they felt that the USSR, Britain, and France should oppose the Fascist "new" order first. In addition, the American bourgeoisie had not yet created for itself the threat of communism as a factor dictating its foreign policy: at that time the USSR was not regarded as a threat by most Americans, and those who already considered it a danger thought they could let the Axis powers take the leading role in the struggle against it. To repeat, the inaction of that period was basically dictated by the view of the Fascist countries, and not of the USSR. The optimum alternative would be if the Axis, the Anglo-French coalition, and communism could all three be weakened without active American intervention. This explains the neutralist and isolationist policy of the United States in the 1930s. Only a few years later the Americans abandoned their neutral-isolationist stance, because in the shortest possible time the international scene underwent a radical change. Isolationism and neutralism became a hindrance in the struggle against the revolutionary transformation of the world, and at the same time prevented the United States from fortifying itself in the vacuum of capitalist power formed by the immediate results of the war.

The contemporary historian, analyzing the reasons for the failure of efforts to ward off the Second World War, cannot excuse the United States of responsibility because of the isolationist mood of the American people. The existence of neutrality laws is not an argument, but only a part of the picture of American foreign policy in the second half of the 1930s, and they did not operate in the impartial way claimed by most American historians. Spain is an example. The United States government could and should have sold arms to the lawful government but did not, thus effectively taking the side of the Fascist rebels. Here American policy cannot be explained by the standard references to isolationism, especially as many isolationists demanded that the embargo on the delivery of arms to the lawfully elected Republican government of Spain be lifted. Speaking about this episode roughly in the same spirit as we do, Basil Rauch, apologist for Roosevelt, finds an absolutely unbelievable way out for a scholar to explain why Roosevelt behaved this way toward Spain—"The question . . . cannot be answered satisfactorily."[50] However, genuine scholarship rejects this bourgeois-positivist agnosticism which is a cover to excuse Roosevelt and Hull. It is perfectly clear that the policy of Washington toward Spain was a deliberate, politically calculated step against the Revolution. Francoism was distasteful, but it was the only force available to oppose the peoples' democracy. It should be remembered that the United States did not recognize Soviet Russia for sixteen years, while Franco-Spain was found fit for democracy sixteen hours after the fall of Madrid.[51]

As we have written earlier, Stalin told the Americans in 1936 that if they would stop making issues over trifles, would stop allowing important matters to go unattended because of petty disputes, both sides could do much to preserve universal peace. Cordell Hull expressed himself in about the same terms, only with much more moralizing and exasperation, to Troyanovsky on 26 March 1939. The secretary of state deplored the fact that the United States, the USSR, Britain, and France did not act as one, did not use "their combined moral influence for peace." He pointed out to the Soviet ambassador that Russia's bad behavior in "small ways" is "seriously handicapping such supremely important efforts."[52]

Where does the historical truth lie? Who was it that actually interfered with the "supremely important efforts," that is, the efforts to stop the aggressors? The facts show that Troyanovsky, not Hull, should have been delivering the rebuke. Between 1933 and 1939 the United States did not advance a single specific proposal for collectively repulsing the aggressors, whether through moral, political, or military means. The Soviet Union, on the other hand, introduced a whole series of such plans. In resisting these proposals the United States was outdone only slightly by Britain and France, and the difference was one of degree, not of kind.

In December 1933 the USSR proposed concluding a Pacific nonaggression pact between the United States, the USSR, China, and Japan. As Litvinov told Bullitt, the next move was up to the United States. For a long time the Americans did not give a definite, final reply. In June 1937, as a result of the growing Japanese threat to China, the Soviet government once more proposed to the Americans that they sign such a pact, even without Japan, in order to curb her aggressive anti-Chinese aspirations. On 29 June 1937, Roosevelt rejected the idea of a Pacific pact, telling Troyanovsky: "There is no faith in pacts." The main guarantee, the president thought, was a strong fleet.[53] He believed that the Japanese would not pass the test of competition on the seas. In July 1937 Japan launched an aggressive war against China.

Munich had shown the whole world that the official bourgeois-democratic West was united in shutting its eyes to Hitler's aggression and channeling it to the East, in the direction of the USSR. The United States lent its support to the Anglo-French Chamberlainites, which could not help but cool Soviet-American relations. On 11 November 1938, Chargé d'Affaires K. A. Umansky sadly reported to Litvinov: "Of late there have been no signs that any substantial improvement in relations with us is intended by Roosevelt."[54] Three days later the peoples' commissar wrote to Umansky in the same melancholic spirit:

> We will take very modest notice in the press of the fifth anniversary of the establishment of relations. It would be hard to speak of the significance of this event and say nothing about the reasons for the absence of any appropriate political effect. And the reasons lie in the complete passivity of the American government, which has traditionally followed an isolationist policy. In spite of the sermon-on-the-mount lectures its presidents deliver about peace, America

cannot disclaim its share of responsibility for the present international situation.[55]

The Anglo-French-Soviet negotiations of 1939 in Moscow offered Washington its last opportunity to make a positive contribution to prewar international relations and to help create a system of collective security in Europe. But the fact that the Americans did not even have an ambassador in Moscow in the fourteen-month period before August 1939 did not promise well for their contribution. At the highest American diplomatic level, only Joseph Davies, who by this time had become ambassador to Brussels, continued to maintain a serious, positive view of the Moscow negotiations. Seeing the lack of progress at this meeting, in April 1939 he proposed to Hull that he (Davies) go to Moscow, and take advantage of his good standing with Stalin and other Soviet leaders to get the negotiations moving. Without his participation, he predicted that they would fail. Davies tried to persuade the State Department to give further support to building the bridge that apparently had been begun between West and East over Fascist Germany. He wrote that "Hitler will not fight now if he is confronted with two military fronts."[56]

But even Davies, who was in the vanguard of the American movement to support the principles of collective security, felt that positive pressure should be put on the Soviet leaders in Moscow, rather than on the Munichite envoys from London and Paris, the Chamberlain and Daladier people. This characterizes very eloquently the entire mood of American diplomacy in those years, for which the Munichites represented the standard of anti-Hitlerism. Something else in Davies' initiative is very significant. He intended to achieve success, that is, to persuade Stalin to meet Britain and France halfway, "without commitments"[57] on the part of the United States. From this it follows that even Davies regarded the safeguarding of peace in Europe, the collective security through mutual commitment, as something that, if not alien to the United States, was in any case somebody else's business.

The president and the State Department declined the services of the ambassador in Brussels, giving the neutrality laws as their reason: "During these days when our neutrality legislation is being considered by the Congress, it is more than ever important not to run any risk."[58]

This, however, did not prevent Roosevelt from meddling in the progress of the Moscow negotiations with advice given to the Soviet ambassador 30 June 1939.[59] First he said that Moscow should have faith in the Chamberlain government. Then he repeated an already familiar dogma of United States foreign policy, saying that Japan was a greater threat to Russia than to America. If the first was an attempt to lead the Soviet government astray, the second obviously contained blackmail. He went on to explain that the Americans were only giving advice, without committing themselves in any way.

Meanwhile Congress, which played an important role in determining the foreign policy of the United States, continued its earlier course of not permitting any steps whatever to contain the aggression. At the same time, other events on Capitol Hill intensified the strain in Soviet-American relations. On 5 July 1939, the influential Congressman Sol Bloom introduced a resolution for the appointment of a special agent (a commissioner) to determine the total amount of debts claimed against the USSR.[60] The matter of the debt was once again proving useful to the enemies of collective security. During the Moscow negotiations, Congress was deciding the fate of neutrality legislation. By repealing it, the United States would have strengthened the forces of the advocates of collective security in Europe, even if she had not joined in it herself. The failure to do so gave new strength to the advocates of appeasement in the British and French governments, and encouraged those who favored an immediate war in the Axis countries.

In August 1939 the new American ambassador, Laurence Steinhardt, at last arrived in Moscow. In a talk with Molotov on 16 August he repeated what Roosevelt had said to Umansky about the Anglo-French-Soviet negotiations. The head of the Soviet government replied:

From the very outset, we have not regarded the negotiations as a matter that must necessarily end with the adoption of some kind of general declaration. We feel that to confine ourselves to a declaration would be a mistake, and unacceptable to us. Today, just as at the beginning of the negotiations, we are trying to get specific commitments for mutual aid to counteract possible aggression in Europe. We are not interested in declarations, we are interested in concrete decisions on mutual commitments to oppose possible aggression. These negotiations have meaning for us only insofar as they result in defensive measures to prevent aggression, and we will not make an agreement to attack anyone. Thus, we feel these talks are important to the extent that they may lead to an agreement on mutual aid for defense against direct and indirect aggression.

To the question whether the USSR had hopes that the negotiations might prove successful, Molotov said he was hopeful, adding, "But, of course, the matter does not depend on us alone."[61]

In fact, it depended more on London and Paris than it did on us. The Chamberlain government and the Daladier cabinet, which followed its lead blindly, rejected the alliance.

By this time the West had already had some experience cooperating with the Soviet Union, and had worked out some distinctive clichés: when for one reason or another it was disadvantageous to cooperate with us, Western leaders invariably raised a ballyhoo about totalitarianism in the USSR, as a maneuver to justify their position. They at once pointed out that all was not well with democracy in Russia, and the gentleman of the West could not have workable relations with such a regime. This was the device used in the 1939 negotiations. Even before 23 August 1939, the anti-Soviet campaign in the United States was intensified. But influential voices in opposition to the anti-Soviet fantasies of the European-American Munichites were also to be heard in America. On 13 August an open letter signed by 400 prominent figures in the world of science and culture was published in the United States. It exposed the falsity of the slanderous attacks on the USSR. Among the signers were Samuel Harper, Corliss Lamont, F. O. Mathiesson, and others. The letter said that "the Fascists and their friends have tried to prevent a united antiaggression front by sowing suspicion between the Soviet Union and other nations interested in maintaining peace." "With the aim of turning anti-Fascist feeling against the Soviet Union," the letter continues, "they have encouraged the fantastic falsehood that the USSR and the totalitarian States are basically alike. By this strategy they hope to create dissension among the progressive forces whose united strength is a first necessity for the defeat of Fascism."[62]

The Roosevelt administration's foreign policy did not rely on either these progressive forces, or on the active anti-Fascists, but on those groups which wanted to bide their time, to avoid frightening the high-handed aggressors too much, to chide them verbally, but to give them no grounds for thinking that Washington and Moscow might enter into joint action.

The failure of the Moscow negotiations, brought about by the Munichites, demonstrated to the Soviet government that there was no one with whom to build a stronghold of collective security. Once again, Moscow experienced the bitterness of disappointment. What was worse, the government of the USSR could not entirely exclude the appearance of some new Munichite design aimed more obviously against us. It must be remembered that during these weeks the Red Army was conducting large-scale military actions against Japan in Mongolia, while Britain was erecting the edifice of a Far Eastern Munich.

Nor did Moscow place any hopes in the United States. "Our attitude," writes Foster Rhea Dulles, "had done nothing to free the Soviet Union of its fear that the Western democracies would encourage Hitler to launch a crusade against Communism as a means of saving their own skins."[63] Dulles continues: "If it was impossible to crush aggression by a united front, Stalin felt the next best thing for Russia was to attempt to divert any immediate German attack from the Soviet Union."[64]

And that is exactly what Stalin did, having no better alternative for getting out of the situation that had arisen. On 23 August 1939, the signing of the Soviet-German nonaggression pact was announced. In the West there arose the usual attack of anti-Soviet and anti-Communist hysteria. Munichites on both sides of the Atlantic had plenty to be sorry about: their efforts to bring the USSR and Germany into collision had failed. But broad circles of respectable people were also drawn into the anti-Soviet campaign. Following the formula that had been prepared for them by these same Munichites, they viewed the step taken by the Soviet government as a deal with Hitler, which betrayed the principles of antifascism and collective security. Some of them later realized that they had been wrong; others still hold to this deluded opinion.

The nonaggression pact with Germany strengthened the position of the USSR—the chief anti-Fascist and peace-loving force in the world. The positive effect of the Soviet move lay not only in warding off the threat of an immediate attack by Germany, but also in the fact that the pact sowed discord in the camp of the Axis powers. It played an especially important diplomatic role in putting a damper on Japanese plans with respect to the USSR. The American ambassador to Poland was one of those who testified to this. On 25 August 1939, he wrote to Hull that the Japanese ambassador in Warsaw had expressed extreme dissatisfaction with the signing of the pact.[65]

In the United States, despite the prevalence of anti-Soviet attitudes in those days, sensible voices were also to be heard in the assessment of the step taken by the USSR. This does not mean only the Communists, who did support the position of the Soviet government. "Moscow and perhaps also the rest of the world," said Professor Samuel Harper publicly on 27 August 1939, "got one real gain from the pact. For to secure Soviet neutrality Germany had had to abandon its pact with Japan, which was perhaps a military alliance."[66] A very truthful assessment of the conduct of the Soviet leaders is contained in a letter Harper received from a scientific worker in October 1939. He said that the Russians had acted correctly in concluding the pact, for the Polish government did not intend to resist the Fascist aggression, and " that Hitler then might turn against the Soviet Union, with the tacit blessing of Chamberlin (*sic*) and Bonnet. Hence the nonaggression pact."[67]

After the outbreak of the Second World War, President Roosevelt, chiding the Congress, told them that he regretted the existence of a neutrality law in the United States, and then added: "I regret equally that I signed that Act." Citing these words, Basil Rauch concludes: "This was perhaps a unique instance of a President in office admitting publicly that he had been wrong."[68]

Thus, the president admitted that American foreign policy during the second half of the 1930s had for the most part been in error. This again shows the validity of the decisive step taken by the USSR in concluding the nonaggression pact. Our country could not remain indefinitely in the dangerous position of appealing for collective security without support from the Western powers, who were trying to push us into a war against the aggressor, while they stood by to see how it would turn out. But the words of the president and the historian who defended him give an unduly self-critical and unduly simplified interpretation of the course taken by the United States government. This was not merely a mistake, but a definite policy, under definite conditions, with a definite goal. It did not prevent the outbreak of the war, for that had not been its purpose. It led the aggressors right up to the borders of the USSR in the East and in the West. But in the end it failed—the USSR did not permit itself to be drawn into the war in 1939. The war began with a conflict within the imperialist camp, and in this sense the ruling circles of Britain, France, and the United States had made a mistake. But this did not mean a triumph for Soviet policy. No, as Moscow had said more than once, the world proved indeed to be indivisible. The events of the late 1930s were indeed tragic, but the tragedy should be understood not as an irrational mystification. It was a natural consequence of the policy of international imperialism, a social phenomenon.

In opposing aggression the government of the United States did not go beyond Roosevelt's "quarantine" speech of October 1937. It did not mobilize itself either diplomatically or militarily nor did it make a serious effort to rearm before the beginning of the war in Europe.

The Roosevelt administration did not want war; it would have been glad to see Germany without Hitler and Japan without the ultra-militarists, and wished somehow to ward off the threat of war. It was for this purpose that in 1933 it proceeded to recognize the greatest Eurasian power which was flanked by Germany in the West and Japan in the East.

But if this is so, then why did the United States stubbornly decline all Soviet proposals to organize a system of collective security before the war? The honor of preventing aggression was deliberately placed on the shoulders of the Soviet people alone. Without question, this indicated Roosevelt's high estimate of both the strength of the USSR and its determination to defend democracy throughout the world. He treated the USSR with as much respect and understanding as he felt was necessary to make it play its proper role in America's balance of power strategy, and no more.

For this reason, relations between the USSR and the United States were bound to improve in direct proportion to the increased threat to the United States from the aggressive powers. Roosevelt's policy expressed this tendency. He was motivated, not by any sympathies for the socialist state, but by a realization of its growing strength, which served as a dependable guarantee of the defense of mankind, including the American people, from the threat of Fascist enslavement.

5

In the Shadow of the "Phony War"

Thus, Nazi Germany took the field to seize world supremacy. It was no great secret that Berlin's confederates—the Axis powers in Europe and Asia—would also take up arms. It was only a matter of time. The main problem for both Moscow and Washington was to gain time for preparations to repel the aggressors. Hence the striking similarity in the policy of the USSR and the United States toward the war that had flared up in Europe.

Both the United States and the Soviet Union announced that they would maintain "neutrality" toward the belligerents. In an address to the American people on 3 September 1939, President Franklin Roosevelt said: "This nation will remain a neutral nation, but I cannot ask that every American remain neutral in thought as well."[1] Berlin had no great illusions about which side had the sympathies of the United States. But the Nazi conspirators, protected by the width of the Atlantic, did not expect anything else from the United States at that time, just as the Americans did not have to fear a direct threat from the Fascist powers. The United States was free to occupy itself with discussions of "isolation" and "internationalism," of the great moral example of a pure America to the sinful world, and other familiar and comfortable things, while its war industry underwent a leisurely expansion, transforming the country eventually into an "arsenal of democracy."

Things were quite different for the USSR, which found itself between two perils—Nazi Germany and militarist Japan. Moscow was not unaware of the "balance of power" policy that the West had been pursuing on the eve of the war, and realized that influential forces there were still hoping for war between the Axis powers and the Soviet Union. The timely conclusion of the nonaggression pact with Germany on 23 August 1939 postponed for a time the inevitable conflict with the aggressors. It was essential to do everything possible to make sure that this time was not wasted, but used to strengthen the defensive capacity of the country.

The war broke out in Europe, where the Wehrmacht, having attacked Poland, was moving swiftly toward the Soviet border. The Polish state collapsed. It was obvious that enslavement was the immediate prospect for the peoples of the Western Ukraine and Western Byelorussia, who had been forcibly incorporated into Poland in 1920. On 17 September 1939 Soviet troops marched into Poland to protect the lives and property of these populations. The Soviet border was moved to the west. Explaining the motives for the actions taken by the USSR, Molotov, president of the Soviet of Peoples' Commissars, said in a radio speech on 17 September 1939: "A situation arose in Poland which required special concern on the part of the Soviet government for the security of its nation. Poland has become a convenient ground for all sorts of fortuitous and unexpected eventualities that might create a threat to the USSR."[2]

The anti-Soviet campaign that was launched in the American press as a result of this action demonstrated clearly the "double standard" by which the United States sometimes judges international actions. The realistic actions of the USSR were condemned from the heights of abstract moral doctrines. The authors of these articles and the American historians of international affairs ignore the curious fact that the United States expected the Soviet Union to go to war with Germany at once, under the most unfavorable conditions possible, something the Americans themselves were not prepared to do. Even the powers that had already declared war on Germany showed no enthusiasm for preventing the Nazi aggression by force of arms. Poland's allies—Britain and France—did not lift a finger to assist the Warsaw regime while it was being crushed.

In the West, the illusory world of a "phony war" prevailed—at least in London and Paris it was expected that Hitler would still change his mind and turn his arms against the Soviet Union.

At Nuremberg the Nazi generals were unanimous in pointing out that only the passivity of the Western allies assured the initial successes of the Reich.

General Alfred Gustav Jodl: "And if we did not collapse in 1939 that was due only to the fact that during the Polish campaign, the approximately 110 French and British divisions in the West were held completely inactive against the 23 German divisions."[3]

General Wilhelm Keitel: "We soldiers had always expected an attack by France during the Polish campaign, and were very surprised that nothing happened. . . . A French attack would have encountered only a German military screen, not a real defense."[4]

Logically, the position of the West was a continuation of prewar policy. Anti-Soviet class inertia made itself felt: blinded by anti-communism, Western statesmen did not see that a direct threat to their countries was in the making. Today, of course, this observation has become commonplace. No less a person than future president Lyndon B. Johnson told the Congress in 1947:

France could have stopped Hitler when he started into the Saar. France and England combined could have prevented the occupation of Austria or even later stopped the Nazis at Czechoslovakia. The United States, England, and France could have prevented the rape of Poland if only there had been a common determination to call a halt to aggression. Japan could have been checked before she got into Manchuria; and certainly she would have been stopped when she declared war on defenseless China. But the siren songs of appeasers convinced us it was none of our business what happened in Europe or the world, and thus France was sacrificed to Fascist ambitions, and England's destiny was fought out in the skies over London.[5]

But more time had to pass before these admissions could be made. In 1939 the "balance of power" policy appears to have brought the first of the dividends one might have expected from it—war was raging in Europe. Feeling very virtuous, Roosevelt called on the people to remember that the United States must remain neutral, and with splendid consistency demanded that Congress change the law regarding "neutrality." On 4 November, after appropriate debate in the capitol, the law was changed, and the principle of "cash and carry" was introduced. Navigation by American ships in the zone of military operations (in the waters off England and France, and in the Baltic Sea) was prohibited.

Many fine words have been written and spoken regarding these measures, especially after the notion of America as the "arsenal of democracy" had begun to be built. At that time the significance of the change in the "neutrality" law was much simpler; it was an expression of that same principle of balance of power politics; it was the interest of the United States that figured first and foremost. An American military historian, Robert Leckie, observes:

> The President told the nation that developing such a trade in munitions would help build national defense, and that by keeping it on a cash-and-carry basis the United States would avoid the kind of incidents at sea which had led to intervention in 1914. "There lies the road to peace!" he exclaimed.
>
> There, rather, lay the road to war. FDR did not think so because he still believed that the Allies were stronger than Hitler. But repeal of the arms embargo effected a deep breach in the isolationist wall, if it was not also an interventionist act. It favored the Allies because, through their control of the seas, they could buy all the war material that they needed, while Germany could not; and implicit in it was the assurance that if the Allies proved weaker than Hilter, as they were, then other radical steps would be taken to prevent their collapse.[6]

Throughout this entire period—from the fall of 1939 to the spring of 1940—the Western powers were busy with anti-Soviet intrigues, some of them still hoping to come to an agreement with the Nazi leaders. Various plans were proposed and discussed, but their essence came down to one thing—to achieve a lull in the West, and then to try to turn the spearhead of aggression against the USSR. The Soviet-Finnish armed conflict gave rise to particular hopes in this respect. Washington, having forgotten its recent insistence, on the very eve of the war, on the necessity for the Allies to fight against Germany, developed a course of energetic action for peace. On 2 December 1939, a "moral embargo" on trade with the USSR was imposed in the United States. At the same time the United States opened a credit account of Finland in the amount of $40,000,000 and sold to it some quantities of armanents. "Volunteer" pilots left America to take part in the war against the USSR on the side of Finland. This coincided not only with the training by England and France of an expeditionary corps to go to Finland, but with preparation of a strike against the USSR from the south. While the Wehrmacht was completing the last arrangements for its campaign in the West, the Anglo-French command was busy with the selection of its most efficient units for war against the USSR.

This was a truly mad venture, dictated by fierce hatred for the Soviet state. As William L. Shirer observed: "One can only speculate on the utter confusion which would have resulted among the belligerents had the Franco-British expeditionary corps ever arrived in Finland and fought the Russians. In little more than a year Germany would be at war with Russia, in which case the enemies in the West would have been allies in the East!"[7] If one needed proof of the irrationality of anti-communism, this is that proof! The political figures of the West really lost their common sense.

In the middle of February 1940 Roosevelt sent two emissaries to Europe—Myron Taylor to the pope in Rome, and Assistant Secretary of State Sumner Welles to the capitals of the belligerent nations—Berlin, Paris, London, and also Rome. The precise goals of these missions have never been adequately explained. Some express the reasonable supposition that the United States had decided to take on itself the initiative of arranging a peace settlement. In Paris and London Welles ascertained that under certain conditions England and France were prepared to come to an agreement. In Berlin the president's envoy was heard out, and the conclusion was reached that the "democracies" had rotted through to their foundations. Welles' visit among other things convinced the Hitler leadership that the West was indeed weak and that one could and should speak to it in the language of arms. But Welles suddenly cut short his activity and was urgently recalled to the United States on 16 March. The reason: On 12 March 1940, peace was signed between the USSR and Finland. The grounds for anti-Soviet intrigues obviously had disappeared.

The German offensive in the West shattered to dust the illusions of the "phony war," a real "fool's paradise." In April 1940 the Nazis occupied Denmark, and began their seizure of Norway. On 10 May 1940 the inevitable occurred—the Wehrmacht struck a blow on the Western front. The Netherlands and Belgium capitulated. Italy entered the war. Shortly after the onslaught of the Wehrmacht, France was defeated.

In Washington, of course, the Fascist dictators were hated and everyone wished with all their hearts for their destruction. The unexpected successes of the Wehrmacht gave rise to oppressive fear across the ocean, not for the fate of the Allies, but now for America's own future. France and Britain of course were fighting for their very lives; but from the standpoint of the American government, it was a campaign to gain time to consolidate the military strength of their own country. They had to act with the greatest haste, to improvise, mainly because a great deal had been recently overlooked when they vainly hoped it would prove possible to turn the war in Europe against the USSR and thus divert danger from the West. In May-June the Congress passed a great number of laws intended to arm the United States to the teeth—a ''two-ocean'' fleet was to be deployed, with twice the number of naval vessels; the number of planes in the Army Air Force was to be increased to 36,000. On 15 June Roosevelt gave the secret direction to begin work on the project that led to the creation of the atomic bomb. In September the United States adopted its first peace-time law providing for selective military service.

If the United States, across the ocean, was in such a hurry, the Soviet Union had to hurry three times as fast—the war was raging on its very doorstep. Remembering the prewar policy of the Western leaders, and keeping in mind the position of the West with respect to the war with Finland, for the time being the Soviet Union could depend only on its own strength. The rout of the Finnish militarists made it possible to move the boundary to 150 kilometers from Leningrad, instead of 32 kilometers. In the middle of 1940 Estonia, Latvia, and Lithuania were reunited with the USSR, and at the end of June, Moldavia, which had been annexed by Romania after the October Revolution, was returned. Thus, within less than a year the USSR had completed the creation of the ''Eastern front.''

When, in 1948, documents from the diplomatic archives of Hitler Germany began to be published in the West, and the usual anti-Soviet campaign resulted, the Information Bureau of the Soviet of Ministers of the USSR published the inquiry *Fal'sifikatory istorii* (Falsifiers of history). It read in part:

> What would have happened if the USSR had not created the ''Eastern'' front even before the attack by Germany, far to the west of the old boundaries of the USSR? If this front had extended not along the line Viborg-Kaunas-Byelostok-Brest-L'vov, but along the old border, Leningrad-Narva-Minsk-Kiev?
>
> This would have given Hitler's troops a chance to gain an area

hundreds of kilometers in extent, bringing the German front closer to Leningrad-Moscow-Minsk-Kiev by 200–300 kilometers; would have enabled the Germans to penetrate deep into the USSR much more quickly; would have hastened the fall of Kiev and the Ukraine; led to the capture of Moscow by the Germans, and of Leningrad by the combined forces of the Germans and the Finns. It would have forced the USSR to turn to a protracted defense, and made it possible for the Germans to free fifty divisions for a landing on the British Isles and a reinforcement of the German-Italian front in the vicinity of Egypt. It is quite likely that the British Government would have had to be evacuated to Canada, while Egypt and the Suez Canal would have fallen under the power of Hitler.

But that is not all. The USSR would have been forced to transfer a large part of its troops from the Manchurian border to the "Eastern" front to strengthen its defense, and this would have made it possible for the Japanese to free up to thirty divisions in Manchuria and turn them against China, against the Philippines, against Southeast Asia in general, and in the last analysis against the American armed forces in the Far East.

All of this would have prolonged the war for at least two more years, and the Second World War would have ended not in 1945 but in 1947 or somewhat later.[8]

The "Battle of Britain" and the mounting wave of Japanese aggression in the Far East left no doubt that the existence of all opponents of the Axis powers, including the nonbelligerent United States, was at stake. The Roosevelt administration introduced into Congress a bill providing for aid to nations that were offering armed resistence to the aggressors (Lend-Lease). The American historian, Thomas A. Bailey, remarked in his typical graphic style: "The scheme was urged by administration sponsors, not on the ground that Britain was deserving of our help, but on the purely selfish ground that if we sent arms to England, the British would keep the war going and we would not have to get into it. We would let Britain fight (with our weapons) to the last Englishman, while we remained fat and neutral."[9] In other words, Lend-Lease was consistent with the highest principles of "balance of power" politics and for this reason alone was bound to be approved by Congress.

On 11 March 1941, the Lend-Lease law was approved. It began with the statement that the aid was being granted to those countries whose struggle against aggression was "in the interest of national defense" of the United States.[10] As early as 1941, Lend-Lease was given out to thirty-eight nations. Harry S. Truman, summing up Lend-Lease, wrote in his memoirs: "The money spent for Lend-Lease unquestionably meant the saving of a great many American lives. Every soldier of Russia, England, and Australia who had been equipped by Lend-Lease means to go into that war reduced by that much the dangers that faced our young men in the winning of it."[11]

If the debates on Lend-Lease took place under conditions of extensive publicity, the Anglo-American staff negotiations that took place simultaneously were surrounded with the strictest secrecy, and it was in these negotiations that the fundamental strategic course of the United States and Britain in the war was worked out. In assessing the general situation in the world, the American and British governments proceeded from the fact that the aggressors had officially joined forces. As far back as 27 September 1940 the Triple Pact had been signed— Germany, Italy, and Japan pledged to cooperate with each other for the establishment of a "new order." They were a threat to the whole world. Those who participated in the staff meetings in Washington in January-March 1941 were unanimous in holding that victory over the Axis powers would be possible only with the participation of the United States in the war; but when America would take up arms remained open.

Having assessed the strength of the enemy coalition, the American and British strategists came to the conclusion that Hitler's Germany constituted the foundation of the coalition. Proceeding from the military axiom that it is essential to strike at the main link in the enemy bloc, the principle, "Germany is enemy no. 1" was formulated, and it was recognized that Germany must be defeated first. As for Japan, if she should take action in the Pacific and in the Far East, passive defense should be maintained up until the successful conclusion of the military operations in Europe. Hence the task of the United States was to concentrate its principal forces in the European theater and at the appropriate time to land an army in Europe for a decisive assault on the Nazi citadel. These principles were stated in the main American-British strategic plan "ABC-1," approved by the staffs on 29 March 1941, and carried out with remarkable consistency throughout the duration of the war.

Soviet leaders, proceeding from different considerations—the defense of their country—reached conclusions similar to those of plan "ABC-1." Recognizing that strategically the main front of the Second World War was Europe, the Soviet government considered it essential to concentrate its maximum forces here. In the interests of preparing a more effective resistance to the Nazi aggression, on 13 April 1941, the USSR signed a five-year neutrality pact with Japan. Although it proved unnecessary to depend on Tokyo's adherence to the obligations of the agreement, and although throughout the duration of the war with the European Axis powers the USSR was forced to maintain up to forty divisions in the Soviet Far East, nevertheless the neutrality pact did to some extent afford hope that war would not flare up here. The conclusion of the neutrality pact was in keeping with the gradually unfolding larger strategy of the anti-Axis coalition.[12]

The threat to all mankind made the Americans more realistic in their relations with the USSR. On 22 January 1941, the State Department announced the lifting of the "moral embargo" on trade with the USSR. In early 1941 the assistant to Secretary of State Sumner Welles warned the Soviet ambassador of the impending attack by Germany against the USSR.[13] For all the value of this information, it had to be considered against the background of the general international situation. There would be no doubt that in the interests of self-preservation, there was a burning desire in the West at this time to hasten the start of the war between Germany and the USSR. In the United States, J. Edgar Hoover's department, the FBI, took steps to properly "orient" the Nazi leadership. For example, strategic misinformation prepared by the FBI was turned over to the German embassy in Washington; it said that the USSR was planning to attack Germany as soon as the Germans would start a big operation on the Western front.

Stalin, like Roosevelt, realized that war with Nazi Germany, which had started along the road to international brigandage, was inevitable. Beginning 1 September 1939, the USSR, exerting tremendous effort, made serious preparations for the impending combat. By the middle of 1941 the total strength of the army and navy exceeded five million men, that is, it had increased 2.8 times over 1939.[14] The latest types of military equipment, first and foremost tanks and airplanes, were being put into serial production.

Admiral N. G. Kuznetsov, who at that time headed Soviet naval forces, writes about this period:

> I believe that Stalin was firmly convinced that war was inevitable, that it was sure to flare up either in the west or the east, or possibly in both places at once. That is why our forces were concentrated simultaneously in both the west and the east. All our borders were being reinforced. Stalin was making extensive and diverse preparations for war on the basis of a long-range schedule that he himself had projected. His calculations were upset by Hitler.
>
> Stalin's suspicions of Britain and America aggravated matters. He had fully ample basis, of course, for believing that they were striving to bring us into head-on collision with Germany. Such a policy on the part of the Western powers was no secret. . . . It seems to me that Stalin began to realize from the beginning of 1941, in the face of very evident facts, that an imminent attack by Hitler was indeed possible. But, realizing that his original estimate of the time available for preparation had been too optimistic, and that our armed forces and our country as a whole were inadequately prepared for war in the months immediately ahead, he tried to do everything possible that might, in his opinion, delay the conflict, and to conduct matters so as to give Hitler no excuse for an attack.[15]

Like Roosevelt, Stalin believed that in any case there would be sufficient time for preparation to repel the aggression. Both committed the very same mistake. The aggressors turned out to be following their own timetable. In this respect, the destinies of our countries were similar—war came to the USSR suddenly at dawn on 22 June 1941, and like lightning from the blue, it struck the United States on 7 December. The scale of the attacks and the geographical situation of the aggressors in relation to the USSR and the United States were different—the Germans were right on the Soviet border, while a great distance separated Pearl Harbor from the United States. From this alone there followed a huge difference in the scope of the military actions and the consequences of the war for each of our countries.

The USSR and the United States Enter the War

News of the incursion of Hitler's hordes into the USSR brought great relief to the White House. Harry Hopkins, closest adviser to Roosevelt, stated with deepest satisfaction: "The President's policy of support for Britain has really paid off! Hitler has turned to the left."[16] The German-Soviet war gave a new impetus to the discussion of strategic questions in the highest councils of Washington.

A day before the attack by Germany on the USSR, the State Department presented to the government recommendations on United States policy in the event of a Soviet-German war. "We should," read the document, "steadfastly adhere to the line that the fact that the Soviet Union is fighting Germany does not mean that it is defending, struggling for, or adhering to, the principles in international relations which we are supporting.... We should make no promises in advance to the Soviet Union with regard to the assistance which we might render in case of a German-Soviet conflict, and we should make no commitment as to what our future policy toward the Soviet Union or Russia might be."[17]

The official announcement by Acting Secretary of State Sumner Welles at a press conference on 23 June 1941, was couched in general terms. He said:

> To the people of the United States this and other principles and doctrines of communistic dictatorship are as intolerable and as alien to their own beliefs, as are the principles and doctrines of Nazi dictatorship.... In the opinion of this Government, consequently, any defense against Hitlerism, any rallying of the forces opposing Hitlerism, from whatever source these forces may spring, will hasten the eventual downfall of the present German leaders, and will therefore redound to the benefit of our own defense and security.
> Hitler's armies are today the chief dangers of the Americas.[18]

Without going into precise details, President Roosevelt spoke out for the United States' rendering assistance to the USSR. When the president expressed himself in this way publicly, the White House received memoranda from the headquarters of the armed forces, from the secretaries of war and the navy. All of them, and also Secretary of the Treasury Henry Morgenthau and Secretary of the Interior Harold Ickes, were convinced that the Soviet Union would be defeated by the Wehrmacht within a matter of weeks. (In the opinion of the secretary of war, "at the earliest within a month, at the latest within three"). They appealed passionately to the president not to let slip the precious opportunity to strike a blow at Germany, while her main forces were tied up on the Eastern front. Henry Stimson begged him to remember that "Germany's action seems like an almost providential occurrence."[19] Ickes turned his eyes to the future: ". . . if we do not do it now, we will be, when our turn comes, without an ally anywhere in the world."[20] These appeals had absolutely no effect on the president, who had faith in the capability of the Soviet people to resist the aggressor. For this reason he declined the insistent requests to have the United States enter the war, giving the Red Army an opportunity for the time being to defend their homeland and world civilization with their own strength.

In July 1941 Roosevelt sent Harry Hopkins to Moscow as his representative. Hopkins became convinced of the determination of the USSR to fight the war, and negotiations were begun to determine exactly what assistance the United States could give to the Soviet Union. But the matter did not go very far during July; for the time being, practically nothing was sent to the USSR. Roosevelt was furious, and as his perspicacious biographer, James M. Burns, writes, he "blew up" at the meeting of the cabinet on 1 August. He pointed out that for a whole month already the Russians had been given the runaround. He didn't want to hear any more about what had been ordered, but wanted to know what had been sent. The cabinet grew quiet, seeing the unusual behavior of the president. An administrator of aid to the USSR was quickly appointed but, as before, almost nothing was done, for, as Burns concludes, "Roosevelt could not make a clear moral issue of aid to Russia because of anti-Soviet attitudes; he could not make a strategic reformulation because he could not bank on Russian survival. His main goal was still simply to prolong Russian resistance. He was committed to a strategy of giving top priority to Britain."[21]

At the same time there was a lot of discussion going on in the United States about what position should be taken with respect to the USSR. The isolationists, tirelessly battling the administration about assistance to Britain, decided that the new war would strengthen their position. They were categorically opposed to any support of the Soviet Union, and appealed to anti-Communist prejudices. Senator Robert A. Taft asserted publicly that the victory of communism in Europe was a greater peril than the victory of fascism. The journal *New Republic* asked: "What are we going to do, fight so as to make Europe safe for Communism?"

Although these and other statements were given wide publicity, they reflected an extreme point of view. The opinion of the solid majority of the American leaders was expressed in the statement of Senator Harry Truman, who pointed out: "If we see that Germany is winning the war we ought to help Russia, and if Russia is winning we ought to help Germany and in that way let them kill as many as possible."[22] Truman, naturally, was expressing himself with his characteristic straightforwardness, but on closer examination it was clear that his point of view roughly reflected Washington policy although nobody in Washington wanted Hitler's final victory. In July 1941 Roosevelt ordered the preparation of plans for specific measures to defeat the enemy. By September the staffs prepared an extensive study, The Victory Program, which was presented for consideration by the government.

The Victory Program provided for the creation of an army of 215 divisions, 61 of them tank divisions. The American generals had visions of gigantic future battles, in which they would lead their troops gloriously into action. At the beginning of September 1941 the staffs reported to the government their view of the kind of action the country should choose: "We must prepare to fight Germany by actually coming to grips with and defeating her ground forces and definitely breaking her will to combat. . . . Air and sea forces will make important contributions, but effective and adequate ground forces must be available to close with and destroy the enemy within his citadel."[23] These proposals, and consequently the entire complex of problems connected with the Victory Program were discussed in the White House. On 22 September the final decision was made to send a large part of the armament and equipment manufactured in the United States to the opponents of the Axis powers. This brought to nought the staff plans for deploying an army of 215 divisions. The United States government was declaring itself firmly in favor of conducting the war indirectly, with others doing the actual fighting.

On 14 August 1941, after Roosevelt's meeting with Churchill, the Atlantic Charter was promulgated—a document proclaiming in general terms the democratic aims of the war. Washington considered it necessary to formulate them, for with its entry into the war the USSR acquired once and for all the character of an anti-Fascist, liberating power. Without question, the Atlantic Charter was a response to the program of struggle against fascism that had already been advanced by

the Soviet government. At the same time, through a piece of sub-
tlety—neither Roosevelt nor Churchill signed the document (it was
simply transmitted to the press)—the United States was left with its
hands free. It was not legally bound by the Atlantic Charter. Roosevelt
went along with this, also, because if it had been otherwise, it would
have been necessary to have the document, as an international agreement, confirmed by the Senate, and this would inevitably have called
forth an empty controversy with the isolationists.

The fact that Germany was busy with the war against the Soviet
Union made it possible for the United States to take a more resolute
position in the Atlantic. On 7 July American troops landed in Iceland;
United States naval vessels constantly plied in waters where German
submarines were operating. Even before the beginning of the German-Soviet war, before it had become clear what it might lead to,
Hitler had ordered that encounters with American vessels be avoided.
But incidents were bound to occur. On 4 September a German
submarine unsuccessfully attacked an American destroyer, which, in
turn, dropped depth bombs on it. On 11 September, in a very
bellicose speech, Roosevelt called the submarines of the Axis powers in
the Atlantic "rattlesnakes," and announced that in waters west of 26°
west longitude they would be attacked without warning, for the
American fleet within the limits of this zone would henceforth protect
convoys bound for England. The command of the German fleet urged
Hitler to take retaliatory measures. The führer categorically forbade
undertaking anything before a "decisive turning point in the Russian
campaign," which, according to him, should be some time in the late
autumn.

The heroic struggle of the Soviet people spoiled the plans of the
Nazi leaders, which permitted the United States to take new offensive
measures without risk. In October, as a result of the sinking of two
American destroyers, the government demanded a change in the
neutrality law so as to permit the navigation of United States vessels in
the zone of military action and to permit arming them. As the *New
York Times* quite correctly observed, the neutrality law rendered
Germany as much assistance as a thousand submarines would have
done: not a single American transport could proceed directly to
England. On 14 November Congress passed into law the changes
requested by the administration. Paul Joseph Goebbels' propaganda,

of course, came down with choice abuse on Roosevelt, but nothing more than verbal attacks followed—Germany, mired on the Eastern front, was not willing to risk acquiring still another opponent. Soviet soldiers, who at that time were defending Moscow, saved the lives of thousands of American sailors serving in the Atlantic, while Roosevelt was able to throw about martial appeals without fear of drawing the United States into the war.

In fall of 1941, when the failure of the Hitler blitzkrieg was completely certain, Washington was at last convinced that the Soviet Union would hold out at least through the winter. This put the rendering of material assistance to the Soviet people in the interests of the United States on a practical basis. The psychological climate in the country was also changing—the manly struggle of the Red Army aroused the admiration of millions of Americans. Public opinion polls showed that 73 percent of Americans hoped for a Soviet victory.[24] The arguments of the isolationists against assistance to the USSR were rejected by the majority of the American people.[25] On 7 November Roosevelt extended Lend-Lease to the Soviet Union. In his official letter to the administrator in charge of implementing Lend-Lease the president said: "Today I have ascertained that the defense of the USSR is important to the defense of the United States." It was the 140th day of the Great Patriotic War.

Up to the end of 1941 Lend-Lease deliveries from the United States to the USSR amounted to $545,000, or less than 0.1 percent of all Lend-Lease deliveries from the United States for that year. In addition, the United States shipped armaments and war materials to the USSR for payment in cash in the amount of $41,000,000. This was the extent of American aid during the most difficult year for the Soviet people, 1941, when we held out, depending only on our own strength. But that year the world listened to a lot of inspiring talk against Fascist tyranny issuing from the noble United States.

Washington's fundamental strategy was to delay direct participation in combat operations as long as possible, in any case, to be the last in line among the great powers to enter the war. It was the goal for which American diplomacy was struggling. Hitler's eastern campaign reduced the danger from Europe to zero. If before 22 June 1941, the Atlantic was a potential American front, the entry of the USSR into the war changed it into an area of small concern for the United States.

Henceforth relations with Japan became of paramount importance. To avert war with her would represent the achievement of the highest goal of the American government—to remain outside the sphere of combat, an implacable enemy of the Axis powers, but deciding for itself when and against whom to take up arms.

Complex American-Japanese negotiations were in progress from the beginning of 1941. Tokyo wanted the United States to recognize the predominant role of Japan in Asia, but the American government of course could not agree. In fact there was nothing to negotiate about, but both sides were procrastinating: the Japanese, mainly in the interest of completing their preparations for war; the Americans, partly for the same considerations, but mostly in an effort to make clear, tactfully, to the Japanese militarists, who were losing their heads, that a war with the United States would not serve their interests, and that other promising prospects were open to Japan. These negotiations were so involved that they have given rise to considerable difference of opinion among American historians. There have been many interpretations of Washington's actions at that time. Some still believe that Roosevelt, knowing Japan's intention to attack the United States, deliberately provoked it, that he arranged Pearl Harbor so as to "trick" the peace-loving American people into the war. These assertions have nothing to do with historical fact, and the efforts of some American historians to prove this curious thesis can only arouse bewilderment bordering on amusement. The matter was much simpler.[26]

Roosevelt did everything possible to avert war with Japan, resorting at times to kindness, at times to threats, depending on the circumstances. There was only one thing that he did not do—he did not caution Japan against attacking the Soviet Union. At the same time, there were competent American military experts who, viewing the war as a combined effort, demanded urgently that the government warn Tokyo against aggression to the North. They were seriously concerned about the consequences of a thrust at the back of our country at the time when the outcome of the entire war was being decided on the Soviet-German front. When United States Army Intelligence learned in the fall of 1941 that Roosevelt was preparing to meet with Japanese Premier Fumimaro Konoe, the head of the secret service told the administration:

This Division is of the opinion that neither a conference of leaders nor economic concessions at this time would be of any material advantage to the United States unless a definite commitment to withdraw from the Axis were obtained from Japan prior to the conference. The immediate objective of the United States is to weaken Hitler in every way possible. A Japanese guarantee not to attack Russia in Siberia would free Russia, psychologically and militarily, for stronger opposition to Hitler. With this in mind, a definite condition precedent to such a proposed conference should be a complete withdrawal by Japan from the Axis and a guarantee, backed by substantial evidence of sincerity, not to attack Russia in Siberia.[27]

This document, dated 2 October 1941, was one of a series of similar memoranda presented to the White House by the military. The government took no action on them, although the war was approaching very rapidly. On 16 October a government of extreme militarists under Hideki Tojo was formed in Japan. American political figures had no illusions about the consequences of Tojo's accession to power. At this time Roosevelt wrote to Churchill that American relations with the Japanese had definitely deteriorated, and that he thought that "they were making their way toward the North." In briefing the command of the Pacific fleet in Hawaii, Admiral Harold R. Stark, commander-in-chief of the United States naval forces, pointed out on 16 October: "The resignation of the Japanese cabinet has created a grave situation.... In either case hostilities between Japan and Russia are a strong possibility."[28] And what action was the United States intending to take in this event? In Washington the supreme command of the American armed forces decided in a series of meetings to continue the same tactics—to stall for time. The final conclusion of the military, reported to the government on 5 November, read: "In case of Japanese attack against Siberia ... the United States should not declare war."[29]

With every day that passed, a stream of disturbing reports flooded Washington; Japan was definitely moving into positions for attack. The suspicion arose that the Japanese warlords were planning to move toward the South. The United States government decided to slow things down by proposing to Tokyo that they agree to a **modus vivendi**, a sort of three-month truce. Negotiations about this began, but here the White House experienced a shock—on the morning of 26 November word was received that large contingents of Japanese troops were moving south! This meant that Tokyo was getting ready to launch an attack on the British or Dutch possessions (Washington did not dream of the possibility of an attack on American possessions), which the United States had already warned about at various times. The question remains open as to what form of action the Americans would have chosen if the Japanese had attacked the British or Dutch colonies alone. Afterward, none other than Cordell Hull remarked to Admiral Stark: "I don't know whether we would have been in the war yet if Japan had not attacked us."[30] All of this is the kind of thing on which it is difficult to make a final judgment. It is clear, however, that the American government reacted to these Japanese moves in an extremely pathological manner, for it was turning out that the long-awaited campaign to the North might not take place.

"The president," writes James MacGregor Burns, "fairly blew up—'jumped up into the air, so to speak,' Stimson noted in his diary. To the president this changed the whole situation, because 'it was evidence of bad faith on the part of the Japanese that while they were negotiating for an entire truce—an entire withdrawal (from China)—they should be sending their expedition down there to Indo-China.' "[31] The formula for a truce that Roosevelt had proposed was discarded that same day. In its stead Hull wrote a ten-point program in which Washington set forth its most extreme demands. Hull told Stimson that he was through with everything, "I have washed my hands of it and it is now in the hands of you and Knox—the Army and the Navy."[32] Actually, the American proposals that were turned over to the Japanese representatives on 26 November had the character of an ultimatum; in essence, they came down to a demand that Japan voluntarily restore the situation in the Far East as it had existed on 18 September 1931, that is, before the Japanese seizures began. There was no chance that this ultimatum would be accepted by the Japanese militarists, who were ready to go to war.

The American note of 26 November had another aim—to help resolve in one stroke the doubts that were tormenting Tokyo about where to direct its aggression. American political leaders were convinced that the Japanese campaign to the North would begin once the USSR had been weakened on the Soviet-German front. This conclusion was not based on speculation, but was the result of reading and analyzing deciphered Japanese wires, in which the plans of Japan were set forth in general form. Late in the fall of 1941 it appeared that the time had come: the German armies were approaching Moscow. Consequently the condition that the Japanese leaders themselves had set for beginning the war against the USSR had been fulfilled—it looked as though an attack would meet with no resistance in the Soviet Far East. Meanwhile, the American declaration was supposed to show that a Japanese strike in the South was expected and that the United States was prepared to retaliate against this advance with a strike of their own. Under these conditions, the American leaders judged that the Japanese would find it easy to choose between attacking the weakened Soviet Union and the armed United States, which, according to the 26 November note, was assuming the role of protector of the British and Dutch.

This entire line of reasoning, which must have occurred to the keepers of national wisdom in the offices of the American capital, was quite unconvincing to the political figures in Tokyo. They assessed the power of the USSR much more sensibly than did those in the republic across the ocean. No matter what they kept saying in Berlin, Tokyo was not at all convinced that the USSR had already suffered a decisive defeat, and saw no necessity to change its temporizing position with regard to the war. Even more important, the Japanese militarists were afraid of missing an opportunity to seize territory in the South, discerning with equal accuracy the resources of the powers that were preparing to defend these regions. There was not the least doubt in Tokyo that the fleet and the army of the emperor would be able to smash the British and Dutch without much trouble.

The Japanese government did not expect to inflict total defeat on the United States and force it to capitulate single-handedly. Their aims were much more realistic—to drive the Americans out of their possessions in the Pacific and to push the outposts of the Empire of the Rising Sun far into that area. Further prospects depended on the course of the entire war of the Axis powers against their opponents. In any case, as they proceeded in the direction of seizure by armed force, the Japanese rulers did not think that the war in Europe could end with the triumph of Soviet arms, and with the total defeat and surrender of Hitler's Germany. In this sense, the Soviet Union, by fighting the Axis powers in Europe while maintaining its neutrality in the Far East up until the summer of 1945, determined the course of the war in the Pacific.

During the last days before Pearl Harbor the American government was piously convinced, as before, that the storm of war would not break out over the United States. The numerous reports of extensive movements of Japanese armed forces were interpreted as proof that Japan would attack the USSR very soon. This firm conviction in the minds of top-ranking American statesmen was responsible for the unprepared state of the American garrisons in Hawaii and other islands, and above all the Philippines, a weakness which had grave consequences.

All of this had not escaped the notice of vision of American historians, and it is hardly necessary for us to preach specially to our colleagues across the ocean on this score. We will simply refer to the way this matter is treated for the Soviet reader in N. N. Yakovlev's book, *Zagadka Pirl-Kharbora* (The puzzle of Pearl Harbor): "It is clear that in this matter American official historians do not think creatively. They only lament, as do William L. Langer and S. Everett Gleason, 'Until and unless additional evidence comes to light, the role of the President as well as Secretary Hull will remain a subject of speculation.'"[33] Or, as Samuel Bemis declared pessimistically, historians would argue about these negotiations for a hundred years.[34] Nevertheless, no matter how annoying the blunders in American documentation may be, the historian can and must judge from the facts. And the facts indisputably tell us that the ultimatum of 26 November was the "big stick" with which the United States was striving to achieve its goals, in this case, to ward off the Japanese threat at the expense of others.

If this thesis is not accepted, then one should either agree with those political speculators in the United States who accuse Roosevelt of having deliberately used the Pacific fleet to lure a Japanese attack and provide grounds for drawing the American people into the war, or else with those who suspect that an epidemic of mass insanity occurred in Washington: although it was known that war was coming, no precautionary measures were taken there. But the foreign-policy leaders of the United States "were of sound mind and strong memory."[35]

To moralize about these events now long passed serves no purpose, and would only impede realistic judgments. Even if one were to speak of the lessons of Pearl Harbor, they are instructive only in that they show to what blunders the blind pursuit of the "balance of power" policy can lead. Life is much more complex than stillborn schemes, especially ones heavily colored with ideological prejudices.

Reflections on American Strategy

The United States found itself in the war not of its own volition, not at the time and not in the circumstances that were planned by the American leadership. The beginning of combat operations, except for the Pacific theater, did not require the country to make an immediate serious military effort. Even the reinforcements that were sent for the war against Japan were by no means large. In short, the United States had every opportunity to adjust its military apparatus relatively free of any great obstacles, and by December 1941 it had already reached impressive proportions.

By the end of 1941 the annual production of the American aviation industry had reached 25,000 machines. Corresponding progress began to appear in other branches of military production as well; the tank industry, for example, must have produced 8,500 new models annually.

Neither the armed forces nor the war industry experienced any financial difficulties in the implementation of their plans. War expenditures in 1940 totaled $8,400,000,000, as compared with $924,000,000 in 1936, and the first session of Congress in 1941 appropriated $33,000,000,000 for war purposes. Meantime, in connection with the end of the next fiscal year on 30 June 1941, the War Department reported that it had not been able to use $1,300,000,000 of the previous appropriations by Congress. During the prewar years Congress had formed the habit in general of allocating more funds than the government requested, although Roosevelt cannot in any way be put in the category of presidents who were not concerned about the defensive capacity of the country.

In considering the general situation of the United States on the eve of the war, the competent war observer, Hanson W. Baldwin, wrote after it had already reached its conclusion:

The assertion that we were unprepared has been applied, with almost monotonous repetition, to the state of American armed forces before World War I, before World War II, in fact before all our wars. But the statement is sophistry. For what were we unprepared? Preparedness is relative, not absolute; there are degrees of preparedness. Before the Second World War this nation had a navy equal to any and the best long-range bomber in the world; the National Guard had been federalized, conscription had started, and the factories of the country already had commenced the manufacture of war orders. Nevertheless, we were, of course, "unprepared" for the war that developed. We shall always be similarly unprepared; for there is no such thing as absolute preparedness and it is futile to strive for it.[36]

In any case, one thing is clear: the United States had at its disposition sufficient power to render immediate military assistance to the opponents of the Axis powers, and first and foremost in the European theater of military action. This was not done for the sound reason that the big strategy of the United States was built on the calculation that it would appear on the scene when the enemy had been weakened sufficiently at the hands of others. This manner of action was, of course, consistent with "balance of power" politics. It was esteemed at the top level of national wisdom in peacetime, and with the coming of war became simply invaluable from the standpoint of American interests.

The strategic doctrine worked out by the United States during the 1930s in essence translated these political considerations into military language, word for word. The American staffs took their point of departure from the fact that the approaching war would be a coalition war; there remained only to estimate the quantitative and qualitative investment that the United States should make in the conduct of such a war. Although each of the three armed services had its own rough plan (the culmination of the strategic planning of the army was the Victory Program), the connection between "balance of power" politics and the armed struggle was contained most clearly in the doctrine of the United States Air Force. During the 1930s the American air force was under the command of the army chief of staff, but the air force commanders conducted a persistent struggle for complete autonomy. They grasped early the theory of the Italian general, Giulio Douhet, formulated at the very beginning of the 1920s, that strategic bombing played the decisive role in the attainment of victory. In the period just before the war, Douhet's theory was elaborated in the United States, taking into account the priorities of the targets of strategic bombing. The final conclusion, approved by the air force staffs, amounted to the fact that destruction of the enemy's transportation system and of the power installations would bring him to his knees. It was proposed to accomplish this through the action of heavy, well-armed bombers that would not require cover by fighter planes. American industry produced the B-17 bomber, which got the name Flying Fortress, and the buildup of the strategic air force began.

The supporters of strategic bombing infected with their enthusiasm serious military figures who had no contact with aviation by virtue of the kind of service they were in. Equipment with B-17 bombers called forth such optimism in the high command of the American armed forces as to verge on the absurd. As Leckie observes, ''MacArthur's confidence sprang ... from his enthusiasm for the B-17 high-level bomber the famous Flying Fortress, Marshall also believed wholeheartedly in the Flying Fort. Three weeks before Pearl Harbor, he declared that the Forts based in the Philippines represented the greatest concentration of heavy bomber strength in the world! He claimed that the B-17s could defend the Philippine coastline without sea power and could counterattack by setting the 'paper cities' of Japan on fire. He was Douhet pure and unadulterated, maintained a year after its signal failure in the Battle of Britain.''[37]

The tenacity of Douhet's views can be explained not by the obstinacy of the American commanders, but by the fact that it appeared to the political leadership in Washington that acting on them would make it possible for the United States to achieve maximum results at minimum cost. In short, it was supposed that the Allies would provide armies of many millions of men, while the contribution of the United States to the coalition war would consist mainly of strategic bombings. Doubtless Roosevelt shared these views. Although the president was an admirer of naval power as interpreted by Admiral Mahan, he came inevitably to the conclusion that the Flying Fortress had replaced the battleship, to which, in his day, Mahan ascribed the decisive role. And Mahan's theory, worked out at the end of the nineteenth century, had in view safeguarding the ''balance of power'' policy, using the technological means that were available at that time. Hence the victory of the proponents of strategic bombings on the eve of the war.

In a special study on the subject it is stressed that "the theory of strategic bombings was embodied completely in the fundamental prewar plan of the Air Force, which can be best evaluated as a modified Douhet doctrine." In accordance with this plan there was envisaged the creation of an air force having 100,000 planes, and a personnel of 2,100,000, trained to carry out air attack with strategic bombers. On the eve of the war, measures were carried out consistently for the achievement of all the above. In his message to Congress on 16 May 1940, Roosevelt pointed out that he wanted to produce at least 50,000 planes a year. Moreover, he considered that the country needed an Air Force numbering 50,000 planes. In March-April 1941 there was created a united air force command and the position of assistant secretary of the air force was established; in June the army air forces were created, and the plan officially incorporated in the general plan for the conduct of the war. Finally, when combat operations began in February 1942, General Henry H. Arnold, commander of the army air forces, became a full and equal member of the Committee of the Chiefs of Staff.[38]

This was how the general strategic conception of Washington appeared. While the opponents of the Axis forces were fighting a war (with the limited participation of the United States in the war in the Pacific), America continued to arm, rendering such material assistance to its allies as could be alloted without detriment to the building of its own armed forces. Meanwhile, the United States Air Force was becoming a mighty striking force, for which a substantial part of the military budget would be required (during the years of the war an average of 40 percent of the military expenses of the United States went for aviation). The Allies were carrying the main burden of the ground operations; the United States would step in when it could strike a decisive blow, but at the end of the war, having suffered minimal losses, it would have at its disposition the mightiest and most modern armament, which its partners in the coalition would perforce have to take into account. The immense air forces, tempered in battle with the enemy, would serve as a proper warning to all.

A prerequisite for carrying out this policy was the guarantee that the United States would have its hands free within the limits of the anti-Hitler coalition that was taking shape. Although after Pearl Harbor the United States became a fighting participant in the coalition,

Washington was anxious not to become legally an ally of the opponents of the Axis powers, not to take upon itself any specific commitments with respect to the conduct of the war. Roosevelt attached paramount importance to this matter, trying to find a flexible formula in which the incompatible could be combined—unity in the struggle against the Axis powers and freedom of action for the United States.

At the end of December 1941 Winston Churchill came to Washington to discuss strategic problems. However, Roosevelt delivered to him first of all the draft of a political document prepared by the State Department which treated in general terms the necessity of fighting against the common enemy. If during the First World War the United States had categorized its place in the camp of the opponents of the German bloc as that of an "associate power," thereby emphasizing that it did not share the war aims of the Entente powers, now Roosevelt proposed the term *United Nations*, which made it possible to avoid using the term *Allies*, with all of the consequences that followed from that. By reserving to itself the right to be first to sign the corresponding declaration, the American government emphasized that it intended to place itself at the head of the "United Nations."

The pretensions of the Washington officials were clearly apparent, but a most cruel war was raging, and the declaration proposed by Roosevelt stated a most important principle: countries that were invited to sign the document committed themselves to cooperate with each other and not to conclude a separate peace. Furthermore, the declaration was flexible in that it did not commit each partner to fight against all of the Axis powers. Each government party to it had to employ its full resources, military or economic, against those members of the Tripartite Pact and its adherents with which such a government was at war.

On 1 January 1942, the United Nations Declaration was adopted in Washington, and signed by representatives of twenty-six nations, including the USSR. This document formally consolidated the existence of the anti-Hitler coalition.

Having discussed at the conference in Washington in December 1941-January 1942 the strategy in the war against the Axis powers, Roosevelt and Churchill confirmed plan "ABC-1." The plan, which was without question rational from the point of view of the problems of the coalition war against the Axis powers, was confirmed on somewhat different grounds than were being followed when it was adopted approximately a year before the events that have been described. As Dwight Eisenhower, head of the War Department group on planning of military actions in the Pacific, pointed out, in the coalition war the "strategic axiom" is that the weakened forces of the dismembered enemy must be routed first of all. Eisenhower considered that "the aggregate military might" of Germany with its satellites was greater than the might of Japan, but that nevertheless Japan was still relatively stronger than they, for she was not tied up in war against the Soviet Union.[39]

Therefore, in the interests of economizing their resources, the United States and Britain should not develop any intensive combat actions in the Far East and the Pacific. After having established all this, a super idea dawned on Washington—to try to saddle the USSR with the war against Japan as well, as if it were not enough to be holding the main front of the Second World War, fighting against Hitler's Germany! As early as December 1941 Roosevelt turned to the Soviet government with an insistent proposal to take part in "joint planning" on the Far East. Meanwhile, General MacArthur was adjuring Washington from the Philippines not to let slip the "golden opportunity" to strike a blow at Japan from the North, by inviting the USSR to participate in the war. Just how this was to be done, the general did not say, trusting it to American diplomacy. The United States manifested willingness to "assist" the USSR by sending a formation of American bombers to the Soviet Far East. This course of action would inevitably have drawn the Soviet Union into the war against Japan. No action was taken by the Soviet government on these appeals.

The position of the Soviet Union corresponded to the highest interests of the coalition war against the bloc of the aggressors, including plan "ABC-1." The participation of the USSR in the war against Japan at that stage would have required additional contingents of troops for the Far East, which could have been taken only from the Soviet-German front. This, in turn, would have prolonged the combat operations against Germany, the principal enemy of the United Nations. As a result, the duration of the entire Second World War would have been extended significantly, for it would have been difficult to crush Japan before the European Axis powers had been defeated. The tactical gains that the United States and Britain might have made if the USSR had entered the war against Japan at that time would have been canceled by the strategic losses. The leaders in the United States and Britain, who throughout the duration of the Great Patriotic War never stopped trying to induce the USSR to take part in the military actions against Japan, did not grasp the self-evident truth.

Soviet Impact on Axis Strategy

On the very day that the Japanese pilots were making short work of the American fleet in Pearl Harbor, the offensive of the Red Army at Moscow began. By spring 1942, Hitler's troops, which at the beginning of December had crept nearly to the gates of Moscow, had been hurled back 150 to 300 kilometers. This was the first strategic defeat of the Wehrmacht in the Second World War. The myth that Hitler's Germany was invincible had been shattered. Hitler, who was irate, removed scores of generals, including the highest in command, from their posts.

The dismissal of the generals, unprecedented in German military history, could not, however, compensate for the catastrophe on the Eastern front. According to Marshal M. A. Zakharov, ''During the period of the battle at Moscow from 1 October 1941, to 31 March 1942, the German-Fascist army lost 650,000 men killed, wounded, missing in action, and taken prisoner. For comparison we may point out that during the entire military campaign on the Western front the German armed forces lost 27,000 men killed.''[40] The losses in military equipment were also tremendous—1,300 tanks, 2,500 pieces of ordnance, and 15,000 motor vehicles and others.

It was at Moscow that the difficult sunrise of victory for the United Nations began. Hope sprang up that not only would the forces of aggression be stopped, but that they would be turned backward. But victory was still a long way off.

In the first half of 1942 the attention of the United States was riveted on the Pacific, where the Japanese had routed the forces resisting them with fantastic swiftness. The dizzying successes took the Japanese leadership by surprise. In Tokyo there was inclination to believe that they had fallen wide of the mark in making their war plans, that they should have envisaged more substantial goals. Where to strike?

According to the agreement between the European Axis powers and

Japan on 12 January, the demarcation line between their operations was at 70° west longitude; in other words, the dividing line passed somewhat to the east of the Ural range, then through the western boundary of India and directly south through the Indian Ocean. The command of the Japanese fleet, which was responsible for victory, proposed a bold plan in early spring of 1942—to move to the west, seize Ceylon, turn it into a base for subsequent operations, and proceed westward to join the Nazi somewhere in the Near East. The realization of this plan (the advance was within the capabilities of the Japanese fleet, which had suffered almost no losses from the beginning of the war) would have been fraught with grave consequences for the United Nations. However, such an offensive required sizable contingents of land forces.

In March, at a meeting with the emperor, the plan was raised for discussion and turned down—the command of the army, preparing an offensive against the USSR, announced that it could not produce the necessary number of soldiers. Germany, in its turn, having committed all to the Soviet-German front, could not detach sufficient forces for an advance in the region of the Near East, where the Germans were fighting with relatively limited forces. Thus, the Soviet Union had a decisive influence on the course of events in the entire Second World War, including the Pacific. The strategic planning of both of the belligerent coalitions invariably proceeded from recognition of the obvious fact that the principal theater of military actions was the Soviet-German front, that everything else in final analysis was derived from conditions on that front.

At the beginning of 1942, just when the American troops were suffering a series of defeats, the Red Army, having smashed the Hitlerites at Moscow, instilled the peoples of the United Nations with hope. Nothing in General MacArthur's past gives any basis for suspecting him of being especially sympathetic to the USSR. But it was he who declared in a salutory telegram to Moscow on the occasion of Red Army Day on 23 February, "The world situation at the present time indicates that the hopes of civilization rest on the worthy banners of the courageous Russian Army. During my lifetime I have participated in a number of wars and have witnessed others, as well as studying in great detail the campaigns of outstanding leaders in the past. In none have I observed such effective resistance to the heaviest blows of hitherto undefeated enemy, followed by a smashing counterattack

which is driving the enemy back to his own land. 1
grandeur of this effort marks it as the greatest military ach.
history.''[41]

The preparation by the Japanese army for war against t.   .iet
Union not only undermined the very possibility of conducting large-
scale combined operations, but also doomed the fleet to actions that
did not have great strategic sense. The superior skill of the American
command in the war against Japan, and the courage and determination of the personnel of the United States armed forces in the war in
the Pacific made it possible to repulse the new thrusts of the aggressor.

At the beginning of June the Japanese fleet suffered a defeat at
Midway Island which had the gravest consequences for the future
actions of Japan. Having lost a significant part of their striking
power—their aircraft carriers—the Japanese admirals no longer dared
to mount large-scale offensive operations outside the radius of the
action of their coastal aviation. From now on the war on the seas had to
and did become protracted. Its outcome was being decided by the
relative military-industrial potential of the opponents, in which all
advantages were on the side of the United States. It was only a matter
of time.

Stalingrad, Kursk, and the United States

In May 1942, Franklin Roosevelt, reviewing the position on the fronts
in the Second World War, wrote to Douglas MacArthur: ''In the
matter of grand strategy I find it difficult this spring and summer to
get away from the simple fact that the Russian armies are killing
more Axis personnel and destroying more Axis material than all
the other twenty-five United Nations put together.'' MacArthur
agreed with Roosevelt and called for maximum aid to the Soviet
Union.[42]

MacArthur's opinion reflected the point of view of the American
generals, who feared for the fate of the United States if the Red
Army could not hold the front. The American commanders reasoned
as professionals, proceeding from purely military considerations.
Eisenhower pointed out that the outcome of the entire war depended
on the struggle of the Soviet Union. Hence, in the interests of
''keeping Russia in the war,'' it was essential to render assistance to
the USSR, first through Lend-Lease, and second through ''beginning

at the earliest possible moment operations that would draw away from the Russian front a substantial number of ground troops and air power of the German army." A competent soldier, but at that time not yet experienced in people's political associations, he pointed out that the shortest operationally strategic direction to the center of the military might of Germany lay through northwest France.

The American staffs immediately put together plans to take corresponding action. According to their calculations, beginning in the second half of July, Anglo-American aircraft would start a bombing offensive from the British Isles, and after six weeks there would follow a landing in France. They had to smash the enemy troops in the Calais-Arras-St. Quentin-Soissons-Paris-Deauville region, and basing their operations on this region, deploy further combat operations. The working out of the plans for these operations was completed in the early spring of 1942. No one in the high command of the American armed forces had any doubt that they could be carried out. From the strategic point of view that was the surest way to guarantee the victory of the United Nations in the shortest possible time. The Soviet government, putting before Washington and London the question of a second front, was proceeding from similar considerations.

American historiography does not deny this. In his study of the military history of the United States, Leckie observes: "Militarily, there could be no better plan to invade France and place Hitler between the two fires that would destroy him. Politically, nothing could be more disastrous, for it would leave Stalin and Communism free to pounce on [the] nations of Central and Eastern Europe."[43]

The American generals, at that time fighting to assure the earliest possible engagement with the enemy, did not take into account these considerations by the political leadership, which was by no means seeking to crown the victorious American troops with laurels immediately. The generals had visions of gigantic battles in which they, the military, would make themselves famous, while the political figures were thinking of the losses that the American armed forces would inevitably suffer in these battles, and consequently, of the fact that the United States would find itself weakened at the end of the war. The staffs were haunted by a nightmare: the Red Army would not hold the front, and victorious Germany would turn its entire might against the United States; hence the insistence with which they pressed for the beginning of the American offensive. The political figures did not take such a tragic view of circumstances and proceeded from other considerations.

There is hardly need to analyze in detail all of these conditions, which have been explored in Soviet historiography.[44] It is sufficient to recall the conversation of Roosevelt with his son Elliot at the end of January 1942. The commander-in-chief of the armed forces of the United States explained the essence of the strategy of Washington, in a form that was intelligible to a captain in the air forces, as follows: "Just figure it's a football game," the father answered. "Say we're the reserves sitting on the bench. At the moment, the Russians are the first team, together with the Chinese, and, to a lesser extent, the British. . . . Before the game is so far advanced that our blockers are tired, we've got to be able to get in there for the touchdown. We'll be fresh. If our timing is right. . . . I think our timing will be right."[45]

Here lies the genesis of the entire history of the second front! When it would be opened depended on that notorious "moment" when the forces of the principal opponents on the field of battle would be undermined decisively. For the time being, however, there was a tendency in Washington to make verbal announcements about the imminent opening of a second front, misleading the enemy and raising the spirits of their ally. The governments of the United States and Britain carried this too far. As a result of the negotiations with the Soviet delegation that visited Washington and London in May-June, corresponding assertions were made publicly. The Soviet-American communique on the subject of the negotiations said: "Full agreement has been reached on the urgent problems of creating a second front in Europe in 1942."[46]

Unfortunately, the enemy was not much misled. The Hitler leadership assessed the words of the communique coolly. The head of the German general staff, Franz Halder, noted down Hitler's words at the meeting with the commanders on 3 July, at the height of the most powerful offensive of the Wehrmacht on the eastern front: "Washington only consoles and assures. There is no actual second front. The proposal is to reckon on 1943. The behavior of Churchill is the best evidence. A diversionary maneuver in the West? Doubtful; obviously there will be no serious assurances given to Russia. More likely they will warn them of the necessity to go on fighting."[47] In other words, the commanders could drive their troops to the East without fear, without a glance backward to the West. At the beginning of the summer, troops of Germany and her satellites totalling 6,200,000 men, 5,400,000 of them German, were brought in against the USSR. Out of 239 divisions and four brigades which the Reich had at its disposal at that time, 182 divisions and four brigades, or 76.3 percent of all the troops, took part in the summer campaign against the USSR.

As in a conjurer's trick, the fundamental substance of Soviet-American relations was concentrated in the problem of the opening of the second front, or, to be more precise, in the nature of the military cooperation between the United States and the USSR. In the summer of 1942, at a time when the Soviet Army was engaged in battles with the advancing German forces that were of unprecedented gravity, the United States and Britain announced that the opening of a second front was being postponed until 1943. Meanwhile, in order to ensure transport for the second front, the Soviet Union agreed to a reduction in the delivery of Lend-Lease in 1942, first from 8,000,000 to 4,100,000 tons, and finally to 2,500,000 tons. The Western Allies, instead of mounting an invasion on the European continent in the fall of 1942, landed in North Africa, where they got bogged down in battles with a relatively insignificant force of German-Italian troops.[48]

The scale of the battles in North Africa, which were dragged out until May 1943, looked more than modest by comparison with the scope of the battles on the Soviet-German front. It took the American-British forces half a year to break the resistance of twelve German and eight Italian divisions. And in the fall of 1942 the USSR was fighting against 258 divisions and sixteen brigades of Germany and her satellites.[49]

The head of the American army staff, General George Marshall, writes in his account of the Second World War, "This generation of Americans can still remember the black days of 1942 when the Japanese conquered all of Malaysia, occupied Burma, and threatened India while the German armies approached the Volga and the Suez. In those hours Germany and Japan came so close to complete domination of the world that we do not yet realize how thin the thread of Allied survival had been stretched. In good conscience this nation can take little credit for its part in staving off disaster in those critical days."[50]

During this critical period, when Hitler's troops had made their way to Stalingrad and the foothills of the Caucasus, Roosevelt sent a series of warm messages to the Soviet government. On 19 August he wrote: "The fact that the Soviet Union is bearing the brunt of the fighting and losses during the year of 1942 is well understood by the United States and I may state that we greatly admire the magnificent resistance which your country has exhibited."

On 5 October Roosevelt sent "heartiest congratulations on the magnificent achievements of the Soviet armies." On 9 October he added: "The gallant defense of Stalingrad has thrilled everyone in America," and on 19 November he observed: "I do not have to tell you to keep up the good work." This was the day that the Soviet troops assumed the offensive at Stalingrad and began to drive the enemy west.

On 14 December Stalin wrote: "Permit me also to express my confidence that time is not passing to no purpose and that the promises about the opening of a second front in Europe that were given by you, Mr. President, and by Mr. Churchill with respect to 1942, and by now in any case, with respect to spring 1943, will be fulfilled." On 28 December Roosevelt reported about a joint resolution of Congress expressing "deep and eternal gratitude" to all of the allies of America. Two days later he expressed his "admiration for the courage, stamina, and military prowess of your great Russian armies," and in another message on the same day he did not forget to mention the naval forces of the USSR, expressing "appreciation of the part your gallant Navy is also contributing to the Allied cause." On 8 January 1943, he added: "My deep appreciation for the continuing advances of your armies. The principle of attrition of the enemy forces on all fronts is beginning to work." Stalin responded by asking why the operations of the Allies in North Africa had slowed down, "they say, not for a short time, but for a long time."

On 24 January, when the USSR was scoring more and more victories and after the conclusion of the conference in Casablanca, Roosevelt announced that the Allies were going to try to achieve the "unconditional surrender" of the Axis powers. This meant, as Gabriel Kolko, a contemporary American student of military diplomacy of the United States, has observed, that "At that time, of course, any surrender imposed on Germany would have had to be largely as a result of

Russian bloodshed.''[51] The USSR placed on the altar of victory still more victims for the sake of the triumph of the United Nations' cause; the United States contributed a resounding slogan—to fight until the "unconditional surrender" of the enemy.

Reporting to Stalin on the decisions adopted at Casablanca, on 27 January Roosevelt stressed that the contemplated operations "together with your powerful offensive, may well bring Germany to her knees in 1943." Three days later Stalin inquired about the specific details of the projected operations. On 6 February a message was received in Moscow in which the commander-in-chief of the armed forces of the United States congratulated the USSR "on the brilliant victory" at Stalingrad and expressed confidence that by their example the Soviet people would rouse all of the United Nations to a new resolution to finish off the enemy.

The battle at Stalingrad, unprecedented in history, ended with the crushing defeat of Germany and her satellites. In the course of this battle, five enemy armies—two German (the sixth and fourth tank forces), two Romanian (the third and fourth), and the eighth Italian force—were annihilated. In a total of more than 100 divisions, the enemy losses in the winter campaign of 1942–43 reached 1,700,000 men; 3,500 tanks, 4,300 fighter and transport planes, 24,000 pieces of ordnance, 75,000 motor vehicles, and so forth were destroyed. Soviet troops advanced 600 to 700 kilometers to the west. The turning point in the course of the entire Second World War was begun at the Volga.

This is obvious, but, as Soviet Marshal A. M. Vasilevsky writes, "the bookstores of the bourgeois West continue to be flooded with the most varicolored 'studies' in which the events that took place on the Volga and in other parts of the Soviet-German front are elucidated in a biased and tendentious way." Some of the authors of such studies, the American General Walker, for example, reach the point where the battle of Stalingrad never took place at all. This general declared that the battle on the Volga was nothing but a Communist propaganda fiction. It would appear that such a statement could be made only by a man suffering from psychological imbalance. Let us turn to the text of one document. It is kept, along with other relics, in the museum of the hero-city after which the battle of the Volga is named. This is a document of Franklin Roosevelt, president of the United States. Here is its text: "In the name of the people of the United States of America, I present this scroll to the City of Stalingrad to commemorate our admiration for its gallant defenders whose courage, fortitude, and devotion during the siege of September 13, 1942 to January 31, 1943, will inspire forever the hearts of all free people. Their glorious victory stemmed the tide of invasion and marked the turning point in the War of the Allied Nations against the forces of aggression."[52]

Victory was bought dearly, with torrents of the blood of the Soviet people. The enemy was still strong, and manifested frenzied resistance. The end of this unprecedented battle could have been hastened by a more active participation in the combat actions by the United States and Britain.

On 9 February Roosevelt announced that the second front would be opened in August 1943. On 16 February Stalin expressed the wish that the time of the opening of the second front might be "shortened as much as possible" and the blow be struck "as early as spring or at the beginning of the summer." He also reported that from the end of December, that is, from the moment that the Allied offensive in Tunisia was halted, the Germans had transferred twenty-seven divisions to the Soviet-German front. On 22 February Roosevelt complained about the "unexpected heavy rains" in North Africa that had halted the Allied offensive, and wished the Soviet army "further successes, which are an inspiration to us all." On the following day, the president wished "to pay tribute to the Russian people" and explained: "The Red Army and the Russian people have surely started the Hitler forces on the road to ultimate defeat and have earned the lasting admiration of the people of the United States."

On 16 March Stalin reported that, inasmuch as the Allied offensive in North Africa did not take place in February-March, Germany had transferred thirty-six divisions from the west. And he further warned, "from the standpoint of the interests of our common cause, of the grave danger of further delay in the opening of the second front in France."

On 5 May Roosevelt wrote that in the estimation of the American staffs, "Germany will deliver an all-out attack on you this summer," and concluded the message: "You are doing a grand job. Good luck!"

On 4 June Roosevelt reported that the United States and Britain had put off the opening of the second front until 1944. To this, Stalin replied on 11 June:

> As is apparent from your communication, these decisions are at variance with those decisions that were taken by you and by Mr. Churchill at the beginning of this year, concerning the time of the opening of the second front in Western Europe. . . . This decision of yours creates exceptional difficulties for the Soviet Union, which for two years already has been conducting a war against the main forces of Germany and her satellites with extreme effort on the part of all its forces, and leaves the Soviet army, which is fighting not only for its own country but also for its allies, with its own forces, in virtually single combat with the forces of a still very strong and dangerous enemy.

The Soviet government could not subscribe to such a decision on the part of its allies.

Roosevelt responded on 22 June in connection with the second anniversary of the beginning of the Great Patriotic War, with a perturbed written message to Moscow. He pointed out that the growing power of the United Nations "testifies to the spirit of unity and sacrifice necessary for our ultimate victory."[53]

In the summer of 1943 Hitler's command concentrated 232 divisions on the Soviet-German front, and on 5 July struck a blow in the region of the Kursk salient with a force of fifty divisions. That was the last major German offensive, which this time did not achieve any success. The Soviet troops not only repulsed the enemy onslaught but launched a large-scale offensive of their own.

The Hitler leadership brought the most massive forces into action in the battle of Kursk—the shock troops reached a strength of 900,000 men. They had 2,700 tanks, 2,000 planes, 10,000 pieces of ordnance. The most modern models in military equipment at Germany's disposal (including the heavy Tiger tanks) were introduced.

In the course of the battles at Kursk, which were unprecedented in their violence, the enemy lost more than 500,000 men, 3,500 planes, 1,500 pieces of ordnance, 1,500 tanks. In this battle the backbone of the Wehrmacht tank troops was broken; the Wehrmacht was no longer able to undertake any large-scale offensive operations in the East. "At the height of the battle of Kursk," writes Marshal Vasilevsky, "our allies made a landing in Sicily, and on 17 August crossed over from there into Italy. Would they have been able to do this if they had had facing them even half the forces with which we clashed in our country in the summer of 1943? I think the answer is obvious."[54] In Sicily, it took the armies of the United States and Britain thirty-eight days to disperse the incapacitated Italian units and to drive German divisions from the island, which evacuated, taking with them their heavy equipment.

The year 1943 concluded the fundamental turning point in the course of the Great Patriotic War. In heavy fighting, the Soviet soldiers moved 1,300 kilometers in the south and 500 kilometers in the center of the Soviet-German front. Two thirds of the Soviet territory that had been temporarily occupied by the Hitlerites was liberated. The decisive role of the Soviet armed forces in the war was obvious: until the middle of 1944, 75 percent of all German ground forces were situated on the Soviet-German front, while only 6.2 percent of the German troops were in action against the Western Allies on all fronts at various times. The losses on the part of the Allies were distributed accordingly.

This development of events in the course of the coalition war, so far as the distribution of the burden among the Allies was concerned, was a consequence of the deliberate strategy of Washington. However, in the middle of 1943 the chosen course began to appear questionable to influential Americans. As early as May 1943, Henry Stimson observed that if the Soviet Union should smash the enemy mainly with its own forces, ". . . that will be dangerous business for us at the end of the war."[55] In August he wrote to Roosevelt: "The British theory . . . [is] that the only heavy fighting which needs to be done will be done by Russia. To me, in the light of the postwar problems which we shall face, that attitude toward Russia seems terribly dangerous."[56] Finally, Averell Harriman, who had been appointed ambassador to the USSR, in one of his first reports from Moscow in November, wrote: "Our whole permanent relations [with the USSR] depend in a large measure on their satisfaction in the future with our military operations."[57]

In 1943 the American leaders, the military leaders first of all, found out another circumstance that was regrettable for them: the alignment of forces within the anti-Hitler coalition was changing rapidly in favor of the Soviet Union. In part this was to be explained by the way in which the United States had conducted the war. Having ascertained that the Soviet Union was carrying the chief burden of land operations, Washington consistently curtailed building up its army. By the middle of 1943, they considered it possible to limit themselves to an army of one hundred divisions (actually, at the end of the war the United States had eighty-nine divisions). This made it possible to conduct the war on the basis of a policy of "guns and butter." It is true that enormous resources—up to half of the military budget—went for aviation, the effectiveness of which, especially of the strategic bombers, was fundamentally exaggerated by the American military.

The burden of the war fell to the lot of the Allies, foremost the USSR. This was perfectly well known to the high command of the armed forces of the United States. If at the beginning of the Great Patriotic War the American staffs made an extremely pessimistic assessment of the military potential of the USSR, by the middle of 1943 their views had undergone an abrupt change. They had before their eyes the collapse of the offensive strategy of Germany in a series of campaigns against the USSR; the scope of the Red Army victories was enormous. Against this background, the achievements of the forces of the Western Allies appeared less than modest.

In the middle of 1943, American strategists demanded with redoubled energy that the government be very wary in its relations with the Soviet Union. The joint chiefs of staff prepared the following recommendations for the Quebec Conference of Roosevelt and Churchill in August 1943: "Russia's postwar position in Europe will be a dominant one. With Germany crushed, there is no power in Europe to oppose her tremendous military forces.... The conclusions from the foregoing are obvious; since Russia is the decisive factor in war, she must be given every assistance and every effort must be made to obtain her friendship."[58] In the eyes of the American generals, this policy appeared wise also because they were faced with having to bring to a conclusion the war with Japan, victory over which without the participation of the USSR seemed costly, and would have required much time.

To be sure, the American generals recognized the wisdom of the projected course—to husband their own forces, as one of the leaders of the army staff, General Thomas T. Handy, put in March 1943: "We must be strong enough militarily at the peace table to cause our demands to be respected."[59] But the military might of the Soviet

Union remained a fact, and there was nothing to be done about it. The alignment of forces within the anti-Hitler coalition determined the possibilities of American foreign policy. It was within these limits that American diplomacy worked, striving to utilize political means to foster the interests of Washington.

The situation on the fronts in the second half of 1943 urgently demanded that the United States conduct active operations on the continent of Europe. If it did not, then not only Germany, but France as well, would have been liberated by the Soviet armed forces. Realizing this, official Washington returned to the age-old operational-strategic course. An end was put to the escapades in the Mediterranean basin that had been contrived in the main at the insistence of Winston Churchill.

The Significance of the Second Front

At the time it was clear to anyone and everyone that it was the Soviet Union that was cutting down Germany—the main power in the enemy coalition—in the most serious battles. Soviet troops were moving westward irresistibly. With the enormous victories of the Soviet Union at the end of November and the beginning of December 1943, a conference took place in Teheran of the heads of the governments of the USSR, the United States, and Britain at which the leaders of the Western Allies at last announced that the second front would be opened in 1944.

The basis of this decision lay first of all in political motives—not to permit Soviet soldiers to be the ones to liberate the whole of Europe. Extensive preparations for operation "Overlord" began— the invasion of Northwest France. At the same time operation plan "Rankin" was worked out—a swift occupation of key points in Germany, if for any reason the resistance of the Hitlerites should suddenly collapse in the West. The American leadership attached paramount importance to the occupation of positions that protruded farthest to the east.

As early as March 1943, General George Marshall, Army chief of staff, expressed the greatest concern in a memorandum to the president that the troops of the Western Allies might "fall behind" the Soviet armed forces in the advance in Europe. If that happened, he predicted postwar chaos in Europe. In November Roosevelt pointed out at the meeting with the joint chiefs of staff that "There would definitely be a race for Berlin. We may have to put United States divisions in Berlin as soon as possible." Hopkins, who was present at the meeting, suggested that "we be ready to put an airborne division into Berlin two hours after the collapse of Germany."[60]

Foreseeing the possible cessation of German resistance in the West, the American-British troops destined to take part in plan "Rankin" prepared to occupy Germany. The plan itself was being constantly corrected, taking into account changes in the military situation, and the contingents of troops that were to take action in accordance with this plan remained in full readiness up to the beginning of 1945, when at last it became clear in Washington and London that the anticipated events never did ensue.

On 6 June 1944, what had been long promised occurred—the Western Allied troops invaded Normandy. A second front appeared that was a second front not only in name but in fact. Although the American-British armies far outnumbered the German forces, the operation developed extremely slowly; the Allies advanced with the greatest caution, expecting strong counterattacks. These did not follow, for as early as 23 June, the USSR, faithful to its duties as an ally, began a very large-scale offensive that pinned down the overwhelming part of the German reserves. Harriman explains: "People forget that there were at the time about two hundred Nazi divisions and about fifty satellite divisions on the Eastern Front. Our plans were based on the premise that we could not land successfully in Normandy if there were more than about thirty mobile German divisions in the West of Europe. Therefore the transfer of a relatively small number of divisions from the Eastern Front to the west could have been disastrous."[61]

The gigantic onslaught of the Soviet armed forces pinned down the principal resources of Germany; its eastern front was on the verge of collapse. Half a year after the landing of the Allies in Normandy, the Hitlerites transferred fifty-nine divisions and thirteen brigades to the Soviet-German front, and removed twelve divisions and five brigades. During this period 108 enemy divisions were completely annihilated, and heavy losses were inflicted on another 128 divisions. During this same period the American-British troops routed approximately sixty enemy divisions. In the central part of the front Soviet troops battled their way over more than 600 kilometers, and by August emerged at the Vistula. General Heinz Guderian, appointed chief of the German general staff, wrote about this offensive as follows: "On the Eastern front, events were developing that directly hastened the day of a monstrous catastrophe. . . . In the main directions [Warsaw and Riga] it looked as though the offensive would continue without interruption. . . . We incurred huge losses. . . . All available forces were thrown into the disintegrating front."[62]

In Western Europe American and British troops were advancing in places that were accessible to them. Later, American and British historians naturally greatly exaggerated the importance of the campaign in France. F. Mellentin, the German general-tactician, who participated in the events directly, observed with respect to this interpretation: "The offensive of the Soviet forces in the summer of 1944 was one of the most important events of the war, and as a military operation it considerably surpassed the invasion of Normandy in scale. Between 1 June and 31 August 1944, the German armies in the west lost 293,802 men. During this same period our losses in Russia numbered 916,860 men."[63] When the Soviet armed forces were carrying the overwhelming share of the burden of the war, the advance of the American-British troops in France exceeded the earlier expectations of the staffs. On 15 August the Allies landed in southern France and made their way northward with practically no resistance.

Before the landing in Normandy, Eisenhower's staff, planning the operation in Europe, contemplated reaching the German border on the 330th day after the invasion, that is, on 2 May 1945. Actually, the border had already been reached on 11 September 1944, and by the middle of September the Allied forces had left behind them not only northern France but also most of Belgium and Luxembourg, and had entered the Netherlands. These successes, and also the news of the plot against Hitler on 20 July, even though it was unsuccessful, gave rise to a sharp rush of optimism in Washington and London. At the beginning of September, the joint American-British intelligence committee advised its governments that the organized resistance at the western front would collapse not later than 1 December, and probably even earlier.

About this time, General Marshall invited a group of selected journalists, spread maps before them, and for the duration of two hours delivered a tirade on the enormous victories of the Western Allies. Arthur Krock, who was present at this press conference, noted that Marshall constantly contrasted the position on the western front with the results of the summer operations on the Soviet-German front. Marshall even expressed "disappointment" at the scope of the victory of the Soviet army. Marshall was in the habit of talking like that. He usually complained to the correspondents that the USSR did not understand why the Western Allies were conducting the war so slowly. But Marshall stressed, "[The Russian Army has] nothing to think about but roads, railroads, mountains, and rivers. Hell, we have everything to think about—air, sea, trackless mountains—...."[64]

All this, of course, is nonsense, for the Soviet troops were fighting against the main forces of the enemy; however, Marshall's opinions are important to the understanding of the psychological atmosphere that enveloped Washington and London in the fall of 1944.

When it appeared that the downfall of the enemy was near and victory was at hand, the thinking of the United States leaders turned to postwar matters. Even that realist, Roosevelt, for a short time lost his sense of proportion. In all probability he imagined that the advance of American and British troops to the east at least to the point of occupying of all of Germany would completely eliminate all concern about European problems. In September 1944, at a meeting in Quebec, Roosevelt and Churchill initialed the "Morgenthau plan," which envisioned turning Germany into a primarily agrarian country, which meant the thorough destruction of the German economy, first of all the industrial complex of the Ruhr. But very soon it turned out that the preconditions of the plan—the collapse of German resistance in the West—were not realized. The United States and Britain abandoned the "Morgenthau plan," which, in the history of the war, remained a striking proof of what would have happened to Germany if they had been able to dictate their conditions for peace. Beyond any doubt, it would have been a Carthaginian peace.

Meanwhile, the military situation turned out inauspiciously for the United States and Britain. In Europe the Hitlerites were able to take their troops approximately to the borders of the Reich, partly to the quickly restored system of prewar fortifications—the "Siegfried line." The efforts of the troops of the Western Allies to advance to the Reich ran up against savage defense. The commanders of the American-

British armies blamed the delay not only on the enemy, but also on their own commissaries, which had not succeeded in arranging the supply of the troops along lengthy communication lines—the front was supplied mainly from the ports that were in the region of the initial invasion. The service behind the front, in turn, notified the captains and generals that it could not improve the supply unless it had access to a deepwater port nearer the front line. This port could be only Antwerp. Eisenhower ordered that all efforts be concentrated on gaining control of the mouth of the Scheldt, but they succeeded in completing this operation only in November, and Antwerp was able to begin to handle vessels only at the very end of that month. The delay on the Western front, which was practically an impasse, prompted the combined chiefs of staff to take up the question whether it would not be possible to overcome the impasse by an offensive in Italy. The command in that theater gave a dissapointing reply that the withdrawal of the German troops from Italy would depend mainly on the Russian offensive rather than on the actions of General Harold R. L. G. Alexander's armies.

Extremely unfavorable news was coming from Asia. Although the American armed forces had achieved impressive victories on the sea and in the air, and were gradually drawing nearer to Japan, no end to the war was in sight. In Japan preparations were being made for protracted resistance not only on the islands of the metropolis, but also on the continent of Asia. The war against the United States and Britain was being fought and lost by the Japanese fleet and naval aviation; the army, many million strong, took almost no part in the combat operations. It demonstrated its capabilities when it opened a large-scale offensive in China in March 1944. Its purpose was to drive the Chinese troops away from the coast and to create a solid line of land communications from Singapore to Manchuria. The Japanese captured a territory approximately two million square kilometers in area, with a population of sixty million people. From then on, blockade from the sea had no decisive significance for Tokyo. The Japanese forces captured several scores of American air bases that had been built in China with enormous difficulty in anticipation of an air offensive against the Japanese islands. The disaster in China created immense difficulties for the subsequent conduct of the war in the Far East.

The Western Allies conducted the enitre war in such a way that the main burden of land operations fell to the lot of the Soviet armed forces. The United States and Britain considered it possible to maintain relatively limited land armies, turning their main attention to the deployment of aviation, in accordance with the strategic conceptions that have already been described. In the autumn of 1944 the Western Allies reaped the bitter harvest of their policy. Of the eighty-nine divisions that the United States had at its disposal, eighty-seven were in action in the European and Pacific theaters. There were practically no reserves left. The British, who by the end of 1944 had used their manpower resources almost to the limit, found themselves in an even more difficult position; they began to disband some of their units in order to reinforce others. The situation was further complicated by the peculiar organization of the Western Allies' armed forces. In the American army, for example, only 30 percent of the personnel were in fighting units.

The Hitlerite leadership strove to take advantage of the impasse in the West to achieve their long-standing goal—to bring about dissension in the anti-Fascist coalition. It was decided to strike a blow against the troops of the Western Allies in a weakly defended sector—in the Ardennes, to move swiftly toward the sea, to seize Antwerp, and, having pinned the left wing of the enemy to the seaboard, to arrange another Dunkirk. Hitler announced to his commanders, optimistically: "In all history there has never been a coalition composed of such heterogeneous partners with such totally divergent objectives ... ultracapitalist states on one side and ultra-Marxist states on the other. . . . These are states whose objectives diverge daily and anyone who, if I may use the phrase, sits like a spider in his web and follows these developments can see how hour by hour these antitheses are increasing. If we can deal it a couple of heavy blows, this artificially constructed common front may collapse with a mighty thunderclap at any moment."[65]

Armed with these political instructions, the generals of the Wehrmacht led their troops into battle on 16 December 1944. Despite the general enormous superiority of forces in the west, the Americans and the British were unable to hold the front in the Ardennes. The width of the breach reached 100 kilometers, and the Hitlerite troops moved in to a depth of up to 90 kilometers. The sudden attack threw the entire Allied front into disarray; reserves were thrown into the

Ardennes; nervous tension was building in the staffs. Eisenhower sent telegram after telegram to Washington, demanding that reinforcements be sent quickly. At the instruction of Marshall, even the garrisons in Alaska and in the Panama Canal Zone were "scoured." On 14 December the British government still reckoned that the war in Europe would be ended by 30 June 1945; at the beginning of January, a new date was accepted as the basis of military planning—31 December 1945.

But at the end of 1944 only about one third of the German armed forces was fighting against the Allies in the West and in Italy. And they were able to place the American-British armies in a difficult situation. An envoy from Eisenhower's staff was quickly sent to Moscow—Britain's Chief Air Marshal Arthur W. Tedder. Roosevelt, in a message to Stalin on 24 December, stressed the urgency of the matter and asked that the head of the Soviet government discuss with Tedder the situation at the western front and coordination with the eastern front.

Taking into consideration the complex position of the Western Allies, the Soviet offensive was speeded up beginning on 12 January 1945. The entire Soviet-German front was set in motion—from the Carpathians to the Baltic Sea. The Germans were forced to fall back everywhere. At the first news of the Soviet army offensive, the Hitlerite leadership hurriedly transferred great shock forces to the east from the Ardennes region, and put an end to aggressive action there. The position on the western front for the United States and Britain was improved.

As German General Kurt von Manteufel (one of the commanders in the Ardennes) stressed later, "the headlong advance of the Red Army brought to nought the consequences of the respite achieved by the Ardennes offensive, and made the rapid end of the war inevitable. And so the gain of time on the Western front turned out to be deceptive."[66] When it was realized in Berlin that the scheme of provoking a paralysis of the Western Allies had failed, another plan was adopted—to yield territory before the advancing Americans and British, and to throw all forces to the east—against the Red Army. In February 1945, for example, the eastern front received 1,675 tanks and self-propelled guns, whereas the western front got only 67. By March, the equivalent of 26 divisions of uncoordinated German units were defending themselves on the western front, while 170 divisions were fighting in the east.

However, at the beginning of 1945 the Western Allies most probably did not understand the political game of the enemy. They could not seem to recover from the shock they had experienced in the Ardennes. The advance into Germany was renewed only at the end of March.

Yalta and After

Urgent problems of the coalition war demanded that another meeting of the heads of the governments of the three big powers be held, and this took place in February 1945 in Yalta. The very choice of the place of the meeting—on Soviet territory—was evidence of the absolute recognition by Washington and London of the decisive role of the USSR in the war. Being educated men, Roosevelt and Churchill deemed it appropriate to call the conference by the code name "Argonaut"—they could feel themselves to be the direct successors of the Argonauts. These came to the Black Sea in olden days in search of the golden fleece, while Roosevelt and Churchill came to ask the USSR to straighten out the complex situation on their fronts in Europe and Asia.

During the years when McCarthyism was raging in the United States, the decisions made at Yalta were explained as "archtreason"; speculative efforts were made to "expose" the sinister designs of the president who stood for the preservation of cooperation with the Soviet Union in combat. At that time, on 17 August 1951, Averell Harriman found it necessary to come out with a statement about the "secret story" of the Yalta Conference. Reminding the people, who had been poisoned by the fumes of anticommunism, of the real state of affairs in the position of the United States at Yalta, Harriman pointed out: "The great danger existed that the Soviet Union would stand by until we had brought Japan to her knees at great cost in American lives, and then the Red Army could march into Manchuria and large areas of northern China.... The military authorities estimated that it would take eighteen months after the surrender of Germany to defeat Japan and that the Soviet participation would greatly reduce the heavy American casualties which would otherwise be expected."[67]

Of course, such designs were alien to the Soviet Union, which saw in the shattering of Japan the fulfillment of its obligation as an ally participating in the anti-Fascist coalition. Militarist Japan had been a long-standing and perfidious enemy of the USSR in the Far East; her defeat was dictated by Soviet national interests. At Yalta, the Soviet delegation explained that the USSR would enter the war against Japan two to three months after the conclusion of combat operations in Europe. At the same time, it was stipulated that the rights of Russia in the Far East would be restored—Southern Sakhalin would be returned to the Soviet Union and the Kuril Islands would be turned over to it. This, moreover, was entirely in keeping with the principles of the policy set forth by the United States and the other powers in the Cairo Declaration of 1 December 1943, concerning the fact that Japan would be driven from territory that it had seized by force or that was under threat of the use of force.

As far as the government of the United States was concerned, it welcomed these agreements, not only with regard to immediate military problems, but also having in mind the prospects that lay ahead for limiting the possible advance of the USSR by means of legally formulated agreements. As Harriman emphasized, the conditions under which the USSR entered the war "limited the Soviet advance toward the East,"[68] from the American standpoint. For similar reasons, the United States approved with great willingness the boundaries of the occupation zones in Germany as outlined in preliminary form. At the time of the Yalta Conference the American-British armies were far from forcing their way across the Rhine, while the Soviet forces, having reached the Oder, stood at the gates of Berlin. Under these circumstances, the assessment by the American staffs that at the end of the war Soviet soldiers would occupy a large part of Germany were not unreasonable. The agreement by the United States to the boundaries outlined for the occupation zones in Europe pursued the same goal as in the Far East of setting a limit to the advance of the Soviet armed forces.

At the conference important decisions were adopted, both on the conduct of the war and on the democratic organization of the world after it was ended. The prevailing atmosphere at the conference was one of aspiration—in Roosevelt's words, "to make the world safe for at least fifty years." The atmosphere of the conference is well conveyed in the words of Stalin, who observed during the course of the discussion:

> Churchill has expressed fear that people might think the three great powers want to dominate the world. But who contemplates such domination? The United States? No, they do not have this in mind. [Laughter and an eloquent gesture on the part of the president.] England? Also, no. [Laughter and an eloquent gesture on the part of Churchill.] Thus, two great powers are removed from the sphere of suspicion. There remains the third. . . . the USSR. So the USSR aspires to world domination? [General laughter.] Or perhaps China aspires to world domination? [General laughter.] Clearly talk of aspiration to world domination doesn't mean a thing.[69]

In the communique about the results of the conference it was pointed out: "Our meeting in the Crimea has reaffirmed our common resolution to preserve and strengthen during the period of peace that lies ahead that unity of purpose and action that has made victory possible and certain for the United Nations in the present war. We believe that peace is a sacred obligation of our governments before their people, and also before the peoples of the world."[70]

The Yalta Conference demonstrated to the world that it was possible for nations with different socioeconomic systems to cooperate. First and most important, it showed that in American-Soviet relations there must prevail a respect for each other's legitimate interests, without which it is impossible to reach decisions on the basis of compromise.

Appearing before Congress with a speech on the results of the conference, Roosevelt singled out this side of the matter especially. Speaking of the principles recognized in the declaration on liberated Europe that was adopted at Yalta, he observed: "The final decisions in these areas are going to be made jointly; and therefore they will often be a result of give-and-take compromise. The United States will not always have its way a hundred percent—nor will Russia nor Great Britain. We shall not always have ideal answers—solutions to complicated international problems, even though we are determined continuously to strive toward ideal. But I am sure that under the agreements reached at Yalta, there will be a more stable political Europe than ever before."[71] Roosevelt assured Congress that the meeting of the heads of the three great powers was crowned with great success. "I come from the Crimea Conference with a firm belief that we

have made a good start on the road to a world of peace. . . . The Conference in the Crimea was a turning point—I hope in our history and therefore in the history of the world."[72] Success was achieved because the
results of the battles against fascism, won first of all by the Soviet Union,
were stated at the conference table. The decisions made at Yalta, which
were the culminating point of the cooperation between the USSR and
the United States during Roosevelt's presidency, have been subjected
to violent attacks in the West for almost three decades now. If one
takes into account the fantastic charges dictated by pure animal anti-
communism, the criticism of Roosevelt usually comes down to the fact
that because of his poor state of health he is supposed to have yielded
some positions to the Soviet Union and had not realized the possible
consequences of the decisions reached at Yalta. This criticism is completely divorced from the real situation that existed in February 1945;
its point of departure is the desire to "replay" the results of the past
war.

At lectures given by Averell Harriman in 1969 on problems in
Soviet-American relations, he was asked straight out: "If you could
relive history, what changes would you make in the United States
foreign policy during the wartime conferences and what effect might
that have had on the future?" He replied:

> Well, I don't think much would have been different. You can argue
> a lot of different things. People blame Eisenhower for not going to
> Berlin, but there had been a decision made in which the occupa-
> tional zones of Germany were set. It was considered important that
> we should not meet and clash with the Russians, that we should
> decide in advance the zones each would occupy to avoid that
> possibility. The agreed zones were considered to be very favorable
> by our chiefs of staff at the time they were decided upon. They
> thought the Russians would be much further in Germany than they
> got and that we would not have gotten as far as we did. It did not
> work out that way.

Harriman pointed to the essence of the problem—circumstances on
the fronts at the end of the military actions in Europe—and declared
categorically: "There was no way we could have prevented any of these
events in Eastern Europe without going into the war with the Russians."[73] Of course, Roosevelt also realized this.

On the twenty-fifth anniversary of the Yalta Conference, the *New*

York Times published the reminiscences of Harriman and Charles Bolen, two participants in the meeting of the heads of the governments of the USSR, the United States, and Great Britain. Both insisted vigorously that American diplomacy obtained the maximum possible at that time. "They contended that it was a myth to say that Yalta was a 'sellout.' ... The theory of a 'sellout' has been expounded by such United States historians as Charles and Mary Beard as well as by many non-Communist Eastern European leaders in exile."[74] Harriman and Bolen reflected a point of view that is firmly enough established in American historiography as a result of the efforts mainly of the school of "realpolitik." Long ago, Hans Morgenthau had already noted that the plans for restoring capitalism in the countries of Eastern and Southeastern Europe were doomed to failure, for even at the time of the Yalta Conference, "It was not possible either to force or to persuade the Red Army to retreat."[75]

George Kennan also categorically objected to assertions that Roosevelt had supposedly made excessive concessions to the Soviet Union at Yalta. "There was nothing the Western democracies," he wrote, "could have done to prevent the Russians from entering these areas except to get there first, and this they were not in a position to do. The implication that Soviet forces would not have gone into Manchuria if Roosevelt had not arrived at the Yalta understanding with Stalin is surely nonsense."[76]

As for the later attacks on Roosevelt personally, to the effect that he was allegedly naive and did not know what he was doing, such assertions do not withstand critical examination. The contemporary "revisionist" trend in American historiography has shown convincingly that the president knew perfectly well what he was doing—he was striving to compensate through political means for the failures of the military. "[It] is almost absurd to think," observes William A. Williams, "that a man with Roosevelt's mastery of political infighting was naive. He may have overestimated his power or his skill, but he was not naive. Significantly, too, Roosevelt had *not* abandoned, at the time of his death, the intention of reasserting American power and influence in Eastern Europe."[77]

Finally, a word about the assertions that his illness allegedly prevented Roosevelt from understanding completely what it was that he was signing his name to at Yalta. On the twenty-fifth anniversary of the day of Roosevelt's death, his personal physician, Howard G. Bruenn, in the *Annals of Internal Medicine*, published an account of the health of the president during the last year of his life. Bruenn observed him almost daily during this period, and it was he who signed his death certificate. An editorial of this journal says: "The principal conclusion that emerges from Dr. Bruenn's article is that President Roosevelt was well able, both in spirit and intellect, to perform his duties and make his decisions." At the same time that this conclusion regarding Roosevelt's health was published, James McGregor Burns explained to a correspondent for the *Washington Post*: this evidence "will force us to revise most interpretations of the significance of Roosevelt's medical condition during his final year." In Burns' opinion, Roosevelt committed himself to carry out the coalition strategy jointly with Russia "and was going to see it through, at least as long as the war lasted."[78]

Roosevelt was a most complex individual, and the foreign policy of his administration was no less complex, if not more so, than he was. He himself had in view first and foremost the interests of the United States, in which he unfailingly included the maintenance of normal, and subsequently also friendly, relations with the USSR. As Burns observes,

> With his unconquerable optimism he felt that he could do both things—pursue global ideals and national *realpolitik*—simultaneously. So he tried to win Soviet friendship and confidence at the same time as he saved American lives by consenting to the delay in the cross-channel invasion, thus letting the Red Army bleed. He paid tribute to the brotherly spirit of global science just before he died even while he was withholding atomic information from his partners the Russians. . . . So the more he preached his lofty ends and practiced his limited means, the more he reflected and encouraged the old habit of the American democracy to "praise the Lord—and keep your powder dry" and the more he widened the gap between popular expectations and actual possibilities. Not only did this derangement of means and ends lead to the crushed hopes, disillusion, and cynicism at home but it helped sow the seeds of the cold war during World War II.[79]

This is possible, and it is even most likely that it is exactly so. But as the Roosevelt years recede ever farther into history, it becomes increasingly obvious that it is precisely the political realism that distinguished him that led the United States to cooperation with the USSR in the face of a common enemy. Roosevelt managed to overcome many prejudices and attempted to construct the relations between the United States and the Soviet Union on the basis of their mutual interests. Roosevelt's efforts in this regard were highly estimated in the USSR.

Victory in Europe, Victory in the Pacific

In the second half of March the American-British troops at last began their offensive in the west, putting eighty divisions into action. It was very soon discovered that German resistance in the West was fundamentally a token resistance; the pace of the advance of the American and British forces was limited not by the might of the enemy (there was practically none), but by the hypercautiousness of the command, inevitable obstructions on the roads, and the logistic difficulties. Two American armies crossed the Rhine north of the Ruhr, with a loss of fourteen men! At that very time on the eastern front, the Wehrmacht was fighting bitterly. Meanwhile, some of the leaders of the Reich were desperately trying to establish contact with the United States and Britain so as to achieve at least a unilateral surrender on the western front, so that there would be no hindrance to the occupation of the greater part of Germany by American and British forces. When news of one round of such negotiations—in Berne, at the beginning of April 1945—became known, the Soviet government expressed understandable concern.

On 3 April 1945, in a message to Roosevelt pointing out that these negotiations were undermining trust between the Allies, Stalin wrote: "And so it turns out that at this moment the Germans have actually brought to an end the war against Britain and America on the western front. At the same time, the Germans are continuing the war against Russia—the ally of Britain and the United States." Roosevelt replied two days later that allegedly "no negotiations took place" in Berne, and that "Our advances on the western front are due to the terrific impact of our air power resulting in destruction of German communications, and to the fact Eisenhower was able to cripple the bulk of the

German forces on the western front while they were still west of the Rhine.''[80]

In reply to this, on 7 April Stalin pointed out:

> It is hard to agree to the proposition that the lack of resistance on the part of the Germans on the western front is to be explained only by the fact that they find themselves crushed. The Germans have 147 divisions on the eastern front. Without detriment to their cause, they could have withdrawn fifteen to twenty divisions from the eastern front and transferred them to assist their troops on the western front. The Germans, however, did not do this and are not doing it. They continue to fight with frenzy against the Russians for some obscure station called Zemlyanice in Czechoslovakia, which they need as much as a dead man needs a poultice but surrender without any resistance such important cities in the heart of Germany as Osnabrück, Mannheim, Kassel. You will admit that this behavior on the part of the Germans appears more than strange and unaccountable.[81]

In the most severe battles, the Soviet forces advanced to the west, bringing liberation to the peoples of Europe. By the middle of April they had driven the Hitlerite troops out of Hungary and most of Czechoslovakia, and had entered Austria. On 13 April Vienna was taken. On the northern wing of the Soviet-German front, Eastern Prussia and Eastern Pomerania were captured. The end of the Reich was near at hand, having reached its last days under the thrusts of the Soviet armed forces. Meanwhile, on the western front the American-British armies were encountering practically no resistance, were advancing, and were taking possession of important regions which the Hitlerites were surrendering almost without battle. Hundreds of thousands of soldiers of the Wehrmacht were obediently putting down their arms before them. Some leading lights in the United States, and Churchill in England, jubilant over these victories, pressed for advance as far as possible to the east, in any case taking Berlin and Prague.

The actual military situation clipped the wings of the armchair strategists. Eisenhower grudgingly explained to Washington the practical difficulties of the advance on Berlin, that was being recommended insistently. The Allied command was striving first of all to reach Lubeck, so as not to permit the Soviet troops to liberate Denmark, and also to strike a blow in the southeast, so as to capture the notorious "Alpine redoubt." Eisenhower's staff was undoubtedly taking into consideration that if they were to try to advance to the east in the direction of Berlin, the Allies would find themselves in the immediate rear of the Soviet-German front and some fighting would be inevitable. American strategists estimated that this operation would have cost the Allies at least 100,000 men.

Hitler's command had anticipated such a course of events, having decided at any price to hold the front on the East and offer no resistance on the West. The German General Busse who was in command of the section of the front on the Oder, that is, where the offensive of the Soviet troops on Berlin was expected, assured Goebbels, who had arrived to see him, that a Russian breakthrough was impossible. He was "holding out until the British kick us in the ass."[82] In general, in the assessment of the situation in Moscow, such a course of events was felt to be not out of the question. When the Berlin operation was being planned at general headquarters, Stalin, having shown the Soviet military chiefs the report about attempted secret negotiations between the German agents and representatives of the Allies, observed: "I think that Roosevelt will not violate the Yalta agreements, but Churchill, now, he might stoop to anything."[83] The Soviet armed forces could not delay their drive on Berlin. At any moment, in pursuit of political advantage, the troops of the Western Allies might move toward Berlin.

After the death of Roosevelt on 12 April, Harry S. Truman became president of the United States. Churchill redoubled his efforts, striving to induce the Americans not only to speed up their advance to the east, but also to retain the territories that the American-British armies would capture beyond the limits that had already been agreed on for the occupation zones of Germany. But the government of the United States realized that such rash actions might blow the coalition to bits, to say nothing about the fact that on the purely military plane, the tasks proposed by Churchill were beyond the capabilities of the sprawled-out Allied armies. Truman foresaw grave political complications. Recalling this period, he wrote: "After the defeat of Germany there still remained Japan. To bring Japan to her knees would require the transfer of many troops from Europe to the Pacific. To be sure, I agreed with Churchill that it would be desirable to hold the great cities of Berlin, Prague, and Vienna, but the fact was that, like the countries of eastern Europe, these cities were under Russian control, or about to fall under her control.''[84]

On 16 April the Soviet advance on Berlin began. The Soviet command concentrated the largest-scale forces for the final operation of the war in Europe; 7,500 combat planes alone were thrown against the alignment of the enemy at Berlin. The capital of the Fascist Reich was surrounded, and on 25 April, units of the First Ukrainian front united with the American forces at the city of Torgau on the Elbe. In Berlin, crack Hitlerite units fought with the persistance of the doomed. The Soviet forces suffered great losses in the battles for Berlin—about 300,000 dead and wounded. The American forces lost a little over 9,000 men during the advance from the Rhine. This was the result of deliberate tactics on the part of the Hitler leadership, which practically opened the front on the west.

The Germans continued to fight to the end against the Soviet armies, and at the same time to put down their arms before the Western Allies. Unlike the Soviet command, which would accept nothing but unconditional surrender, the British and American staffs not only accepted the surrender of German units in separate sections, but also permitted German soldiers and officers, fleeing from the Soviet army, to pass through their lines. This was a flagrant violation of the agreements among the Allies which stipulated the surrender of the German troops to whichever ally it was against whom they were conducting combat operations.

On 7 May, representatives of the United States, Britain, and France accepted the unconditional surrender of Germany at Eisenhower's general headquarters in Reims. This spectacular move was to create the impression that the Reich had been defeated mainly by the Western powers. The Soviet government would not agree that the war was brought to an end in Reims. On the same day Stalin informed Marshal G. K. Zhukov:

> Today the Germans signed an act of unconditional surrender in the city of Reims. The main burden of the war was borne on the shoulders of the Soviet people, and not on those of the Allies. Therefore the surrender must be signed before the High Command of all of the countries of the anti-Hitler coalition, and not before the High Command of the Allied forces alone. Nor do I consent to the

signing of the act of surrender not in Berlin, the center of the Fascist aggression. We have agreed with the Allies to consider the signing of the act in Reims as a preliminary protocol of surrender.[85]

On 9 May, in Karlshorst, the eastern part of Berlin, German Field Marshal Wilhelm Keitel signed the final act of unconditional surrender by Germany, before the representatives of the command of the USSR, the United States, Britain, and France. The war in Europe had ended.

But the Soviet troops had to continue to fight for several days longer in the south of Germany and in Czechoslovakia, where the German troops were trying to withdraw to the west. On the night of 9 May, Soviet formations entered Prague, liberating the capital of Czechoslovakia. Nonetheless, a large German force was trying to cross into the American zone. "The command of the American troops," wrote Zhukov, "violating their obligations as Allies, did not block the withdrawal of the German-Fascist troops into their zone, and even assisted it. We observed the same phenomenon in the British sections. The Soviet command entered a protest to the Allies, but no action was taken on it."[86]

This was an expression of the "tough policy" adopted by Washington during the last months of the war in Europe. As Germany's end drew near, the leading figures in the United States, comparing the actual results of the war with those they had anticipated, saw that the United States was by no means all-powerful, that one could by no means leave the Soviet Union out of one's reckoning. The powerful upsurge in anti-Fascist sentiment evoked by the victories of the Soviet armed forces, that were of worldwide historical importance, led the peoples of Eastern and Southeastern Europe to set out on the road to building a new life. Plans to restore the "sanitary cordon" along the western borders of the USSR collapsed.

The peoples of these countries were repudiating regimes that the United States and Britain, under the banner of "democracy," were attempting to restore there once more, while the USSR had sufficient opportunity to guarantee that the violent enemies of socialism would not rage on its borders once again. It was here that the essence lay of the discord that clouded Soviet-American relations as early as the end of the war in Europe—on the Polish question, for example. Those in the United States who had gotten into the deplorable habit of reasoning in terms of the "American century," did not want to resign themselves to this. The leadership of the State Department and the American embassy in Moscow insisted on a tough policy toward the Soviet Union.

During the last weeks of his life, Roosevelt probably began to lend an ear to these voices. As his daughter, Anna, wrote concerning what took place in the White House on 24 March, "The president was in his wheel chair as we left the room and both Mrs. Roosevelt and I walked at his side. He was given a message which I learned later was a cable from you [Harriman] which had been decoded. He read it and said, 'Averell is right; we can't do business with Stalin. He has broken every one of the promises he made at Yalta.' He was very upset and continued in the same vein on the subject. These were his exact words. I remembered them and verified them with Mrs. Roosevelt not too long before her death."[87]

When Truman found himself in power, clever politicians and some military officials found him an avid listener who agreed with them. During the days when the world was celebrating the victory over the European Axis powers, Under Secretary of State Joseph Grew was convinced that "A future war with Soviet Russia is as certain as anything in this world can be certain. It may come within a very few years."[88] Secretary of the Navy James Forrestal considered that it would be better to fight the Soviets then than later. President Truman gave considerable weight to this kind of advice.

But the president had to take into consideration the fact that the conclusion of the war with Japan remained to be faced. The invasion of the Japanese islands, in the estimation of the American staffs, would have cost a million men, and the war in the Pacific would have continued for at least eighteen months after the V-Day in Europe. The command of the American armed forces considered the participation of the USSR in the war absolutely necessary, and informed the government accordingly. And so, if we do not count the clearly unfriendly act of cutting off Lend-Lease deliveries to the USSR on 8 May, Truman was forced to adhere outwardly to an even friendly position toward the Soviet Union.

There was an additional consideration known to only the highest leaders in Washington—work on an atomic weapon was being completed in the United States. Henry Stimson adjured the president to postpone an "engagement" with the USSR until the moment when the atomic bomb, or, as the secretary called it, the "trump card," would be in the hands of the United States. In anticipation of the first test of the atomic weapon, Stimson induced Truman to delay the meeting of the heads of the three governments, the USSR, the United States, and Britain, so as to appear at the meeting fully armed. And finally, an openly hostile policy toward the USSR at that time would not have had the support of the people of the United States either. It was no secret that it was precisely the Soviet Union that had rid the world of the Fascist plague.

Also, the war in the Pacific was continuing. Despite the loss of almost their entire fleet and grave losses of aircraft, Japanese resistance was not weakening. The Japanese command used thousands of "kamikaze" suicide-pilots, who inflicted serious damage. And on the Japanese islands in Asia there was an army of seven million that was taking almost no part in the Pacific war, which was being conducted mainly by the fleet and the air force. The combat actions in the Pacific were being conducted and lost by the admirals, while the generals were burning with the desire to show what the emperor's army was capable of doing in the defense of its native islands. Under these circumstances an invasion would have taken the form of a monstrous slaughter on both sides.

The Soviet armed forces saved the peoples of Japan and the United States from a bloody epilogue. On 8 August, faithful to its obligations as an ally, the Soviet Union entered the war against Japan. The operations unfolded in Manchuria, where the Kwantung Army, numbering 1,200,000 men, was positioned behind strongly fortified regions. Although the Japanese forces were inferior to the Soviet army in both numbers and in the quality of their armament, smashing them was a difficult problem, for the crack divisions of the Japanese army were drawn up in Manchuria.

The Soviet command brought into action against the Kwantung Army a formation totaling 1,500,000 men, with 5,500 tanks, 3,800 planes, and 26,000 pieces of ordnance.[89] In a lightning campaign, the Soviet troops broke the backbone of the Japanese forces. The prisoners alone numbered 594,000 of the enemy soldiers and officers. The utter defeat in Manchuria brought to nought Tokyo's plans to conduct a protracted war. Despite the frenzied appeals of fanatics, the Japanese government was forced to proceed to unconditional surrender.

During the days when the fate of Japan was decided, it was known in Washington that the USSR was entering the war in the Far East. On Truman's orders, atomic bombs were dropped on Hiroshima on 6 August and on Nagasaki three days later. The use of the atomic weapon was of no military significance; it had a different purpose— to demonstrate it, and to try to intimidate the Soviet Union. That is how American atomic blackmail had its start.

Although Tokyo had already declared its willingness to surrender unconditionally on 14 August and the Japanese troops had begun to give themselves up to the Americans, the Soviet armed forces had to continue fighting until the end of August, eliminating the last centers of resistance. On 2 September 1945, on the deck of the *Missouri*, which had entered Tokyo Bay, the act of unconditional surrender by Japan was signed. The Second World War had come to an end.

The Dawn of Peace

The years of the Second World War were marked by cooperation between the Soviet and the American people in combat. So far as Washington was concerned, it was based on the clear realization that this was the only possible policy for America. Roosevelt's admin-istration had already assessed the scope of the Soviet victories properly on the Volga and at Kursk, and on the basis of these victories had come to the appropriate conclusions.

Washington understood distinctly the alignment of forces in the anti-Hitler coalition. The West was the weaker side, and the political possibilities of the United States were dependent on its military potential. When in the autumn of 1943 Cordell Hull left for the first conference of the ministers of foreign affairs of the USSR, the United States, and Britain, General John Deane came with him as his military adviser. The high military command of the armed forces—the Com-mittee of the Joint Chiefs of Staff—in their instructions charged Deane with the responsibility of constantly reminding Hull of the inseparable interrelationship between political proposals and military capabilities, taking into consideration that when Germany was de-feated the powerful Soviet military machine would be in a dominant position east of the Rhine and the Adriatic, and the Soviet Union would be able to impose whatever territorial settlements it desired in Central Europe and the Balkans. There is nothing surprising in the fact that corresponding decisions were made in Moscow.

In 1941-45 the USSR and the United States stood shoulder to shoulder in the war against the Axis powers although their contribution to the ultimate defeat of the aggressors proved to be different. Twenty million Soviet people gave their lives for the sake of achieving victory over the enemy. The United States lost 400,000 killed on all fronts. In other words, for every fifty of our people lost, one American was lost. At the rate of exchange of that time, the war cost the USSR $485,000,000,000 ($128,000,000,000 in destruction inflicted during the occupation, and $357,000,000,000 in military expenses and various losses as the result of the war). The cost of the war to the United States was $330,000,000,000, including Lend-Lease.

In order to destroy the enemy, the Soviet Union had to strain its resources to the limit—in 1941-45, 68 percent of all Soviet industrial production went for war purposes (in the United States up to 40 percent). From 1 July 1941 to 1 July 1945, the Soviet military economy produced 108,000 war planes, 95,000 tanks and self-propelled guns, 348,000 mortars, 6,000,000 submachine guns and machine guns, 12,000,000 rifles, and a corresponding quantity of other military equipment and ammunition (for example, almost 600,000,000 shells and mines).[90] The USSR, possessing a considerably smaller economic potential than Germany, together with her satellites and the German-occupied countries in Europe, far outdistanced Germany in the production of armament and ammunition.

As is known, during the years of the war the United States rendered Lend-Lease assistance to the USSR in the amount of approximately $10,000,000,000. From the United States (together with deliveries from Britain) there were received 9,600 pieces of ordnance, 18,700 planes, and 10,800 tanks, which constituted 5, 12, and 10 percent, respectively, of the production of these kinds of military equipment in the USSR.[91] In addition, the United States sent the USSR raw materials, foodstuffs, and means of transportation. Lend-Lease was a definite help to the Soviet people during the war years. Its total volume constituted about 4 percent of gross Soviet production in the years 1941-45.

Toward the end of the war the anti-Hitler coalition grew stronger; the growth in solidarity of the three main Allies on questions of war and peace can be compared only with the growth of the military might of the Soviet Union. Notwithstanding the fact that even at that time some reactionaries in the United States were talking of the necessity of a "tough policy" toward the Soviet Union, responsible political leaders in Washington also saw clearly the danger of these proposals. On 16 May 1944, in special recommendations to the State Department, the joint chiefs of staff called the attention of its leadership to the "phenomenal growth" in the military might of the USSR. After the war, wrote the military, there would remain three great powers—the USSR, the United States, and Britain. In the event of a conflict with the Soviet Union, "The disparity in the military strengths that they could dispose upon that continent would, under present conditions, be far too great to be overcome by our intervention on the side of Britain. . . . We could not, under existing conditions, defeat Russia. In other words, we would find ourselves engaged in a war which we could not win. . . ."[92] On 3 August 1944, the joint chiefs of staff in new recommendations to Hull stated more precisely: victory in the war would create in the world "[a profound change] in respect of relative national military strengths, a change more comparable indeed with that occasioned by the fall of Rome than with any other change occurring during the succeeding fifteen hundred years. . . . The relative strength and geographic positions of these two powers preclude the military defeat of one by the other, even if that power were allied with the British Empire."[93]

With the alignment of forces among the winning powers as it had taken form by this time, there could be no other way except for the cooperation between the USSR and the United States to continue. Roosevelt, the realist, realized this perfectly well. This explains the declarations of his government in favor of international cooperation. Although as early as the first months following Roosevelt's death loud voices began to resound in the United States telling of the necessity to end cooperation with the Soviet Union, the American supreme command continued to adhere to the former point of view. During the period of preparation for the Potsdam Conference of the heads of governments of the USSR, the United States and Britain, the responsible political leaders of the United States could not raise any doubt concerning the professional opinion of its commanders. They applied considerable effort to the end of not provoking a crisis in American-Soviet relations through any hasty actions. The American government knew that Churchill proposed immediately taking a provocative position toward the Soviet Union which, by the way, did not reflect the opinions of the British professional military. On 24 May 1945, chief of the British Imperial General Staff, Field Marshal Alan Brook, wrote in his diary: "This evening I went carefully through the planners' report on the possibility of taking on Russia should trouble arise in our future discussions with her. We were instructed to carry out this investigation. The idea is, of course, fantastic and the chances of success quite impossible. There is no doubt that from now onward, Russia is all-powerful in Europe."[94]

American statesmen, on the contrary, thought that a meeting of the heads of the governments of the United States and the USSR should precede the trilateral conference. At the beginning of June 1945, Truman sent his personal representative to London. The envoy, Joseph E. Davies, was charged with delivering to Churchill a message from Truman in which he said, among other things: "The President was gravely concerned over the serious deterioration in the relations of the Soviets with both Britain and the United States.... The President had reason to believe that the situation was the more serious because of Soviet suspicion that now Britain and the United States, along with the United Nations, were (to use the Prime Minister's own phrase) 'ganging up' on them."[95] Churchill attacked the very idea of a conference between the United States and the USSR, and, observed Davies, "he was bitterly hostile to the Soviets."[96] The envoy, having listened to Churchill's malicious speeches about the USSR, was forced to declare to him: "I had wondered whether he, the Prime Minister, was now willing to declare to the world that he and Britain had made a mistake in not supporting Hitler, for as I understood him, he was now expressing the doctrine which Hitler and Goebbels had been proclaiming and reiterating for the past four years in an effort to break up allied unity and divide and conquer."[97]

Truman's representative gravely warned Churchill: "To assume that we could win through a 'tough' approach, in my opinion, would involve a terrific risk."[98]

In Washington the true alignment of forces in the world on the eve of the Allied victory was perceived far better than it was by Churchill. The American leaders knew that talk of the "aggressiveness" of the USSR was fiction, that a threat to peace in the postwar world could originate only in the West. But a military adventure against the USSR would end in inevitable catastrophe. In going to Potsdam, the American delegation was following the recommendations of the joint chiefs of staff, first of all the recommendations of 16 May 1944, which were reproduced in their entirety and confirmed in the instructions from the State Department on 28 June and 7 July 1945. Proceeding from a recognition of the military might of the USSR and taking into account Churchill's personal views concerning the conduct of international affairs, the State Department insisted: "We should direct our best efforts toward smoothing out points of friction between Great Britain and Russia and fostering the tripartite collaboration."[99] Such were the motives that prompted the United States to enter into joint decisions on German and other questions at Potsdam. The balance in strength between the USSR and the United States, which was a consequence of the enormous victories of Soviet armament during the war years and was recognized in Washington, led to the proclamation of the democratic principles in the postwar structure of the world.

The Folly of the Cold War

Some Trends in American-Soviet Relations

The genesis, development, and consequences of the cold war will undoubtedly intrigue generations of future historians. They will probably express astonishment at how reason could fail in an age when mankind had come close to discovering the secrets of the atom, penetrated the cosmos, and the scientific-technological revolution was transforming the planet before our eyes. We simply have to say that the development of international relations had lagged far behind the accomplishment of the human mind during this time. Where do the causes lie?

A great number of books have been written about the cold war both in the United States and in the USSR. Even on Capitol Hill attempts were made to find its causes.[1] Many charges and countercharges have been uttered; over the course of decades the positions of the two sides historiographically have been opposite. Only in the most recent years has a certain rapprochement in the points of view regarding the causes and progress of the cold war begun to appear. What Soviet historiography has always maintained has come to be shared (with certain reservations, and for purposes of which more will be said below) by the "revisionist" school of American historiography. Memoirs have appeared during recent years—those of George Kennan, Dean Acheson, Arthur Krock, Cyrus Sulzberger, and some others, and, ironically enough, the book by loving daughter Margaret Truman about her father—have shed light on the motives of American policy.

In any case, what led Washington into the most dangerous error with respect to the Soviet Union has been ascertained with a reasonable degree of authenticity. On the heels of the victory over fascism in the Second World War, a "totalitarian model" of socialism was developed in the United States, and anything that did not fit into this far-fetched scheme was repudiated out of hand. Through the concerted efforts of a number of Sovietologists, a perverted picture of Soviet society and of the motives of the policy of the USSR was being created. As Professor Hans Morgenthau remarked, with a great deal of wit: "The Kremlin was perceived as the headquarters of the devil on earth, causing all that was wrong with the world and more particularly, scheming the destruction of the United States."[2] The "totalitarian model" served anti-Communist propaganda rather well, but it did unprecedented damage to the national interests of the United States, for they proved to be unequal to the realities of a multipolar world. This is why the process of reappraising values with respect to the USSR, which is continuing to this day, has turned out to be so pathological.

Actually, how could the policy of the USSR have been interpreted reasonably when, for example, the popular textbook by Richard Allen, written to extend the understanding of communism, offers a paranoid interpretation of even well-known terms in the field of international life? If one is to believe the "Selected Glossary of Communist Terms" that embellishes Allen's book, then to the USSR, *aggression* supposedly means: "Any act which serves to impede Communist achievement of a goal; also any action by 'imperialist' nations attempting to defend their own interests when dealing with weaker nations." Or, another pearl, *"Progressive*—adjective used to describe anything which assists the Communist cause, or which injures the interests of the West."[3] One may protest that it is doubtful whether this "textbook," published under the aegis of the Standing Committee on Education against Communism, American Bar Association, has any relation to the practical needs of American foreign policy.

Unfortunately, the facts show that the people to whom the conduct of these relations was entrusted did not depart far from Allen—of which Dean Acheson reported eloquently, but, alas, after the fact, in his memoirs. He described the controversy between international scholars and the State Department at the end of the forties. "The former," wrote Acheson, "challenged the belief which I shared with the planners that the Kremlin gave top priority to world domination in their scheme of things. They contended that we attributed more of a Trotskyite than Leninist view to Stalin. . . . A decade and a half later a school of academic criticism has concluded that we overreacted to

Stalin, which in turn caused him to overreact to policies of the United States. This may be true.''[4] Acheson has in mind the "revisionists." But the main thing is that, according to the authoritative evidence of a man who was "present at the creation" of United States policy at that day, obviously Washington was guided not by facts but by prejudices. It was inconceivably difficult for sensible people to achieve anything— the bigwigs in the State Department (as Acheson relates) simply drove out dissidents. And that was all.

During the years when the "totalitarian model" prevailed completely in the thinking of the leaders of American foreign policy, they formed the deplorable habit of looking for the secret springs behind the actions of the USSR. No attention was paid to the manifestly senseless nature of the usual explanation, so long as it could be fitted into the preconceived notions. Thus, among many prominent members of the State Department, including several ambassadors to the USSR, the book by Astolphe de Custine, *The Russia of Nicholas*, acquired great popularity. What Custine saw in the Russia of Nicholas I in 1839, was extrapolated to the contemporary Soviet Union. The American ambassador to the USSR, Walter Bedell Smith, made it his handbook; George Kennan drew inspiration from this muddy source; and Foy Kohler (United States ambassador to the USSR in 1962-66) not only esteemed the book as a practical guide but also built his memoirs, published in 1970, around it!

"The longer one lives in modern Russia," Kohler instructed his countrymen in the voice of an expert, "the more one realizes the fallacy of trying to understand this country with the misconception that it started just fifty years ago. The point was brought home to us first and with lasting force in Moscow in 1948, when we discovered the writings of the Marquis de Custine. We owed this discovery to the 'find' in a secondhand bookshop of a copy of an abridged edition of his writing in Russian.''[5] This is how the professional diplomat proposed that the Americans "understand the Russians," choosing these words for the title of his memoirs.

To a historian, the above approach is an amazing example of intellectual blindness, but it was made the basis of the practical policy of the United States and in many ways contributed to the origin of the cold war. Anything that was said or asserted in Moscow met with the greatest suspicion in Washington. Conclusions were reached not on the basis of facts but on the basis of previously formed stereotypes. As for them, one example illustrates the problem. On 4 December, Senator James D. Eastland of Mississippi, explained on Capitol Hill: the American people "must realize that Russia is a predatory aggressor nation, and that today she follows the same fateful road of conquest and aggression with which Adolf Hitler set the world on fire."[6]

At the beginning of 1946 regular elections to the Supreme Soviet were being held. On 9 February Stalin came out with a preelection speech. In it he summed up the period since the previous elections, which included the Second World War. During its course, Stalin stated, "the anti-Fascist coalition of the Soviet Union, the United States of America, Great Britain, and other freedom-loving nations, was formed, which later played the decisive role in the business of crushing the armed forces of the Axis nations." After giving the allies of the USSR—the United States and Britain—their due, Stalin passed on to the plans for reconstruction of what had been destroyed and the continuation of peaceful construction in our country. He pointed out: "particular attention will be paid to expansion of the production of consumer goods, to raising the standard of living of the workers by the consistent reduction of prices of all goods, and to extensive construction of all kinds of scientific-research institutions that may make it possible for science to develop its powers.... As for more long-term plans, the party intends to organize a new powerful development of the national economy that would make it possible for us to raise the level of our industry, for example, to three times the prewar level."[7]

What is there to say about this speech? A calm program speech in a land facing complex problems of postwar reconstruction, a land grieving over the loss of twenty million of its countrymen who gave their lives so that the world might live. As Margaret Truman tells us now, the reaction to this speech at high levels in the United States was very sharp. The interpretation of the speech in Washington at that time can arouse only the deepest amazement.

Margaret Truman writes: "On February 9, 1946, the Russian dictator had made a speech in Moscow on the eve of a so-called election. It was a brutal, blunt rejection of any hope of peace with the West. Stalin blamed World War II on capitalism, and declared that as long as capitalists controlled any part of the world, there was no hope of peace. The Soviet Union must rearm, and forget all about producing consumer goods. He called for trebling Russian production of iron, steel, and coal and doubling all production to 'guarantee our country against any eventuality.'"

A few days later a long dispatch from George F. Kennan, the chargé d'affaires in Moscow, arrived in the State Department. An expert on Russia who had been studying that country for twenty years, Kennan analyzed the Russian approach to the world, not from the viewpoint of communism but from the more profound viewpoint of Russian history. "At the bottom of the Kremlin's neurotic view of world affairs is the traditional and instinctive sense of insecurity," he wrote—an insecurity based on the feeling which Russia's Communist rulers shared with the czars that "their rule was relatively archaic in form, fragile and artificial in psychological foundations, unable to stand comparison or contact with political systems of Western countries." Stripped of their Marxist justifications, Kennan said that the Soviet leaders would "stand before history, at best, as only the last of that long succession of cruel and wasteful Russian rulers who have relentlessly forced the country on to ever new heights of military power in order to guarantee the external security of their internally weak regimes." In the opinion of the White House, adds Margaret Truman, Kennan "[e]ssentially ... didn't tell us anything we didn't already know."[8]

This necessarily extensive excerpt from Margaret Truman's book shows graphically the mechanism by which false and dangerous conclusions about the Soviet Union were reached in Washington. In essence, the statements gathered by Margaret Truman come down to the fact that Truman, according to her, was striving to reach an understanding with the USSR, while the ill-intentioned Soviet government was creating threats to the world and to the United States.

What was the actual situation? We turn to the past in this case not with the object of prolonging the controversy of the period when the cold war was at its height, that has left our jaws sore. It is simply necessary to recall a number of facts.

The Atomic Bomb

After the above heart-rending account of the "threat" supposedly contained in Stalin's speech of 9 February 1946, it is appropriate to ask

who it was that began to rattle the saber when the rumble of armaments had scarcely died down. A notable landmark on the road to
charging up the war hysteria was the famous speech of Winston
Churchill in Fulton, Missouri, on 5 March. On the platform behind
the speaker's back sat an unusually animated Truman. The president
of the United States had deemed it his duty as matter of courtesy to
make the thousand-mile trip from Washington to present the important guest to his countrymen.

The speech in Fulton was not only a personal venture of the British
ex-premier's, but to some extent a joint affair of Churchill's and
Truman's. The fundamental ideas contained in this speech were a
matter on which they had agreed. Churchill urged close Anglo-
American alliance, shed tears over the alleged "iron curtain" that had
fallen in Europe, and demanded that relations with the USSR be
cleared up immediately, for, he said, "Our difficulties and dangers
will not be removed by closing our eyes to them. They will not be
removed by mere waiting to see what happens. . . . What is needed is
a settlement, and the longer this is delayed the more difficult it will
be."[9] Churchill obviously had in mind the possibility of the loss by
the Americans of the monopoly they had at that time of the atomic
weapon. To give it up, he stressed, would be "criminal madness."

Churchill's speech called forth enormous indignation throughout
the world. The American and British governments deemed it expedient to dissociate themselves from it officially. But *Newsweek*, one
of the leading journals in the United States, could not resist observing
the hearty applause Truman had given the speaker in Fulton. "Could
have been omitted without damage to either protocol or country,"[10]
wrote the journal, didactically. In an interview with *Pravda* on the
Churchill speech, Stalin observed: "As a matter of fact, Mr. Churchill
and his friends in England and the United States are laying before the
non–English-speaking nations something like an ultimatum: acknowledge our supremacy voluntarily, and then everything will be all right,
otherwise war is inevitable. . . . Beyond all question Mr. Churchill's
aim is a war aim, a summons to war against the USSR."[11]

In Washington at that time the belief had spread that the United
States could pursue any course it wished in foreign policy, since they
had the atomic bomb at their disposal. Only this can explain the
astounding change in the views of the United States government

about the possibility of cooperation with other nations as equals. Going before the American people in a radio address on 8 May 1945 on the occasion of the German surrender, Truman said: "We can build such a peace only by hard, toilsome, painstaking work—by understanding and working with our Allies in peace as we have in war."[12] A little more than half a year had passed when the president proclaimed on 19 December 1945: "Whether we like it or not, we must all recognize that the victory which we have won has placed upon the American people the continuing burden of responsibility for world leadership."[13]

During the months that separated these statements, the war had ended, and bright prospects had opened before the world, but the rulers of the United States found the atomic bomb in their hands. The monopoly of the atomic weapon turned the age-long thesis of the theory of "manifest destiny" that the United States was "destined" to lead the world into a practical program, at least for its most aggressive wing.

As was known, the spur to the development of the atomic weapon in 1940-45 was the Fascist threat to the United States. In the 1950s General Leslie Groves, who during the period of the war had headed the Manhattan Project—the laboratory and factory in Los Alamos where the first atomic bombs were manufactured—introduced an amendment into the copybook presentation. Groves pointed out, "I think it important to state that there was never, from about two weeks from the time I took charge of the project, any illusion on my part but that Russia was the enemy and that the project was conducted on that basis. I didn't go along with the attitude of the country as a whole that Russia was a gallant ally. I always had suspicions and the project was conducted on that basis. Of course, that was reported to the President."[14]

Sometimes people speculate about what Roosevelt would have done after the war, having the atomic bomb. Edward Teller, the American physicist and a sworn enemy of communism, who had taken part in the work on the bomb, thinks: "I cannot rid myself of the thought that President Roosevelt may have planned to use the existence of the atomic bomb, after the war, as a powerful driving force toward world government."[15] These opinions cannot be verified for, as William A. Williams has observed, "The charge, later made by some, that

Roosevelt should have gazed three months into the future of atomic physics is absurd.''[16]

American political figures thought that the atomic bomb would permit the United States to dictate any conditions, to alter the military alignment of forces. The capabilities of the new weapon were attested in every way. From the windows of bookstores throughout the United States there stared books with frightening titles: *No Place to Hide*, *The Absolute Weapon*, and so on. The greatest tectonic force that had ever come down on the earth, a catastrophe, a world cataclysm, flood, destruction, and disaster, all merged together—these were the terms in which the stories of Hiroshima and Nagasaki were told. On 12 February 1946, Virgil Jordan, president of the National Industrial Conference Board, appeared at a dinner in Philadelphia before 500 business representatives. After having complained that ''the war has left us facing an encircling world of beggars or robbers'' and that the Soviet Union was allegedly threatening the United States, he proposed that we ''proceed to the inescapable task before us swiftly.'' Jordan announced that the United States must demand of all countries of the world disarmament to the level of ''local constabulary,'' establish control over how this disarmament was carried out, and meanwhile ''let us make, keep, and improve our atomic bombs for this imperative purpose; and let us suspend them in principle over every place in the world, where we have any reason to suspect evasion or conspiracy against this purpose; and let us drop them in fact promptly and without compunction whenever it is defied.''[17] Jordan's speech was published and distributed in a large printing.

George H. Earle, former American minister to Bulgaria, urged that Russia be given an ultimatum to ''get back to her own territory and if they refused I would use atomic bombs on them.''[18] Ferocious articles on the mass murder of Soviet people with the aid of the atomic weapon were never off the pages of the American press. The following is from an article by William Bradford Huie reprinted in the *Reader's Digest* in 1948: ''. . . we are now buying and maintaining two separate, vast, and expensive air forces. One of these air forces can deliver the nuclear weapons to Moscow and is, therefore, an influence for peace.''[19] If Huie was writing about the future, the military observer, George Fielding Eliot, as early as 1949, envisioned striking "quick and hard at the centers of Soviet power, and so shatter[ing] the will and smash[ing] the strength of the Soviet monster."[20]

Officials also took part in fueling the war hysteria, often linking it with preventive war on the part of the United States. George C. Kenney, commander of the American strategic air force, insisted on this in May 1948. Another general, James H. Doolittle, proposed that the United States "be prepared, physically, mentally, and morally, to drop atom bombs on Russian centers of industry."[21] If persons in official positions considered it possible to advocate such views—and a great many similar statements were made—why were these resounding words not turned into deeds?

In 1945 the United States government received a report from a committee of atomic scientists headed by Professor James Frank. The scientists demanded the greatest discretion in making a decision to use the atomic bomb in combat. They thought it better to confine the matter to a demonstration of the new weapon. "The saving of American lives might be outweighed," warned the report, by "a wave of horror and revulsion sweeping over the rest of the world and perhaps even dividing public opinion at home."[22] In 1945 the government rejected their arguments, but what actually happened confirmed that the scientists were correct. The rattling of the atomic weapon evoked growing indignation throughout the world.

Although the American atomic weapon of the late 1940s did foreshadow a revolution in warfare, this was destined to be accomplished by the thermonuclear bomb. The A-bombs of that day and the methods of their delivery—by piloted bombers—could not replace all forms of armed forces without exception. Without question the A-bomb was capable of causing unprecedented destruction. But the experience of the Second World War had demonstrated beyond any doubt that concentrated strategic bombings alone were not able to bring Germany and Japan to their knees. The American generals knew this better than anyone else. Special American and British survey commissions followed on the heels of the Allied armies, striving to study in detail the results of air attack on the Axis powers. This work was of exceptional importance in the eyes of the Anglo-American strategists: the United States and Britain had spent more than 40 percent of their resources on aviation during the years of the Second World War. The United States Strategic Bombing Survey alone left

208 separate published items for the European war and 108 items for the Pacific war.[23] In all of the studies without exception, the conclusion was reached that the strategic bombings were not the decisive factor in either wrecking military production (it increased steadily) or undermining the morale of the population.

The strong feelings aroused by Hiroshima and Nagasaki were not much help in making a sensible analysis. But even in 1946, an American military commission, studying the consequences of atomic bombing, came to the conclusion that the people of Hiroshima and Nagasaki were no more inclined to surrender than those of other Japanese cities, and the military casualties, such as those in the Philippines and Okinawa, played a greater role in persuading the Japanese that they were doomed to failure. American experts calculated that the destruction caused by the atomic bomb at Nagasaki was equivalent to that of 120 B-29 bombers, each carrying a ten-ton conventional bomb; and at Hiroshima, that of 210 such bombers. In raids on some towns more than 1,000 bombers took part simultaneously! Competent military men could not fail to take into account the lessons of the past war, and therefore they inevitably cast doubt on the possibility of winning a future war with an atomic weapon alone, at that stage of its development.

Bernard Brodie, an ardent advocate of strategic bombings, admits with the greatest reluctance that "fission bombs were sufficiently limited in power to make it appear necessary that a substantial number would have to be used to achieve decisive and certain results. That in turn made it possib e to visualize a meaningful even if not wholly satisfactory air defense, both active and passive. . . . Even with fission weapons numbering in the hundreds, there was still a real—and difficult—analytical problem in choosing targets that would make the campaign decisive rather than merely hurtful. . . . Finally, the functions of ground and naval forces, though clearly and markedly affected by the new weapons, still appeared vital."[24] A British instructor in NATO military staff colleges summed up the study of the problem in 1952-55 by saying that now the majority of military commentators realized that the atom bomb was not a universal air force weapon.

This conclusion was reached much earlier by the American generals, and was apparently known to the political figures as far back as the time of the blossoming of the hopes connected with the monopoly of the atomic weapon. But efforts to acquaint the public with their views met with resolute opposition on the part of the government. At the end of 1948, James Gavin, lieutenant general of the United States Army and commander of the celebrated airborne division, wrote an article in which he cautiously raised doubt concerning the conception of the omnipotence of strategic aviation armed with atomic bombs. Recalling the deplorable results of the strategic bombings of the past war, he observed: "The strategic bomber is the ballista to be employed on a global scale. The ballista was but a small part of war power and so is the big bomber."[25] Publication of the article was forbidden by the military censorship. It did not prove difficult to silence the generals, but the opinions of the heretics were taken into consideration in the United States government's approach to the building of the American strike force. Although publicly it was reiterated that the atomic bomb had brought qualitative changes to armed warfare, Washington set out on the course of the quantitative stockpiling of atomic bombs and the means of their delivery—strategic bombers. Talk of quality was left to the man in the street; in preparing for war, it was quantity that was given first consideration.

The relative cheapness of atomic weaponry as compared with maintaining a large army convinced Washington once and for all that American strategy was headed in the right direction. In the final analysis, it was assumed that the atomic armaments race would make it possible to overcome the balance of power between the United States and the USSR that had resulted from the Second World War. However, it was not possible to achieve this.

The correlation of forces between the USSR and the United States—in the broad scheme, between socialism and capitalism—proved to be a more complex problem than the narrow-minded atom-mongers had supposed. Monopoly of atomic arms did not nullify traditional foreign policy.

"Containment" Proclaimed

Conditions in the world during the first postwar years were not very favorable to carrying out power politics. It was simply impossible to explain convincingly the necessity of solving controversial issues by armed force. During the years of struggle against the Fascist threat people learned much that found expression in the strengthening of democratic attitudes. In all countries, on all continents, people experienced a feeling of fervent gratitude to the Soviet Union. The years of cooperation in combat with the Soviet peoples were memorable to the Americans.

The American publicist, Cyrus Sulzberger, who during those years was traveling about the world, entered "with the greatest delight" into his diary the order that he read on 9 March 1946, in the staff of the American sector, quartered in Würzburg (West Germany):

> The Soviet government is an ally of the United States of America.... I will not tolerate any disparaging remarks against our allies.... Millions of Russian soldiers and civilians died to save *our skins*. Just remember that. If propaganda causes you to hate Russians, stop and think. They died for *you too*. If you want to fight again.... Those were the good old days, yes?... It is cold in Russia. Remember that. In case you think I am pinko and you want to write a letter to the B-Bag, let me forestall you. In political thinking I am a conservative Southern Democrat. An ancestor of my name was killed in the War of the American Revolution. But the Russians are our allies. They have guts. They kept hordes of jerries off of us and, by God, I never want to fight again. Think it over. You have been warned. Frank W. Ebey, Lt. Col.[26]

If an officer in the American army could express such thoughts in an official order, it is easy to imagine the attitude of the millions.

This was very well known in Washington, and in planning a policy of putting pressure on the USSR along every line, an effort was being made to give the unattractive goals an appearance of respectability. In September 1946, Truman received a memorandum from Clark Clifford, the result of many months' effort. Having familiarized himself with it, the president asked Clifford how many copies of the document had been made. Clifford replied, ten. Truman ordered them all delivered to him, adding: "This has got to be put under lock and key. This is so hot, if this should come out now it could have an exceedingly unfortunate impact on our efforts to try to develop some relationship with the Soviet Union."[27]

Why, in fact, such precautions? The fact was that what Clifford had written showed clearly that the United States was not in the least striving to achieve normal relations with the USSR. This document,

"The Relations of the United States with the USSR," crystallized the opinion of the command of the armed forces, the State Department, and the principal members of the cabinet. The wordy memorandum (over 100,000 words) opened with the categorical declaration: "The fundamental tenet of the communist philosophy embraced by Soviet leaders is that the peaceful coexistence of communist and capitalist nations is impossible."[28] Having thus distorted Lenin's conception of peaceful coexistence, the author of the document called for carrying out a hostile policy toward the Soviet Union, preparing in case of necessity to unleash war against it.

Here is what the memorandum said:

> The Soviet Union's vulnerability is limited due to the vast area over which its key industries and natural resources are widely dispersed, but it is vulnerable to atomic weapons, biological warfare, and long-range air power. Therefore, in order to maintain our strength at a level which will be effective in restraining the Soviet Union, the United States must be prepared to wage atomic and biological warfare. A highly mechanized army, which can be moved either by sea or by air, capable of seizing and holding strategic areas, must be supported by powerful naval and air forces. A war with the USSR would be "total" in a more horrible sense than any previous war and there must be constant research for both offensive and defensive weapons. Whether it would actually be in this country's interest to employ atomic and biological weapons against the Soviet Union in the event of hostilities is a question which would require careful consideration in the light of the circumstances prevailing at the time. The decision would probably be influenced by a number of factors, and by the Soviet Union's capability to employ similar weapons, which cannot now be estimated. But the important point is that the United States must be prepared to wage atomic and biological warfare if necessary.[29]

The philosophy of "containment," begun by Washington as a foreign-policy course, was set forth publicly in an article, "The Sources of Soviet Behavior," that appeared in the July 1947 issue of the journal *Foreign Affairs*, signed by "X." Shortly afterward it became known that it was George Kennan who was using this pseudonym as a cover. Citing the fact that the Soviet Union had suffered terribly during the years of the Great Patriotic War, the author pointed out that if it were subjected to constant pressure, the USSR would "collapse in less than 10 or 15 years." At the basis of this "projection" lay Kennan's firm conviction that the threat from abroad would entail the necessity of setting aside substantial resources for purposes of defense, which would prove to be a burden beyond the strength of the USSR. For a start, "containment" was rationalized in terms of the Truman Doctrine. The president promised support to the like-minded, and pronounced an anathema against those of opposing views. The president's message was in point of fact an anti-Communist manifesto. Truman had officially announced anticommunism to be the national policy of the United States. His commitment to use the resources of the United States to support welcome regimes "everywhere" caused some confusion.

Later, Kennan, the author of the concept of "containment," regretted that the president had introduced diffuse ideological considerations into the realm of practical politics. Walter Lippman sardonically reminded people that a crusade is not politics. "A policy, as distinguished from a crusade, may be said to have definite aims, which can be stated concretely, and achieved if the estimate of the situation is correct. A crusade, on the other hand, is an adventure which even if its intentions are good, has no limits because there is no concrete program."[30] But the deed was done. To a deafening accompaniment of anti-Communist propaganda the building of military blocs began, and armaments increased.

The creation of NATO heartened Truman. He imagined that a decisive change in the alignment of forces in the international arena was at hand. The creation of large armies by America's allies was put on the agenda. The concept of "shield and sword" arose. Advancing the allied armies—the "shield"—to the fore, the United States, behind this shield, would strike a blow with the atomic "sword." On 20 April 1949, Truman summoned the chief of staff of the air force and requested a detailed report of the plans for an atomic war against the Soviet Union. The general explained to the president, using maps and diagrams, exactly how the strategic air force would operate.

The following day the president gave this directive to the secretary of defense: "Yesterday afternoon I listened with interest to an Air Force presentation of plans for strategic bombing operations, in the event of war, against a potential enemy. I should like to examine an evaluation by the Joint Chiefs of Staff of the chances of successful delivery of bombs as contemplated by this plan, together with joint evaluation of the results to be expected by such bombing.'' The Pentagon immediately reported that such estimates had been compiled long ago and were constantly being revised. On 1 July Truman gathered together a special committee of the National Security Council to consider the state of American atomic arms. Wrote the president, ''As a result of my request, the Special Committee brought this important conclusion to me: that production of atomic weapons should be stepped up. At the same time, they recommended that the newly developed B-26 bomber be given a priority second only to atomic weapons, for the B-26 was designed as a long-range plane capable of delivering our new-type A-bomb on any target in the world.'' The corresponding measures were taken. Washington thought the United States and its allies would prove to have sufficient time to create a preponderance of power over the USSR—the appearance of a Soviet atom bomb was not expected before 1952. Nonetheless the president was in a hurry, concluding every meeting on matters of military strategy with the appeal: ''We should maintain our superiority.''[31]

The gigantic military machine of NATO began to gather momentum. The armaments race entered a dangerous stage: Truman's atomic strategy was growing into a real threat. It is hard to say how events in the world have unfolded if it had not been for the progress of the USSR in the realm of science and technology.

On 25 September 1949, Tass announced the testing of an atomic weapon in the USSR. The White House was seized with dismay. In strict secrecy the president ordered an investigation of the possibility of creating a thermonuclear weapon. The overwhelming majority of the scientists who were members of the advisory committee on atomic energy spoke out against work on the ''superbomb,'' perceiving in it an enormous danger to mankind.

Scanty reports of the arguments over the thermonuclear weapon became public. At a press conference on 20 October, Truman was asked: ''Was the decision to go ahead with it [the atomic program] now influenced in any way by the Russian bomb?'' The president replied: ''No. It was not.''[32]

On the same day that Truman came out with the announcement of the beginning of work on the thermonuclear weapon, he requested the secretary of defense and the State Department to present an estimate of the alignment of forces, taking into account the secret possession by the USSR of an atomic weapon. On 7 April 1950, these departments replied: "Within the past thirty-five years the world had gone through two world wars, had seen two major revolutions, in Russia and in China, had witnessed the passing of five empires and the drastic decline of two major imperial systems, the French and the British. These events had basically altered the historical distribution of power until now there were only two major centers of power remaining, the United States and the Soviet Union."[33]

Of course, the situation that had developed did not suit the top national leaders of the United States. Continuing their analysis, they presented to the president recommendations concerning precisely how to win a victory over the Soviet Union. These recommendations, formulated as directive no. 68 of the National Security Council, determined the foreign policy of Washington for many years. Although the text of the document was not made public for many years its general content was known in paraphrases.

The authors of the directive stressed that the interests of the USSR are "inimical to American ideals," expressed in the desire to have the principles of the Constitution of the United States triumph throughout the world. "We must seek to do this by peaceful means and with the cooperation of other like-minded peoples. But if peaceful means fail we must be willing and ready to fight." Having discussed a number of alternative courses of action possible for the United States, the authors of the directive proposed the following plan:

> [We should] strike out on a bold and massive program of rebuilding the West's defensive potential to surpass that of the Soviet world. . . . Its fulfillment calls for the United States to take the lead in a rapid and substantial buildup in the defensive power of the West, beginning "at the center" and radiating outward. This means virtual abandonment by the United States of trying to distinguish between national and global security. It also means the end of subordinating security needs to the traditional budgeting restrictions; of asking, "How much security can we afford?" In other words, security must henceforth become the dominant element in the national budget, and the other elements must be accommodated to it. . . .

The wealth potential of the country is such that as much as 20 percent of the gross national product can be devoted to security without causing national bankruptcy. This new concept of the security needs of the nation calls for annual appropriations of the order of $50 billion, or not much below the former wartime levels.

Having given the above exposition of directive no. 68, the historian of Truman's administration concludes: "President Truman initialed NSC-68 as 'approved' in April [1950], and it thereupon became official government policy. It was in the process of implementation when the crisis in Korea exploded."[34] The policy adopted by Washington was fraught with enormous danger for the world. Proceeding from its subjective assessment of Soviet intentions, the government of the United States made its decision to rush into a monstrous armaments race—at the moment when directive no. 68 was adopted, the military budget of the United States was $13,500,000,000. Henceforth it was planned to spend up to $50,000,000,000 for this purpose. Although in the end the intention was to unleash a war in case that became necessary, for the time being the policy of "containment," as it was developed in the April decisions of the United States government, was aimed directly at destroying the Soviet Union on the road of competition in the armaments race. Directive no. 68 gave a material foundation to the theoretical arguments of George Kennan (three years before it was implemented), insisting in addition on turning the economic potential of the United States into an instrument of foreign policy.

Truman and the USSR

During these years, when Truman's administration was moving toward an armed confrontation with the USSR, the Soviet government applied considerable efforts to normalize relations with the United States. This was consistent with the basic principle of Soviet foreign policy—peaceful coexistence—and was acutely necessary for the restoration of the Soviet economy, for raising the standard of living of the people. If in America people were chattering without restraint about the Soviet military "threat," in the USSR a systematic reduction in armed forces was being carried out. In 1948 there remained 2,847,000 men under arms in the USSR, compared with 11,365,000 in 1945.

The United States clung tenaciously to its bases in many countries, and under conditions of peace endeavored to secure additional ones, while the Soviet troops, having fulfilled their obligation, were withdrawing from the countries that had been liberated during the years of the struggle against the Axis powers. As early as autumn of 1945, Soviet troops had been withdrawn from Yugoslavia, Czechoslovakia, and Norway; in April 1946, from the Danish island of Bornholm; by the beginning of May 1946, from China and Iran. At the end of 1948 Soviet troops left North Korea, while American army formations remained in South Korea.

The Soviet government strove with all its might to achieve normalization of the international situation. With the utmost patience, literally as one would do with children or with hysterical unbelievers, Soviet representatives at the United Nations explained that the USSR regarded peaceful coexistence as of paramount importance and was prepared to continue cooperation between the powers that had won the war together. The USSR repeatedly advanced proposals that the troops of members of the United Nations be withdrawn from the territories of other United Nations members, and spoke out for a general reduction in armaments and for a ban on atomic weapons. All was in vain, for Washington unswervingly followed its course, once it had chosen it.

The matter approached the point of absurdity. In the 1948 election campaign, Truman even decided to make use of arguments that he was supposedly ready to adjust relations with the USSR. On 4 May, the American ambassador to Moscow, Walter Bedell Smith, appeared at the Ministry of Foreign Affairs of the USSR and made an announcement on behalf of the United States government. In the words of the ambassador, Washington's policy was supposedly one of "self-defense," for the USSR was allegedly trying to exert direct or indirect pressure on the affairs of its neighbors. Specifically, the United States expressed unwillingness to consent to the strengthening of the regimes of the peoples' democracies in East Europe. At the same time, Smith assured that the United States had no aggressive plans with regard to the USSR and proposed a comprehensive discussion and adjustment of the differences of opinion between the USSR and the United States.

In its reply on 9 May, the Soviet government pointed out first of all that "no one has the right to dispute that carrying out democratic reforms is the internal affair of each nation. However, from the above announcement of its Government, it is clear that the United States is of a different opinion and allows itself, for its part, to interfere in the internal affairs of other nations, which cannot help but give rise to grave objections on the part of the Soviet government. The events in Greece are not the only example of such interference in the internal affairs of other nations.'' This statement stressed that the strained situation in American-Soviet relations had arisen as a result of the policy of surrounding the USSR with American military bases, some in countries bordering on the Soviet Union; of forming military blocs against the USSR; of discrimination in trade with the USSR.[35]

In spite of all this, the Soviet government agreed unconditionally to negotiations on improving the relations between the USSR and the United States. In view of the fact that he had taken the initiative in this exchange of views with Moscow, it appeared that Truman had no alternative but to enter into such negotiations. The president, however, hastened to settle the question, announcing that his ''hopes for peace had not increased'' as a result of this exchange of announcements. At this point Henry Wallace, a well-known American political figure at that time, spoke up, coming forward with an open letter. He proposed that the United States and the Soviet Union come to an agreement on a general reduction in armaments and a ban on atomic weapons; on the elimination of military bases on the territory of countries that were members of the United Nations; on noninterference in the internal affairs of other nations; on the development of international trade, and so on.

Stalin's reply of 17 May to Wallace's open letter said:

> I do not know whether the United States government approves of Henry Wallace's program as a basis for an agreement between the USSR and the United States. As for the government of the USSR, it considers that Henry Wallace's program might serve as a good and fruitful basis for such an agreement and for the development of international cooperation, for the government of the USSR considers that, despite the difference in economic systems and ideologies, the coexistence of these systems and the peaceful adjustment of the differences between the USSR and the United States is not only possible but is also absolutely necessary in the interests of general peace.[36]

On 19 May the State Department announced that the matters enumerated in Wallace's letter and in the Soviet reply cannot be discussed between the USSR and the United States.[37] In that case, we may ask why all the ballyhoo, Smith's visit to the Soviet Foreign Ministry, and so on?

All this history shows that the Truman administration had no need for an adjustment in relations with the Soviet Union, but only for talk of one. Of course, one cannot deny the practical value of such talk for the sake of appearances for American political figures of that time— rhetoric about the peaceful aims of the United States served to alleviate the shock that its aggressive course had aroused.

In 1950 the war in Korea broke out. From the first weeks of the conflict, the USSR advanced proposals for its immediate peaceful settlement. When, for example, on 13 July, Jawaharlal Nehru, in an appeal to the USSR and the United States, spoke out officially for the earliest cessation of military actions through negotiations in which the Korean Peoples' Republic would take part, the Soviet government announced that it shared this point of view "concerning the advisability of a peaceful settlement of the Korean question through the Security Council with the obligatory participation of representatives of the five great powers, among them the Peoples' government of China."[38] It was all in vain; the United States got deeply involved in the war in Korea, and the actions of General MacArthur at one time might have turned out to have the gravest consequences. It is known that Washington had a hard time keeping the United States from slipping into war with the Peoples' Republic of China. Why?

In the latest study by Bert Cochran, it is appropriately noted:

> If an unlimited struggle with China was the wrong war at the wrong time, what was the right war and the right time? Here it came out that the administration was rejecting MacArthur's fantasy of an easy victory over China for NSC-68 fantasy of its own. The right war was with Russia, the putative center and powerhouse of the Communist conspiracy and the right time was on completing NATO's and our rearmament. That was why it was necessary, in the midst of the difficulties of the Korean war, to park troops in Europe, to assign a disproportionate part of our resources for strategic air power for the test of wills to come.[39]

Kennan, in the second volume of his memoirs, has conveyed rather well the feeling of despair that gripped him, a sensible person, in the atmosphere of war hysteria that pervaded the Pentagon. American strategists had arbitrarily chosen the year 1952 as the time when the decisive engagement would take place, and were carrying out military preparations with this date in mind. There could be no talk of normal interrelations between the United States and the USSR; the folly of the cold war, which at this time had reached its greatest intensity, absorbed everything. The open military preparations of the United States, to Kennan's horror, obviously having the USSR in view as their object, could not but provoke an obvious reaction.

So he writes about the period when he was the ambassador to Moscow:

> A particularly violent jolt was received one day when one of the service attachés showed me a message he had received from Washington concerning a certain step of military nature that the Pentagon proposed to take for the purpose of strengthening our military posture in a region not far from the Soviet frontiers. I paled when I read it. It was at once apparent to me that had I been a Soviet leader and had I learned (as the Soviet government would have been certain to learn) that such a step was being taken, I would have concluded that the Americans were shaping their preparations toward a target of war within six months.[40]

At the end of August 1952 Kennan sent a lengthy report to Washington, requesting that the provocation be stopped, and that moderation be observed in relations with the Soviet Union. "This document," observes Kennan, "drafted in Moscow many years before the 'revisionists' challenges of the late 1960s to the propriety and integrity of American statesmanship in the postwar period were advanced, constitutes unquestionably the strongest statement I ever made of my views on this general subject of our responsibility for the deterioration of relations between Russia and the West in the late 1940s."[41] The report did not make the slightest impression on American leaders.

Having made the report available to the reader, Kennan concluded:

> Instead of moving along the lines I here urged, the United States government would move, for at least nineteen years into the future, along largely contrary lines.... It would teach itself and its NATO associates never to refer to the most menacing element of our own military potential otherwise than as the "nuclear deterrent" —the unmistakable implication being that the Russians, longing for inauguration of World War III, would at once attack, if not deterred by this agency of retribution. Year after year, nothing would

be omitted to move American air bases and missile sites as close as possible to Soviet frontiers. Year after year, American naval vessels would be sent on useless demonstrative expeditions into the Black Sea—thus, by implication, imputing to the Russians a degree of patience which our own public and congressional opinion would have been most unlikely to master had the shoe been on the other foot. Time after time, as in Pakistan or Okinawa, the maintenance and development of military or air bases would be stubbornly pursued with no evidence of any effort to balance this against the obvious political costs. Political interests would continue similarly to be sacrificed or put in jeopardy by the avid and greedy pursuit of military intelligence.[42]

Kennan's expert analysis leaves no doubt as to who bears responsibility for the deplorable turn of events in American-Soviet relations. There gradually came into being and developed around the United States a powerful inertia to repeat over and over that there was an immediate threat to the country allegedly coming from the Soviet Union. Afterward, General Douglas MacArthur remarked: "Our government has kept us in a perpetual state of fear—kept us in a continuous stampede of patriotic fervor—with the cry of a grave national emergency. . . . Yet, in retrospect, these disasters seem never to have happened, seem never to have been quite real."[43] But what could the ordinary American do when none other than John Foster Dulles structured his famous book, *War or Peace*, published in 1950, around this thesis?[44]

On 26 June 1951, the Congress of the United States adopted the following resolution: "The American people and their Government desire neither war with the Soviet Union nor the terrible consequences of such a war. . . . The American people welcome all honorable efforts to resolve the differences standing between the United States Government and the Soviet Government." The Congress charged the president with bringing the resolution to the attention of the Soviet people.

Truman, however, made known to the Americans his own point of view on the possibility of reaching an understanding with the USSR. In a speech on 17 September, he announced: "A Bolshevik agreement is not worth the paper it is written on. It is only a scrap of paper." In a press conference three days later, Truman was asked the following questions:

"Q.: Mr. President, would it be correct to infer from what you have just said about Russia, that in the future we will place our reliance on force rather than diplomacy in our dealing with Russia?

The President: Under the circumstances it is necessary...

Q.: The other fellow has to use the force first?

The President: I didn't say that. That is what brought on the Korean thing."[45]

Thus, there was no ray of light. Truman invariably saw in the Soviet Union a mortal enemy.

It would not be a difficult task to adduce a great number of facts to corroborate the picture that has been described. Contemporary American historians and publicists are handling this matter quite well. Bert Cochran is absolutely right in the conclusion of his book about President Truman:

> Under the tutelage of his experts, Truman decided against a policy of accommodation and making peace. Like William Pitt who matched the finances and arms of the British Empire against Bonaparte, he dealt out the resources of the American colossus to isolate Russia, put down revolutionary movements, in order to eventually bring down Stalin and his regime. Our leaders did not dare to start a full-scale war with the professed enemy in the Kremlin, and they would not make peace with them....
>
> In his farewell address, Truman tried to justify his fateful decision to the ages. 'When history says that my term of office saw the beginning of the cold war,' he opined, 'it will also say that in those eight years we have set the course that can win it.' That is precisely what history will not say. The course he set, followed with the zeal of knight-errant, under varying battle cries and hallucinatory catchphrases, by four succeeding administrations, and at the costs, financial, social, human, too enormous to fathom, has produced no American advantage, much less victory. One cannot even say that Cold War doctrinaires built up American military powers at the expense of the health and comfort of the citizenry.[46]

The 1950s Revisited

The history of the 1950s and to a considerable extent the 1960s is a sad tale of lost opportunities in the realm of American-Soviet relations. The Calvinist view of the USSR got considerable reinforcement through the efforts of Secretary of State John Foster Dulles. He followed his doctrine piously, expounded with great pomp in a television appearance in January 1953. Having pointed the "Communist Empire" out on a map, Dulles said solemnly: "The Soviet Communists are carrying out a policy which they call encirclement.... At the end of the Second World War, only a little over seven years ago, they only controlled about 200,000,000 people, and today ... they control 800,000,000 people.... Once [having] largely completed their encirclement of the United States, they would be ready for ... the decisive blow."[47] With such an approach, of course, it was difficult to expect a blossoming in American-Soviet relations. Confrontation with the USSR became certain, and political problems came to be regarded only in military terms.

Dulles' rhetoric about "liberation" acquired a sinister meaning, for Washington placed the doctrine of "massive retaliation" at the basis of its relations with the USSR. Its meaning was obvious. Adlai Stevenson pointed out correctly: "We are told, and I am quoting Secretary Dulles, that we have rejected the 'tradition of meeting aggression by direct and local opposition.' We have taken the decision 'to depend primarily upon a great capacity to retaliate instantly, by means and place of our choosing.' ... This means, if it means anything, that if the Communists try another Korea we will retaliate by dropping bombs on Moscow or Peking."[48]

As far as technological means were concerned, Washington believed confidently in the superiority of the United States in the realm of science and technology.

American military bodies began the swift buildup of a fleet of piloted bombers and the replenishment of their arsenals with A-bombs. At first Washington was convinced of the irreproachable rectitude of their chosen course. But in August 1953 it became known that a thermonuclear weapon had been tested in the Soviet Union. Somewhat later, an impressive number of intercontinental bombers were shown in air displays in Moscow. There could be no doubt of the swift progress of the USSR in the realm of modern armament systems.

A real hysteria began in American official circles. Some demanded a preventive war against the Soviet Union. At a press conference on 11 August 1954, the president rejected this idea, pleading the destructive power of thermonuclear weapons. This was a reaction to the appearance in the *Washington Post* of an article by William Bullitt asserting that destruction lay in store for the United States if it did not immediately destroy the industrial center of the USSR. Only the might of the USSR, which had a sobering influence on the extremists in Washington, prevented the United States from going too far along this path.

The next test of strength took place in the autumn of 1956. A counterrevolutionary revolt broke out in Hungary, and in the Near East Israel, together with Britain and France, attacked Egypt. In these critical days the Soviet Union came to the assistance of the Hungarian people and helped them to hold out against the attempted takeover. At the same time, on 5 November, the Soviet government announced the resolution of the USSR to shatter the aggressors in the Near East by the use of force and to restore peace. The USSR proposed to combine its efforts with those of the United States to this end, down to the joint use of armed forces as determined by the United Nations. The warning of the USSR had an effect—the aggressors discontinued their combat operations against Egypt.

Meanwhile, it was decided in the United Nations to move the Israeli troops out of the occupied territories. Eisenhower came out in favor of the United States supporting this decision. His diplomacy did not suit the extremists, and there were quite a number of these in Congress. They demanded that the United States take the part of Israel, refusing to take the troops out of the captured lands.

On 20 February 1957 the president summoned the discontented congressional leaders for an explanation. They arrived, on their guard and embittered. In military style, Eisenhower rapped out: Israel must take its troops out "for its own good." Otherwise the prestige of the USSR in the Arab world would increase sharply, and the West would lose sources of oil in the Near East. The senators and congressmen tried to persuade the president to take precipitate action. The two sides parted company extremely displeased with each other, having agreed only that Eisenhower was to explain his position to the American people in a televised speech. Appearing that same evening on television, after having apologized for his "racking cough," the president hurled menacing words at the USSR. All the same, the main idea of his appearance was that the Israelis must leave the occupied territories.

In all probability, the decision that beginning in July 1957 "Captive Nations'' week began to be observed in the United States, was a concession to the militant anti-Communists. This venture was in no way consistent with the national interests of the United States, but was put into effect by people who were interested in something else. As Kennan wrote:

> It was the existence in our country of one vocal and not uninflu-ential element that not only wanted a war with Russia but had a very clear idea of the purposes for which, in its own view, such a war should be fought. I have in mind the escapees and immigrants, mostly recent ones, from the non-Russian portions of the postwar Soviet Union, as well as from some of the Eastern European satellite states. Their idea, to which they were passionately and sometimes ruthlessly attached, was simply that the United States should, for their benefit, fight a war against the Russian people to achieve the final breakup of the traditional Russian state and the establishment of themselves as the regimes of various ''liberated'' territories. . . .
>
> They appealed successfully at times to religious feelings, and even more importantly, to the prevailing anti-Communist hysteria. An idea of the political power they possessed can be had from the fact that some years later (1959) they were able to recommend to Con-gress through their friends there the text of a resolution—the so-called Captive Nations Resolution—every word of which was written (on his own published admission) by their spokesman Dr. Lev E. Dobriansky, then associate professor at Georgetown University, and to get this document solemnly adopted by the Congress as a state-ment of American policy. This resolution committed the United States, insofar as Congress had the power to do so, to the ''lib-eration'' of twenty-two ''nations,'' two of which had never had any real existence, and the name of one of which appears to have been invented in the Nazi propaganda ministry during the recent war. Thus, the writing of a congressional statement of policy on Russia and Eastern Europe was more than I, with many years of official service in that part of the world, could ever have hoped to achieve.
>
> I could think of nothing worse than what these people wanted us to do. To commit ourselves politically and militarily not only against the Soviet regime but also against the strongest and most numerous ethnic element in the traditional Russian land. . . . This would have been a folly of such stupendous dimensions that even the later venture in Vietnam now pales to insignificance beside the thought of it. . . . I also had some awareness of the limits of our own

power, and I knew that what was being asked and expected of us far exceeded these limits.[49]

In spite of all this, the Soviet Union continued efforts directed toward reducing international tension, and sought ways to normalize relations with the United States. In 1955 the USSR advanced a broad program in the sphere of disarmament, and on 14 May the Soviet government announced the reduction of the armed forces of the USSR by 1,200,000 men. In that same year the USSR proposed that the United States sign an agreement pledging friendship and co-operation. In 1957 there followed further Soviet proposals for disarmament.

Unfortunately, all of these proposals were rejected by Washington out of hand. Eisenhower thought: ''[The Soviet] tactic . . . was to lull Western Europe into a false feeling of security.''[50] In this instance, at any rate, both common sense and logic took a considerable beating.

On 4 October, the day of enlightenment came. The first *Sputnik* was launched in the USSR. The premise on which the course of relations with the USSR was built—belief in the indisputable scientific and technological superiority of the United States—was overturned. Whatever calculations the strategists of ''massive retaliation'' might have made, henceforth they could not ignore the obvious—in the age of rocket-powered nuclear weapons the United States, too, was within reach of retaliatory strikes.

Without question, *Sputnik* awakened Washington to political realities. The agonizing reappraisal of values in the United States at the end of the 1950s and the beginning of the 1960s gradually led to the idea that changes should be made in American policy toward the USSR.[51] These were hopeful signs. As far as the USSR was concerned, there was no necessity for any reappraisal of values, for the Soviet government continued, as before, to adhere to the principles of peaceful coexistence.

From the end of the 1950s the power of the inertia of the cold war became clear. Although common sense demanded insistently that an end be put to the abnormal relations between the United States and the USSR, serious relapses into the former policy constantly occurred.

In 1959 Nikita Sergeevich Khrushchev visited the United States. The Soviet prime minister and the American president held talks in a friendly spirit. A summit meeting was planned for 1960, and a return visit by Eisenhower to the USSR. None of this was destined to be realized.

On 1 May 1960, on the eve of the summit meeting, the U-2 spy plane was shot down over the Soviet Union. The official government statements of the United States were false from beginning to end. They said that the plane "got off course" due to trouble with its oxygen apparatus, and so on. When the Soviet agencies announced that the U-2 plane had been shot down in the region of Sverdlovsk and the pilot taken prisoner, Washington found itself pilloried. Caught red-handed, the United States government would stop at nothing, and announced that espionage flights were "national policy." At a press conference on 11 May, Eisenhower admitted that from the very beginning of his presidency, he had authorized the acquisition of intelligence information by whatever means were necessary. American prestige was seriously undermined, and the summit meeting and Eisenhower's visit to the USSR became impossible.

Later it became known that the U-2 flight was almost deliberately timed in relation to the summit meeting. In a talk with Sherman Adams, who visited him after the U-2 incident, Eisenhower reminded him that the entire program of the flights of these planes were being carried out under his control: "I . . . personally approved every one of those flights."[52]

In the second volume of his memoirs, which appeared five years after these events, the president had only one regret: "The big error we made was, of course, in the issuance of a premature and erroneous cover story. Allowing myself to be persuaded on this score is my principal personal regret. . . . Regarding the U-2 program itself, I know of no decision that I would make differently."[53]

The Kennedy Years

President John F. Kennedy made his debut in relations with the USSR, showing considerable political realism. In May 1961, at the time of his meeting with Khrushchev in Vienna, he admitted that a balance of power existed with the USSR. And following this, without pausing for breath, he tried to change the correlation of forces in favor of the United States. The widely disseminated stock of Kennedy's thinking corresponded to the greatest degree possible with trends that became apparent in the political market of the United States at the end of the 1950s. In a conversation with James MacGregor Burns in the summer of 1959, Senator Kennedy revealed: "The 1960's will be a terribly difficult time. . . . The real dilemma we face is whether a free society, in which each of us follows our own self-interest, can compete over a long period of time with a totalitarian society." Speaking of competing socieconomic systems, Kennedy maintained that "The struggle between Sparta and Athens furnishes a classic case."[54]

Kennedy repeated constantly that if the United States did not have a strong government capable of increasing the rate of economic growth, the Soviet Union would quickly leave America far behind. "Their industrial capacity is expanding nearly three times as fast as ours, at the annual rate of 9.5 per cent. . . . In 1958, for example, Russia produced four times as many machine tools as the United States. Much of our steel output—which has been declining—goes into these autos and appliances, into our homes, office buildings, and shopping centers. But practically all of Russia's growing steel capacity . . . goes . . . to extend their industry at home and those of hopeful nations abroad."[55] Kennedy sounded the alarm about the fact that America's science educational systems and higher education were falling behind: "The Russians were putting twice as much of their resources into education. Their teachers commanded top salaries. Their classrooms contained fewer pupils per teacher. Their curricula were stronger in terms of science . . . they will soon have three times as many scientists, technicians and engineers as we do."[56]

First and foremost, Kennedy insisted on increasing the military power of the United States. Kennedy's arguments about the necessity for increasing the military might of the country latently concealed the aim of forcing the USSR to enter on a new round of the armaments race, which would have weakened the positions of socialist countries in their policy of peaceful competition with capitalism. These positions lay at the basis of the doctrine of "flexible response," worked out by theoreticians close to Kennedy, and approved by him.

The doctrine of "massive retaliation" did not suit Kennedy and his entourage because it reduced the effectiveness of the "balance of power" policy, that is, it narrowed the possibilities of using the contradictions in the world in the interests of Washington. It undermined the value of political actions, substituting a purely military approach for it, which, in the era of rocket-powered nuclear weapons and applied in its full extent (and "massive retaliation" could not have been applied with anything less than this), promised Armageddon. Hence the problem of American foreign policy as Kennedy saw it—to use the maximum effort to find the "Achilles heel" in the socialist camp. He understood this heel to be the relations between the socialist countries. We must, Kennedy insisted, "drive new wedges into each new crack in the Iron Curtain. There is no point now in consolidating the Red Bloc with our talk of massive retaliation—now we must seek ways of dividing it."[57]

Kennedy was firmly convinced that a balance of power between the United States and the USSR was intolerable, that it was essential to achieve a decisive superiority over the Soviet Union. For the sake of speeding up the armaments race he was prepared to misinterpret everything: the first cosmic flight in history, of Yuri Gagarin on 12 April 1961, and Soviet proposals for concluding a peace treaty with Germany and the settlement on this basis of the question of West Berlin. As an ultimate goal of American military buildup, unfolded beginning in 1961, was announced the achievement of the capability of carrying on "two and a half wars" simultaneously. From the first months after the Democratic administration came to power, the United States military budget began to swell rapidly. A comparison with the Eisenhower period is instructive: during the 3,000 days of his presidency, the United States spent $315,000,000,000 for military purposes; over the 1,000 days of John Kennedy's life in office as president—$167,000,000,000. Eisenhower spent approximately $40,000,000,000 annually; Kennedy raised the annual military expenditures to $60,000,000,000.

During this period of Kennedy's presidency, the United States increased the number of its nuclear warheads by 150 percent; tactical air power, disposed in Europe, grew by 60 percent; the number of army divisions increased by 45 percent; the number of transport planes and helicopters increased by 75 percent; the construction of warships increased 100 percent; and the number of units intended for carrying out special operations and antiguerilla warfare increased eightfold. If there were 2,484,000 men in the American armed forces in 1961, in 1968, after the programs of military buildup laid down under Kennedy had been carried out completely, the United States had 3,547,000 men under arms. Summarizing what had been done during these years, Robert MacNamara observed philosophically in the Senate

Armed Forces Committee: "We are, in effect, attempting to antici-
pate production and deployment decisions which our opponents,
themselves, have not made."[58]

After "flexible response" had been approved as a general strategy
of NATO, the military expenses of the corresponding countries rose
sharply. NATO members spent more than $1,300,000,000,000 for
military purposes in 1949–68, $800,000,000,000 in 1960–68.

The rapid buildup of the military power of the United States
without question gave rise to a chain reaction in Washington—the
leading circles tried to get action, having tried to "reverse the trend"
not only in word but also in deed. The warlike "hawks" were only
looking for grounds. This the United States government discovered in
October 1962 in the basin of the Caribbean Sea. In view of the
constant threat of American intervention, the USSR and Cuba in the
second half of 1962 reached an agreement on placing powerful means
of defense in Cuba, including rockets and medium-range bombers.

As a result of this, Kennedy undertook some extremely warlike
actions, openly threatening a thermonuclear war. Although extreme
militarists in the United States supported the president's course, and
the generals and admirals even demanded immediate invasion of the
island, Washington's policy gave rise to general panic not only in the
United States but also among America's major allies. The actions of
the Kennedy government brought the world close to a thermonuclear
war. Common sense triumphed in the course of complex Soviet-
American negotiations. The efforts of the USSR in the matter of
ensuring international peace were crowned with success. The United
States announced that it would not itself carry out an armed intervention against Cuba, and would not permit any country that was a
member of the Organization of American States to do so. The Soviet
Union removed from Cuba the rockets and bombers that had been
placed there. The test of strength that Washington had attempted led
to the guarantee of a peaceful life for the Cuban people.

The outcome of the crisis in the Caribbean embittered and hardened the extreme reactionaries in the United States, who pounced on
Kennedy with attacks. The "hawks" never could understand that the
United States was not omnipotent. The heat of their passions astonished the president. Robert Kennedy, talking with his brother just
after the settlement of the crisis and touching on the attitude of the
extremists toward the actions of the president, observed: "I just don't

think there was any choice, and not only that, if you hadn't acted, you would have been impeached.'' The president became thoughtful and agreed: ''That's what I think—I would have been impeached.''[59] This dialogue testifies eloquently to the atmosphere that had grown up in the United States as a result of the anti-Communist and militarist campaign of many years. Professor Duane Lockard, a contemporary investigator of the question of presidential power, observed: ''No small part of the problem is that mad ideas captivate both the public and the officials. At root is our quasi-imperialistic mentality.... If there is widespread belief in the divine role of the United States as world policeman, if there is acceptance of playing the game of nuclear chicken, if anticommunism continues to be a matter of devout conviction then presidents will be dangerous in domestic and international affairs because they know where their support comes from.''[60]

The Cuban crisis probably opened Kennedy's eyes to the fact that his options were sharply limited. In all probability he decided to unclench the vise, trying to awaken the country to a more realistic turn of thinking. In any case, he saw himself that to remain the helpless prisoner of reckless propaganda slogans was not only unwise, but also mortally dangerous for the United States, although during the first part of his period in power he himself had lent a hand in renewing them. Only after the hard shock in October 1962 did Kennedy begin to reflect seriously on the wisdom of realism in international affairs, first of all in relations with the Soviet Union. Kennedy's famous speech at American University on 10 June 1963 reflected the president's enlightenment. He proposed to reexamine the American position toward the Soviet Union. Peace ''does not require that each man love his neighbor—it requires only that they live together in mutual tolerance.''[61] The necessity of reconsideration, in the opinion of the speaker, was dictated by the fact that a war under the circumstances of the contemporary level of development of military technology grew senseless, and if it should break out, it would be directed in the first instance against the United States and the USSR.

Kennedy was, of course, not calling for putting an end to the foreign-policy course of the United States of that time, or giving up Washington's goals in the international arena. He had something else in view—a reconsideration of the Calvinist approach of the United States to world problems, doing away with the tendency to regard everything in terms of black and white. The speech at American

University was an attempt to assess the development of international relations in the world, which were no longer bipolar, when the traditional place of diplomacy was being restored and new possibilities were opening up for carrying out "balance of power" policy, especially taking into account the contradictions that had arisen in the socialist camp. As Kennedy observed, "the tide of time and events will often bring surprising changes in the relations between nations."[62] In short, the president called for putting an end to subordinating practical politics to abstract ideological principles, formulated by thick-skulled reactionaries, for looking at things in a calmer light. Shortly after the speech at American University, Kennedy's government proceeded on 5 August to sign an agreement in Moscow on the ban of the testing of nuclear weapons in three realms: in the air, on the ground, and underwater.

Sacred Cows and Revisionism

The political realism that became apparent in the realm of American-Soviet relations toward the end of Kennedy's presidency had no great practical consequences during the 1960s. The war in Vietnam cast a dense shadow on the interrelations between the United States and the USSR. A whole library of books already exists in the United States about this war. Its aftereffects are well known to America through the personal experience of Americans, and we can hardly open any new perspectives to them in this respect. The war has receded into the past, leaving a heavy burden of disillusionment and bitterness.

It is a question of something else—a modest attempt to understand its significance for the state of relations between the United States and the USSR. There can be no question but that the heat of passions that resulted from the participation of the United States in the military actions in Indochina arrested a timely evaluation in Washington of the processes taking place in the world. At the beginning of the 1960s, when Kennedy was still president, the armed power of the United States was used in Vietnam, proceeding on the basis of premises that were perhaps appropriate in the world of diplomacy, but which had already at that time lost their significance.

Political bipolarity fettered the thinking of those whom David Halberstam appropriately called "the best and the brightest," a circle of trusted advisers and leaders of American policy under Kennedy and

Lyndon Johnson. Following a chimera (if you please, even the "domino theory"), they rushed toward the unattainable, not seeing that the old methods are inappropriate in the contemporary world. It was exactly the political figures who missed the mark, for "civilians [made] the decision of keeping the military out of the decision making."[63] The war in Vietnam revealed the usurpation by the executive branch in the United States of the prerogatives of the Congress. "In short," observed Arthur Schlesinger, "warfare anywhere on earth could, if the President so judged, constitute an attack on the United States and thereby authorize him to wage 'defensive' war without congressional consent. Under this theory it was hard to see why any future President would ever see any legal need to go to Congress before leading the nation into war."[64]

The predominance of the notion of the prevalence of a bipolar world, over which the presidential power stood guard, permitted of no other assessment of international relations; multipolarity remained the property mainly of theoreticians. The problem of explaining that the political palette has many more colors than black and white fell to a certain extent to the lot of the "revisionists" in American historiography.

Naturally, the theories and assessments of the "revisionists" gave rise to great differences of opinion in the United States. Most of those who worked actively in the realm of American foreign policy at the beginning of the cold war usually have a negative reaction to it. Averell Harriman thinks that "People have tried to rewrite history, but it doesn't matter."[65] Professor Adam Ulam has found that: "Historical revisionism is thus one expression of that intellectual masochism which has colored the discussion of so many problems in American society."[66] Often people find that their arguments coincide with the Soviet point of view. Without question, this is correct—the "revisionists," somewhat tardily, have agreed with Soviet historians regarding who bears the responsibility for the cold war and who is to blame that the reasonable possibilities in American-Soviet relations were not realized.

But with an essential difference—sharing the basic values of American society, the "revisionists" have tried to find the best means of securing them. For reasons different from those of the Soviet historians, they have spoken out in favor of something which on the whole approaches to some extent the Soviet concept of peaceful coexistence. They have accepted the doctrine of the diversity of the world; of respect for the rights of others—of respect for individual rights, if you will; of the danger of searches for immediate and radical solutions to all of the international problems in our era. The leading Soviet historical journal *Voprosy istorii* (Problems of history) printed a lengthy review of the "revisionists" in which it said (already in the period of Richard Nixon's presidency):

> In the realm of ideas, the "revisionists" have only reflected the latest tendencies in Washington's approach to international problems, its transition from a position of "bipolarity" to a system of "balance of power." They, like scavengers in the world of nature, are completing the removal of the debris of old conceptions, discarded because of their uselessness for practical politics, from the deck of the American ship of state. . . .
>
> The "revisionists" are corroborating through historical arguments what political pratice has shown: Global strategy is dangerous for the United States under the present-day correlation of forces in the contemporary world. After an agonizing reappraisal of values, and interminable failures in the international arena, the United States has returned to the traditional "balance of power" policy, which is, of course, being conducted on a different basis; for the scientific and technological revolution introduces grave amendments to international relations and forces a new assessment of the "power factor," the notion of "national power" and other attributes that pertain to the theoretical basis of a foreign-policy course. On the whole, the "revisionists" have shown that the United States is only one among the nations of the world, although this was obvious before then.[67]

The conclusion reached by these historians in the theoretical sphere was that the United States must live within its means, must not nourish messianic projects. In this respect the Vietnam War was a grim lesson. Until this lesson had been mastered, it was difficult to expect any serious changes for the better in Washington in its approach to relations with the Soviet Union.

7

In essence, the entire postwar period was permeated by the persistent striving of the United States to alter the balance of power in the world to its own advantage. Whole libraries of books have been written concerning the efforts of Washington in this direction, in which attempts are made to analyze the policy of the United States since 1945 from different points of view and arriving at different conclusions; but the general conclusion of the researchers raises no doubt and is well known—the cold war had not achieved the goals on which those who initiated it in the West had been counting. At the same time there had become apparent a circumstance that was regrettable for the proponents of the policy of operating from a "position of strength": the destructive power of present strategic armaments had reached such dimensions that it had become impossible to translate force into rational policy. Moreover, the unrestrained arms race had turned out in the end to have serious consequences for the United States itself, having given rise to certain economic and financial difficulties and having created a number of acute problems in its domestic policy.

The problems of nuclear war have been discussed for many years in the United States. A multitude of books have been written concerning its strategic aspects. Efforts have been made to "conceive of the inconceivable," to introduce some sort of "rules of the game" in the event of an armed conflict, for example the strategy of "counterforce" that was developed by Secretary of Defense Robert McNamara. Gradually, however, it has become clear (it is noteworthy that this had taken place on the level of speculation, rather than on the practical level) that for America to conduct a thermonuclear war on the level of a global conflict is simply impossible. No matter what refined conceptions in this connection have been worked out, they have all proved to be delusions, attempts to take the wish for the reality. The arms race alone has proved to be a colossal monument to empty-headed thinking. As the British journalist, Robert Hargreaves, well-versed in United States policy, has observed: "Somehow, the nuclear strategies that had seemed so rational in the early days of the Kennedy administration later led to the most dangerous arms race in the history of mankind. The attempts to achieve a graduated response to the threat of communism that at first had looked so liberal led directly to the bottomless swamp of Vietnam."[1] Apart from the trite talk about how America was ostensibly "defending itself" many thousands of kilometers from its shores, for the most part the Englishman is right—military thinking in the political sphere is fruitless.

In the jungles of the tragic Vietnam War pride resulted in a rift in the doctrine of "flexible reaction"—the doctrine of a "limited war." This showed once more that in our time there is no prospect for settling disputes by force. Life itself has forced us to recognize the necessity not of working out the "rules of the game" for an armed conflict, whether eventual or actual, but of turning our attention to working out such rules within the framework of the policy of coexistence between the United States and the Soviet Union. It was not the subjective intentions of one statesman or another that prompted the change in American-Soviet relations but objective reality.

This is a difficult process, including a struggle against vestiges of the cold war in many areas. It is especially complex and distressing for the United States where for decades theories that had little likelihood of promoting the relaxation of international tension have been widely prevalent. Even in 1967 the thoughtful researcher Robert Osgood, in his preface to George Liska's book, *Imperial America*, found it possible to write: "The United States is now clearly the most powerful state in the world by any criterion; it is the only global power."

There is nothing surprising in the fact that in 1973 the no-less-thoughtful French researcher Raymond Aron cited the words of Osgood when he wrote: "The last sentence, typical of what was being said in the years following the second Cuban crisis, has manifestly ceased to be true if it was true at the time of writing."[2] Whatever date one may set as the date of the achievement of strategic balance between the United States and the USSR, whether according to the American joint chiefs of staff or according to Aron, there is no doubt that this balance does exist. It is in the light of this balance that not only the political relations between our two countries but also scholarly thinking in the United States in the realm of international relations are taking place. The achievements of American historians, firmly based on realistic grounds, are inevitably helping to destroy the mirages that had arisen as a result of blind faith in the omnipotence of America.

During the last decades tenacious searches have begun in the United States for a new approach to relations with the Soviet Union, inasmuch as the postulates that lay at the basis of the cold war had not only proved unsuitable but were in the process of coming to be positively dangerous for America itself. The "realist" school, which has assumed a leading position in the United States, has contributed to this. It was precisely at this time that Henry Kissinger achieved attention as a scholar exactly by insisting that the realities of the present day be recognized.

Today much is being written concerning Kissinger, both as to theory and as to practice; many are trying to ascertain and throw light on his inner world. Henry Brandon, the veteran journalist representing the London *Times* in the United States, found that:

> It is not impossible that in the recess of his mind Kissinger occasionally compared his own situation to that of the Iron Chancellor Bismarck, who, at least after 1871, applied his mastery of the balance-of-power game to protect a vulnerable Prussia against any hostile coalition. The feat of developing good relations with China and the Soviet Union at the same time was alone one that would have been quite a challenge to Bismarck or Metternich; Kissinger succeeded because he knew how to restrain the contending forces by manipulating their antagonisms and how to exploit their aspirations.[3]

One is free to think this way, making final conclusions with respect to processes still in progress. Analogies of this sort are rather dubious. It is well known that after 1871 Prussia was not "defending" herself at all, but rather was measuring the first miles along the road toward the First World War. In this case, however, it is not a question of history; we are interested in the present.

It would appear undeniable that, regardless of the motives, between the sixties and seventies there arose in Washington elements of political realism in the approach to relations with the Soviet Union.

Naturally the establishment of new principles takes its course by way of acrimonious struggle against those who cling to bygone conceptions. A typical example of people of this type was the retired diplomat Charles Bohlen, who in 1973 published memoirs in which he attempted to summarize his forty years of work in the field of Soviet-American relations. These memoirs are permeated with deep pessimism concerning the possibility of improving these relations. And his discourse on this subject is presented in the guise of an "objective" approach. Bohlen declares: "No diplomat in his right mind who has been through nearly four decades of dealings with the Soviet Union would attempt to predict, with any degree of precision, the future of American-Soviet relations." And in the same breath he does that against which he himself cautions. The essence of his "predictions" comes down to the following: "I see little the United States can do except to continue along the lines of the policy that has been generally followed since World War II. This involves, above all, keeping our defenses sufficiently strong to deter the Soviet Union from any possibility of yielding to the temptation of a first strike against the United States. I do not believe we can look forward to a tranquil world so long as the Soviet Union operates in its present form."[4]

One can state with satisfaction that his reasoning lies far afield from what began to be established in American foreign policy at the dawn of the 1970s. In April 1973, in presenting to the Congress the report of the State Department for 1972, Secretary of State William Rogers pointed out in his introductory remarks: "1972 was thus a year of achievement in our efforts to turn away from the rigidity of confrontation and the tensions of the cold war." In evaluating the state of American-Soviet relations he wrote: "Of the many significant developments taking place in U.S.-Soviet relations, negotiations this year on a permanent and comprehensive strategic offensive arms agreement will be the single most important. A successful conclusion of those negotiations will also be of importance to Europe as a whole, further stabilizing strategic relations under which Europe derives its basic protection."[5] The report stressed that as a result of the Nixon visit to Moscow in 1972, Soviet-American relations became better than in any time since the Second World War.

Underlying these relations is the realistic realization by the United States of the present-day alignment of forces in the international arena which is finally becoming a part of the political reality. It is precisely from this position that some responsible American statesmen have been taking their point of departure, and this has been true already for a relatively long time. Thus, as early as May 1961, John Kennedy admitted in Vienna that there existed an equilibrium of power between the USSR and the United States.

The novelty in the approach to the pressing political problems by the Nixon administration consisted not only in the fact that new phenomena were being manifested in the international situation, but also in the fact that the United States began to draw practical conclusions for its policy from long-familiar facts. There was a certain departure from the earlier unrealistic Washington line, a continuation of which boded sharp escalation of the difficulties that the country was experiencing.

The people who had grown up during the years of the cold war were taken aback by many aspects of the Nixon-Ford administrations' policy, which was, however, called forth by objective factors. In attacking this policy, they focused on whatever was most striking, among other things the new system of arriving at decisions at the summit level.

On the whole, of course, the relapses represented by these opinions are the unavoidable price of the struggle between the new and the old. Certainly no one can be surprised that AFL-CIO president George Meany adheres to the old views. At the end of February 1975 *Time* magazine attempted to ascertain his opinion concerning Soviet-American relations. His replies were not unexpected; at Bal Harbour when asked whether he had confidence in Secretary of State Kissinger, Meany quickly replied: "Oh my God, no." Then he added: "I think his policy [the pursuit of detente] has got to lead us to an eventual disaster. His policy is a give-away policy. It's not a relationship between two sovereign nations. . . . I say this is a policy of appeasement, just plain, ordinary appeasement."[6] Meany's deep suspicion of the Soviet Union and its policies has not changed over the years. This is all to be regretted, although such intellectual aberration, the unwillingness to take new facts into account, is what one would expect from people of this type.

So far as Soviet researchers are concerned, in their evaluation of the progress taking place in American policy toward the Soviet Union the main thing to state is that a process of detente is taking place. This has been reflected in the consistently peaceful course of the foreign policy of the Soviet Union and other socialist countries. The program for peace adopted at the Twenty-fourth Congress of the Communist Party of the Soviet Union is being realized before our very eyes. The April 1973 plenary session of the party's central committee set before Soviet foreign policy the task of making irreversible the positive changes taking place in the world arena.

The approach of the Soviet Union to its relations with the United States has not been dictated by circumstantial considerations—it reflects the Leninist line directed toward the peaceful coexistence of nations with opposite social systems. This line is being carried out consistently and unswervingly by the Soviet government. In a speech at the International Conference of Communist and Labor Parties in 1969 General Secretary of the Central Committee of the Communist Party of the Soviet Union Leonid Brezhnev emphasized that peaceful coexistence is an important principle of peaceful socialist foreign policy: "In this we make no exception for a single capitalist government, including the USA."[7] In Brezhnev's report to the Twenty-fourth Congress, it was pointed out: "We proceed from the assumption that it is possible to improve relations between the USSR and the USA. Our principled line with respect to the capitalist countries, including the USA, is consistently and fully to practice the principles of peaceful coexistence, to develop mutually advantageous ties, and to cooperate, with states prepared to do so, in strengthening peace, making our relations with them as stable as possible."[8]

An important stage in the normalization of Soviet-American relations was the summit conference in Moscow in May 1972, while Brezhnev's visit to the United States served to continue and consolidate the change toward normalization that has been indicated. During this period more than twenty agreements were concluded between the USSR and the United States implementing the program for peace and affirming the principles of peaceful coexistence in the relations between our countries. Among these agreements the most important documents are the Basic Principles of Mutual Relations between the USSR and the United States; the Agreement on the Prevention of Nuclear War; the Treaty on the Limitation of Anti-Ballistic Missile Systems; the Interim Agreement on Certain Measures with Respect to the Limitation of Strategic Offensive Arms; the Basic Principles of Future Negotiations in this Area; and others. The mutual advantages of cooperation between the USSR and the United States in the sphere of economics and trade have been noted. In 1972–74 the volume of trade reached $2,400,000,000, which was 4.8 times the volume during the preceding three-year period. Technical, scientific, and cultural cooperation has been expanded.

There is no question that these changes are positive, and they have proved possible because they have objective, firm facts as their basis. The Soviet Union maintains the point of view that the improvement in Soviet-American relations will inevitably lead to an improvement in conditions in the world in general. The notion of ''two superpowers'' is alien to Soviet foreign policy in principle; our diplomacy works in the interests of universal peace and international security.

Regardless of the motives that guide one or another of the American leaders who have come out in favor of normalizing relations with the USSR, it is the fact of that normalization that is essential. From this standpoint the development of American-Soviet relations cannot help but lead to a further reinforcement of the elements of realism and a sensible approach to international affairs on the part of the United States. This opens better prospects not only for the USSR and the United States, but for the entire world as well.

The significance of Soviet-American relations for improving the international situation is emphasized in the resolution of the Political Bureau of the Central Committee of the Communist Party of the Soviet Union, the Presidium of the Supreme Soviet of the USSR, and the Soviet of Ministers of the USSR concerning the results of Brezhnev's visit to the United States. The resolution reads:

If during the postwar decades the tension on Soviet-American relations had an adverse effect on the entire world situation, now, on the contrary, the improvement in Soviet-American relations; the fact that both sides have taken on themselves the responsibility of refraining from the threat or the use of force against each other, against each other's allies, and against other countries; the clearly formulated will on the part of each to respect the rights and interests of all nations are an important element in the radical improvement in the world situation, and open great possibilities for constructive cooperation between all other lands.[9]

However, certain obstacles still lie in the path of improvement in the relations between our two countries. One of these is the deplorable tendency, today associated with the name of Senator Henry Jackson, of making the development of international relations dependent on his personal views and the personal views of some others toward the situation within the USSR.

In December 1974 a new law concerning trade and national credit for export went into effect in the United States. The granting to the Soviet Union of most-favored-nation status and of export credit was made dependent on conditions which had no relation to trade and economic activity. This contradicted the general practice in world trade. Therefore in an official Soviet statement on 19 December 1974, it was rejected. The Soviet government qualified "as unacceptable any attempts from whoever they may come, to interfere in internal affairs that are entirely the concern of the Soviet state and no one else." This pronouncement should not have come as a surprise to anybody who had even an elementary knowledge of the basic principles of Soviet foreign policy.

It is noteworthy to quote here a letter from Foreign Minister Andrei Gromyko to Henry Kissinger, dated 26 October 1974, and published in Soviet newspapers on 19 December, together with the above-mentioned Tass statement. This letter, practically unnoticed by the American press, well in advance to the signing of the trade bill, warned in most forceful words both Jacksonites and those practicing so-called quiet diplomacy that all their plans to exert pressure on the Soviet Union were absolutely groundless. The Gromyko message said:

Dear Mr. Secretary of State,

I believe it necessary to draw your attention to the question concerning the publication in the United States of materials of which you are aware and which touch upon the emigration from the Soviet Union of a certain category of Soviet citizens.

I must say straightforwardly that the above-mentioned materials, including the correspondence between you and Senator Jackson, create a distorted picture of our position, as well as of what we told the American side on that matter.

When clarifying the actual state of affairs in response to your request we underlined that the question as such is entirely within the internal competence of our state. We warned at that time that in this matter we had acted and shall act in strict conformity with our present legislation on that score. . . .

We believe it important that in this matter, considering its principal significance, no ambiguities should remain as regards the position of the Soviet Union.

A little later, Minister of Foreign Trade N. Patolichev also warned:

These actions by the American Congress went contrary to the basic principle of detente—noninterference in the internal affairs of nations and, moreover, they ran contrary to the positions of trade agreement signed which provides for unconditional granting of most-favored-nation treatment. It is quite natural that the Soviet Union could not agree to conduct its trade and economic affairs with the United States on the basis of the legislation in question and did not find it possible to put the trade agreement into force. The adoption of the legislation in question was a step backward in Soviet-American relations.[10]

Needless to say, such an approach is a revival of anti-Communist prejudices in their most acute form. It can lead to no good. The provocative activities of Zionist circles also were noted in the Soviet Union. In the final analysis, regardless of the propagandistic dividends the enemies of detente might reap from all of this, the kind of activity that has been described has an adverse effect in the first instance on the United States itself.

The USSR and the United States are nations with opposite socioeconomic systems. It is not a question of concentrating on the differences—we, the Soviet people, could say many things about conditions in the United States—but rather a question of learning to live in peace on one planet the dimensions of which are being steadily and rapidly reduced by scientific and technical progress. If we were to take the position of Senator Jackson and Co., we would never make our way out of the maelstrom of accusations and counteraccusations. The value of detente, as the USSR understands it, lies in both nations adhering strictly to the principle of noninterference in each other's affairs.

The head of the delegation of the Supreme Soviet, B. N. Ponomarev, during his stay in the United States, in an appearance before
the American Senate on 21 May 1974, announced: "The USSR and the
USA carry a tremendous burden of responsibility, both before their
own peoples and before all of mankind. We understand this responsibility to be not the right of world leadership, or world hegemony,
but a responsibility to work honestly and persistently toward the
prevention of wars, toward a restructuring of the system of international relations on democratic and just foundations, on the beginnings of equality of all nations and peoples, their freedom and
independence, and noninterference in their internal affairs."

From 27 June to 3 July 1974 there took place the third Soviet-
American summit meeting. During this meeting the participants in
the talks came to the conclusion, as the Political Bureau of the Central
Committee of the Communist Party of the Soviet Union, the Presidium of the Supreme Soviet of the USSR, and the Soviet of Ministers
of the USSR emphasized, "of the necessity of firmly sustaining and
bringing to realization the main position noted in the documents
signed in 1972–73."

At the third summit meeting agreement was reached on a series of
essential questions, among them questions on the further limitation of
the antimissile systems of both countries, on the agreed-on limitation
of underground testing of nuclear arms, on renewed efforts to limit
strategic offensive armaments, and so on.

The meeting between Brezhnev and President Gerald Ford in
Vladivostok led to a deepening of the mutual understanding between
the USSR and the United States in the sphere of disarmament. The
practice of meeting at the summit had fully justified itself and was
proving productive.

A very important step toward improving the whole atmosphere of
international relations was made in August 1975, when the leaders of
the thirty-three European nations and those of the United States and
Canada convened in Helsinki after ten years of the political preparations and two years of the immediate preparations. Here the final act
of the European conference on security and cooperation was signed.
The participants of the conference have reaffirmed the inviolability of
the existing European frontiers. Basic principles and foundations have
been worked out for governing international relations conforming
fully with the requirements of peaceful coexistence.

In many ways, the results of the conference are projected into the future. Perspectives for peaceful cooperation have been outlined in a large number of fields—economy, science, technology, culture, information, and development of direct personal contact between people.

It is clear that the climate of international relations depends on the degree of Soviet-American understanding and cooperation. The Soviet Union has demonstrated its readiness to continue to improve and develop our mutual relations. "There are good prospects for our relations in the future as well," said Brezhnev in his report to the Twenty-fifth Congress of the Soviet Communist Party in February 1976, "to the extent to which they continue to develop on this jointly created realistic basis when, given the obvious difference between the class nature of the two states and between their ideologies, there is a firm intention to settle differences and disputes not by force, not by threats or sabre rattling, but by peaceful political means."[11]

The essentially positive development of Soviet-American relations, however, has been complicated by a number of serious factors in recent years. Influential forces in the United States that have no interest either in improving relations with the USSR or international detente as a whole, have been trying to impair it. It has become typical for some politicians to depict the policy of reducing tension in the Soviet-American relations as a "one-way street," as something playing into the hands of Moscow. As Brezhnev commented in his interview on French television in October 1976, Russians are, of course, very pleased that everything positive in international relations is considered in the interests of our country, but he added that detente is necessary for all countries participating in normal international communication. In other words, detente is a two-way and many-way street!

The mutual benefits of the Soviet-American detente were stressed by many Americans as well. The elder statesman, W. Averell Harriman, whose standing in the Soviet Union has always been very high, says: "I decry those who contend that any relaxation of tensions must inevitably benefit the Russians, to our disadvantage. It seems to me we have no choice. In this nuclear age, war is unthinkable. Our interest is bound to be served by relieving tensions as much as we can, by working for what I have called 'competitive coexistence.' I for one do not fear the competition."[12]

In the presidential campaign of 1976 the candidates of both major parties chose to be ambiguous on the Soviet-American relations. As a whole, both have recognized the positive values of detente, but at the same time deviating to a ''strong course,'' ''position of strength,'' and other antidetente vocabulary. Maybe politics required that, but the public opinion of the USSR could not leave unnoticed those pronouncements which went beyond accepted commonsense norms in international relations.

Here are just two examples of how Soviet public opinion reacted to some of the distortions of the USSR position and policies made by the candidates to the presidency and by Secretary of State Henry Kissinger.

GENTLEMEN CANDIDATES, DO NOT OVERSTEP THE BOUNDS OF THE PERMISSIBLE

Now in the United States of America, as is well known, an election struggle is going on between the candidates of the Republican and Democratic parties for the post of president, between the current president G. Ford and J. Carter. Both candidates are using every possible method to show the electors the correctness of their views and political platforms in individual appearances and together on television before huge audiences.

At those times when they dispute problems of the internal life of their own country—that, of course, is of concern only to Americans. However, when the talk is about foreign policy and on issues concerning other states and peoples, in those instances it is impermissible for the candidates for the presidency to say and do whatever comes into their heads. This is no longer a question of the domestic competency of the USA.

Observing the changing fortunes of the electoral campaign in the United States, regrettably one concludes that both candidates have overstepped that limit. And they keep insisting on overstepping it. For example, can the Soviet people evaluate in any way other than as an extremely unfriendly act the reception in the White House of a diverse rabble of various sorts of emigrés—fugitives from the Baltic and other republics of the Soviet Union, Poland, Czechoslovakia, Hungary, and Yugoslavia. In his address before these renegades the candidate of the Republicans, to gain their praise, uttered many slanderous remarks that have nothing in common with a serious statesmanlike approach to international affairs. Later on J. Carter uttered statements of a similar nature.

Even if one discounts for the typical methods of bourgeois countries in the pursuit for the votes of electors, such methods of the candidates are absolutely impermissible and evoke the understandable indignation of the Soviet peoples.

One would like to be assured that in the United States each right-minded person who strives for relaxation of international tensions and peace, for the development of relations with the Soviet Union on the basis of equality and mutual respect, for which the Soviet state unfailingly stands, would positively condemn such impermissible methods.

Pravda, 15 October 1976

THIS IS SEWN WITH WHITE THREAD, GENTLEMEN!

Recently the American secretary of state, in an interview that was broadcast on radio and television, made some pronouncements which would deserve no special attention were it not for the official position of their author. According to the broadcast communications, Henry Kissinger said that "if China is subjected to a massive attack, then exceptionally unfavorable conditions would be created for the security of the entire world." He added also that "an attempt to violate the world's equilibrium by a massive attack on China would not find the United States indifferent."

The Soviet Union was not named in these remarks. However, the entire chorus of voices inimical to our country now catching up this theme, and even the secretary of state himself, leave no doubt that they are speaking about some threat supposedly issuing from the USSR.

One has to ask himself: Why are such statements being made? On this the American press is unanimous: they are uttered to make a favorable impression in Peking. It would be impossible to show more graphically a concealed desire to witness bad relations between the Soviet Union and China, or even better, extremely strained relations with all the consequences that would stem from that.

But there are no longer in the world so many fools who will bite this bait. Nevertheless, the calculation is clearly as follows: What if in Peking, where these statements are primarily addressed, everyone listens to them and a feeling of resentment remains? It is not without reason that the American secretary of state has done this kind of thing before. Just recently he calculatingly tossed out the same clumsy fabrication directed at the same ears.

It is just as though, because it is now the political season in the

United States, anything, regardless of what it might be, so long as it creates enmity in the relations with the USSR, is considered admissible.

The entire world knows that the Soviet Union has not threatened anyone and is not threatening anyone. It has not contemplated and is not contemplating any action against China. Those in Washington know this better than anyone else. The Soviet state consistently is putting into practice the Leninist policy of peace and mutual collaboration among all countries and peoples. This was once again expressed with all possible clarity and emphasis in the just-published speech of the General Secretary of the Central Committee of the Communist Party of the Soviet Union L. I. Brezhnev at the plenum of the party's central committee. The position of the Soviet Union in relation to China was expounded in this speech absolutely clearly and definitely.

The United States secretary of state's revelations are clearly and purely motivated by domestic political considerations. This entire dish, cooked up in the Washington political kitchen, is seasoned with a solid portion of preelection sauce. Apparently, by such devices they hope to score a point, half a point, a quarter-point in the presidential election race. But it is doubtful that this will serve as useful bait for catching votes on the day when the American voter goes to the polls to cast his ballot for the candidate whom he desires to see as president of the country.

To those who resort to political falsification in Washington, one can tell the saying well known to the Russian people: "This is sewn with white thread."

Pravda, 27 October 1976

But we hold to an optimistic view of our relations with the United States. There are powerful objective factors operating in favor of having mutual understanding of the two countries broadened and deepened. It is not by chance that, all the antidetente rhetoric notwithstanding, no major American party nominated in 1976 a candidate who would go away from what had already been achieved along the way of reducing tension in the Soviet-American relations. Henry Jackson and Ronald Reagan are just the two major casualties among the cold war crusaders who proved to be unhappy warriors. There is no substitute for the objective necessity to markedly improve the Soviet-American relations and put them on a stable, constructive, and cooperative basis.

We hope that this is a consensus of public opinion of the United States as reflected during the last elections. As for the Soviet people, our position was once again expressed by Brezhnev on a plenary meeting of the party's central committee on 25 October 1976: "In any case, this must be absolutely clear—our course on broad development of the relations with the United States, on reducing the threat of a new world war, is unchanged."[13]

And if as we stand on the threshold of what will probably be a better future, we have looked back on the past, it is for the basic reason that history teaches us at least what we must not do, what we must avoid. We must avoid an arms race, first of all, and instead of accusations and counteraccusations learn more positive language. May the possibilities which in the recent past have been lost in the wind not be permitted to slip by during our time.

Epilogue

We finished this book in 1976. In June 1978 the publisher asked us to make final corrections before the manuscript went to press. Having reread the Conclusion, we changed nothing. The hopes for better Soviet-American relations that we cherished two years ago we cherish now, even though some may think that the wheel has come full circle. We simply do not believe it. It is impossible to destroy the heritage of the early 1970s in United States–Soviet relations.

But it seems proper to comment upon these developments. We as professional historians deplore the recent impact of anticommunist ideology upon US policy and the use of so-called dissidents by some American politicians. We Soviet people are constantly told by various means—for example, by various radio "Voices"—that "dissidents" represent true aspirations of our country! We witness ever new "operations" by the Western mass media—"Solzhenitsyn," "the issue of human rights," etc. We are constantly taught to try to see a certain beacon of freedom that is to light the way for the whole world, especially for us, allegedly steeped in vice and delusions. One needs, indeed, a strong sense of humor to tolerate this massive campaign.

The greatest pandit, we are told, of course is Alexander Solzhenitsyn. In late 1976, the Novosti Press Agency Publishing House published an essay by Nikolai Yakovlev, *Living in Lie*. It should be quoted at some length because this essay has direct bearing on the problems of our book. Having analyzed Solzhenitsyn's major works, I, Professor Yakovlev, concluded:

> Solzhenitsyn called upon the capitalist world to assume Cato's position—the Soviet Union must be demolished, and since détente contradicts this formula, it must be declared anathema. He flatly

declared that ever since the October Revolution the West, and particularly the United States, had been committing a series of "errors" in regard to the Soviet Union, i.e., tolerated its existence instead of crushing it with the force of arms. This refrain sounds in the *Archipelago*, in "The Calf Butting the Oak," and in all the speeches that Solzhenitsyn has been delivering in the West. The basic thesis of Solzhenitsyn was expressed in concise form during a banquet arranged in his honor by the AFL-CIO leader, George Meany, in Washington's Hilton Hotel on 30 June 1975. "The failure to support the czar, the recognition of the USSR in 1933, the collaboration with the Soviet Union during the war," Solzhenitsyn declared, ". . . were immoral compromises" with communism.

He thought nothing of besmirching the memories of Winston Churchill and Franklin Roosevelt, reviling them for their collaboration with the Soviet Union during the war, despite the fact that this action was solidly based on the national interests of Britain and the USA. According to Solzhenitsyn, the two great statesmen were guilty of "shockingly obvious nearsightedness and even stupidity" in dealing with the Soviet Union, particularly America after it "had in her hands the atom bomb."[1] In his reminiscences about the latter part of the 1940s Solzhenitsyn remembers how he and his friends "laughed at Churchill and Roosevelt."[2]

. . . Solzhenitsyn works like a hysterical beaver producing masses of salable copy with the single hope of promoting the fastest and sharpest confrontation between the Soviet Union and the West (including, if necessary, a thermonuclear war). Oh God, he moans, surveying the past, how much you have missed! Why did you conduct yourself so stupidly during the last war!

Nor does he spare his criticism in speaking about Hitler's Germany. In the third volume of the *Archipelago* this theme, mentioned in his previous writings, reaches a violent crescendo. "If only the invaders had not been so hopelessly crude and arrogant," he wails, ". . . we would not have been forced to mark the twenty-fifth anniversary of Russian communism."[3] In other words, the Germans would have defeated the USSR by 1942. The scoundrel does not mention the obvious: had not the Red Army held the front in that glorious and tragic year, there would have been no one around today to read his libels. Under fascism all literate humanity would have gone up through crematorium chimneys, with the exception of the "master race," and Solzhenitsyn himself at best would have been reduced to the status of an obscure "Volksdeutsche."

"And the West, the West!" Solzhenitsyn moans. Why "did not the Western allies enter the war for freedom in general, but only for their own Western freedom, only against the Nazis? Would it not have been more natural for us [meaning Solzhenitsyn, no doubt—Author] to believe that our allies were faithful to the principle of freedom—and would not abandon us?" In his paranoiac delirium, mixing up everything, he babbles on: "In 1941 the population of the USSR naturally considered that the advent of a foreign army meant the overthrow of the communist regime, there was just no other meaning in such an advent. They awaited a political program—a liberation from Bolshevism."[4] Solzhenitsyn's meaning is crystal clear—you, the Western democracies, should have joined the Nazis in a united action against the USSR—to Mr. Solzhenitsyn's pleasure.[5]

Here we come to the last point—"freedom," the meaning of "human rights," all that is now being hotly debated in the West; and we, the Russians, are invited to draw salutary lessons from torrents of words. Recent celebrations of the United States bicentennial helped us all to realize the precise meaning of this high-sounding discussion. We never concealed the fact that our countries represent opposite socio-economic systems. The major difference is private property. As Professor Jack P. Green reminded distinguished listeners in a lecture delivered at Oxford University:

Equality of opportunity thus meant to the Revolutionary generation the preservation of the individual's equal right to acquire as much as he could, to achieve the best life possible within the limits of his ability, means, and circumstances. Every man was to have an equal opportunity to become more unequal.
. . . Although the Revolution generated a widespread examination of the social ramifications of the general concept of equality and even converted a few to the ideal of equality as social leveling—an ideal that has often resurfaced in American political life during times of economic and social distress over the past two centuries—the commitment to equality of opportunity and the admiration . . . for those people who had successfully taken advantage of that opportunity perforce meant that equality could not be widely regarded in America as implying "the equalization of property, or the invasion of personal rights of possession."[6]

Thus emerged the American political tradition that Richard Hofstadter, more fully than any other historian, has propounded in his history of the United States from colonial days down to the end of the Franklin D. Roosevelt administration. He emphasized the theory of "accord": "However at odds on specific issues, the major political traditions have shared a belief in the rights of property, the philosophy of economic individualism, the value of competition; they have accepted the economic virtues of capitalist culture as necessary qualities of man."[7] The right to get rich at the expense of others occupies a prominent place in this philosophy of "human rights." Needless to say, this philosophy is alien to the values of the socialist society, where an end was put, once and for all, to exploitation of man by man.

We highly respect the American Revolution and the men who led it; for their time it was a mighty step forward, especially in comparison with eighteenth-century Europe. And we remember our Revolution of 1917. At that moment the Russians chose their way. They knew that there were other ways of organizing society.

Samuel N. Harper, a leading authority on Russia, a special adviser to the American ambassador to the Provisional Government, tried in 1917 to explain the significance of the American Revolution to a group of revolutionary soldiers in Russia in these words:

> I found the illustrated supplement of a leading Petrograd newspaper devoted to America and her entry into the war. The frontispiece was a portrait of George Washington: and, thinking to use this as an entering wedge, I approached a group of Russian soldiers ... to begin the conversation by calling attention to the fact that Washington was the father of the American Revolution and I was distinctly embarrassed when one of the soldiers remarked: "Prosperous looking gentleman." The conversation never got off the ground.[8]

Our state was established by the Great October Socialist Revolution, defended in the Civil War and World War II. We fought for the principles embodied in the Soviet Constitution of 1977:

> All power in the USSR belongs to the people (Article 2).
> The foundation of the economic system of the USSR is socialist ownership of the means of production.... No one has the right to use socialist property for personal gain or other selfish ends (Article 10).
> Earned income forms the basis of the personal property of Soviet citizens.... Property owned or used by citizens shall not serve as a means of deriving unearned income (Article 13).

The source of the growth of social wealth and of the well-being of the people, and of each individual, is the labor, free from exploitation, of Soviet people (Article 14).

As for the basic rights and freedoms of the citizens of the USSR:

Citizens of the USSR enjoy in full the social, economic, political, and personal rights and freedoms proclaimed and guaranteed by the constitution of the USSR and by Soviet laws.

They have the right to work; to rest and leisure; to health protection; to housing; to enjoy cultural benefits; are guaranteed freedom of scientific, technical, and artistic work (Articles 40-48).

. . . Citizens of the USSR are guaranteed freedom of speech, of the press, and of assembly meeting, street processions, and demonstrations (Article 50).

Citizens of the USSR are guaranteed inviolability of the person. No one may be arrested except by a court decision or on the warrant of a prosecutor (Article 54).

Citizens of the USSR are guaranteed inviolability of the home. No one may without lawful grounds enter a home against the will of those residing in it (Article 55).

The privacy of citizens and of their correspondence, telephone conversations, and telegraphic communications is protected by law (Article 56).

Such are major features of the new Soviet Constitution. One can easily see the difference between our two systems.

The United States and the Soviet Union embody two opposite social systems in the world: capitalism and socialism. The advocates of each of the the two contending systems are convinced their own social and economic system best serves the cause of all mankind. This dispute began a little more than sixty years ago and may be resolved only if it continues within definite limits, in peace and with respect for each other's legitimate interests. Clearly, each country sets great store by its achievement and can say a great deal about the other's shortcomings and failures. But it is essential that they should prove their point by material progress; it will take a long time until the world can see which side is right.

We have gained enough experience to see that we have a great deal to learn from each other. Crass individualism, which was once praised unquestioningly in the United States, has now given way to a more enlightened view of the role which the state has to play in social and economic spheres. It would be enough to recall the heated debate on the New Deal to see that the American legislators could not turn their eyes from the Soviet social achievements. No one in America is likely to deny the fact that it was the first Soviet sputnik that jogged into alertness the lethargic American officials responsible for education and science. These officials naturally saw it as a challenge only in the military field and stepped up armaments. However, the outcome was a substantial improvement and expansion of the educational system in America. Much impetus also came for science. In other words, socialism can set an example.

To take the human rights problem seriously, and lest there be misunderstanding in this respect, we should say very frankly that the Soviet people share a widely held view that American society has not been able to solve its domestic racial and civil-rights problems, and for this reason only, Americans should hold their horses before rushing into "human rights" drives elsewhere.

We have touched on this subject not because the recently activated "crusades" are of any appreciable danger to the socialist principles of the Soviet Union. Not at all! And many of the initiators of those campaigns undoubtedly comprehend this.

We would like Americans to understand that all those "crusades" create additional and artificial barriers to solving many great and most pressing problems that are on the agenda of Soviet-American relations. The *Pravda* editorial of 17 June 1978 has reminded us once more of how great the problems confronting both our countries are, and how dangerous any politicking in this field is.

We write these words on 22 June 1978. Every citizen of the USSR and millions around the globe have a particular feeling when they see the date 22 June on their calendars. The Soviet people are doing all they can to keep the annals of world history free from such tragic dates. Therefore Moscow has been so serious and tireless in promoting the course of peaceful coexistence, slowing down the arms race, and achieving general disarmament.

We are resolutely against the "superpower" concept. But it has been the obvious truth that our two great nations share too much responsibility in international relations, in preserving world peace, to allow unscrupulous, irresponsible, and vested interest groups to distract them from fulfilling truly historical tasks.

Notes

Chapter One

1. Norman E. Saul, "The Beginnings of American-Russian Trade, 1763-1766," *William and Mary Quarterly* 26 (1969): 596-600.

2. V. I. Lenin, *Collected Works*, vol. 28 (Moscow, 1965), p. 68.

3. N. N. Bolkhovitinov, *Stanovlenie Russko-Amerikanskikh otnosheniy, 1775-1815* [The formation of Russian-American relations, 1775-1815] (Moscow, 1966), p. 377.

4. Thomas A. Bailey, *America Faces Russia: Russian-American Relations from Early Times to Our Day* (Ithaca, N.Y., 1950), p. 2.

5. *The State of the Union Messages of the Presidents, 1790-1966* (New York, 1966), p. 112.

6. N. N. Bolkhovitinov, "Iz istorii Russko-Amerikanskikh nauchnykh svyazey v XVIII-XIX vekakh" [From the history of Russian-American scientific ties in the eighteenth-nineteenth centuries], *SShA: ekonomika, politika, ideologiya* [USA: economics, politics, ideology], no. 5 (1974), pp. 17-25.

7. N. N. Bolkhovitinov, *Doktrina Monro* [The Monroe Doctrine] (Moscow, 1959).

8. Clarence A. Manning, *Russian Influence on Early America* (New York, 1953), pp. vi-viii.

9. Foster Rhea Dulles, *The Road to Teheran: The Story of Russia and America, 1781-1943* (Princeton, N.J., 1944), p. 44.

10. This point of view has been expressed in Soviet literature also. See S. B. Okun', *Rossiysko-Amerikanskaya Kompaniya* [The Russian-American Company] (Moscow-Leningrad, 1939), pp. 81-82.

11. N. N. Bolkhovitinov, "Russkaya Amerika i provozglashenie doktriny Monro" [Russian America and the enunication of the Monroe Doctrine], *Voprosy istorii* [Problems of history], no. 9 (1971), pp. 79-80; John Quincy Adams, *Memoirs of John Quincy Adams*, 12 vols. (Philadelphia, 1874-77), 6:163.

12. *State of the Union Messages*, p. 218.

13. Dulles, p. 44.

14. N. N. Bolkhovitinov, "Zaklyuchenie torgovogo dogovora mezhdu Rossiey i Soedinennymi Shtatami, 1832 g." [The conclusion of the trade agreement between Russia and the United States, 1832], *Istoriya SSSR* [History of the USSR], no. 1 (1974), pp. 153-67.

15. Stanley S. Jados, ed., *Documents on Russian-American Relations: Washington to Eisenhower* (Washington, D.C., 1965), pp. 8-11.

16. Norman E. Saul, "Beverley C. Sanders and the Expansion of American Trade with Russia, 1853-1855," *Maryland Historical Magazine*, Summer 1972.

17. Frank A. Golder, "Russian-American Relations during the Crimean War," *American Historical Review* 31 (1926): 467.

18. *State of the Union Messages*, pp. 296, 446.

19. Ibid., p. 777.

20. Dulles, p. 46.

21. Bailey, p. 51.

22. N. N. Bolkhovitinov, "Dekabisty i Amerika" [The Decembrists and America], *Voprosy istorii*, no.4 (1974), p. 97.

23. N. G. Chernyshevksy, *Polnoe sobranie sochineniy* [Complete collected works], 16 vols. (Moscow, 1939-53), 3:353.

24. M. M. Malkin, *Grazhdanskaya voyna v SShA i tsarskaya Rossiya* [The Civil War in the United States and czarist Russia] (Moscow-Leningrad, 1939), p. 38.

25. Max M. Laserson, *The American Impact on Russia: Diplomatic and Ideological, 1784-1917* (New York, 1950), p. 173.

26. "Documents Relating to Russian Policy during the American Civil War," *Journal of Modern History* 2 (1930): 603-7.

27. "Grazhdanskaya voyna v SShA i Rossiya: K prebyvaniyu Russkikh voennykh korabley v SShA, 1863-1864 gg." [The American Civil War and Russia: Concerning the sojourn of the Russian naval vessels in the U.S.A., 1863-64], *Novaya i noveyshaya istoriya* [Modern and recent history], no. 6 (1973), p. 90.

28. E. Adamov, "Russia and the United States at the Time of the Civil War," *Journal of Modern History* 2 (1930): 586-602. This is a translation from the Russian of an article by the Soviet historian, E. A. Adamov.

29. *State of the Union Messages*, p. 1125.

30. T. M. Batueva, "Prokhozhdenie dogovora o pokupke Alyaski v Kongresse SShA v 1867-1868 gg." [The passage of the agreement to purchase Alaska by the U.S. Congress in 1867-68], *Novaya i noveyshaya istoriya*, no. 4 (1971), pp. 117-24.

31. Frederick L. Schuman, *American Policy toward Russia since 1917* (New York, 1928), pp. 21-23.

32. Laserson, p. 306.

33. Ibid. pp. 303-4.

34. N. A. Borodin, *Severo-Amerikanskie Soedinennye Shtaty i Rossiya* [The North-American United States and Russia] (Petrograd, 1915), p. 299.

35. V. G. Korolenko, *Povesti i rasskazy* [Tales and stories] (Moscow, 1953), p. 476.

36. Dulles, p. 74.

37. I. K. Mal'kova, "Istoriya i politika SShA na stranitsakh Russkikh demokraticheskikh zhurnalov Delo i Slovo" [The history and politics of the U.S.A. on the pages of the Russian democratic journals *Deed* and *Word*], *Amerikansky yezhegodnik, 1971* [American yearbook, 1971] (Moscow, 1971), pp. 273-94.

38. I. P. Dement'ev, *Ideynaya bor'ba v SShA po voprosam ekspansii (na rubezhe XIX-XX vv.)* [The ideological battle in the United States over expansion at the turn of the twentieth century] (Moscow, 1973).

39. William Appleman Williams, *The Tragedy of American Diplomacy* (New York, rev. ed., 1962), p. 27.

40. *State of the Union Messages*, p. 1767.

41. William Appleman Williams, *American-Russian Relations, 1781-1947* (New York, 1952), p. 28.

42. Dulles, p. 77.

43. Pauline Tompkins, *American-Russian Relations in the Far East* (New York, 1949), p. 5.

44. *Krasny Arkhiv* [The Red Archives], 52 (1935): 133.

45. Ibid., p. 141.

46. Williams, *American-Russian Relations*, p. 45.

47. Richard B. Fisher, "American Investment in Pre-Soviet Russia," *American Slavic and East European Review* 8 (1949): 90-105.

48. V. A. Val'kov, *SSSR i SShA: Ikh politicheskie i ekonomicheskie otnosheniya* [The USSR and the U.S.A.: Their political and economic relations] (Moscow, 1965), p. 10.

49. V. V. Lebedev, *Russko-Amerikanskie ekonomicheskie otnosheniya, 1900-1917 gg.* [Russian-American economic relations, 1900-1917] (Moscow, 1964), p. 97.

50. Ibid., p. 42.

51. Ibid., pp. 123-24.

52. Bailey, p. 215.

53. Leonid I. Strakhovsky, *American Opinion about Russia, 1917-1920* (Toronto, 1961), pp. x-xi.

54. Cyrus Adler and Aaron M. Margalith, *With Firmness in the Right: American Diplomatic Action Affecting Jews, 1840-1945* (New York, 1946), p. 265.

55. Bailey, p. 218.

56. M. Pavlovich (M. P. Vel'tman), *RSFSR v imperialisticheskom okruzhenii, vypusk tretiy: Sovetskaya Rossiya i kapitalisticheskaya Amerika* [The RSFSR encircled by imperialism, third issue: Soviet Russia and capitalist America] (Moscow-Petrograd, 1922), p. 25.

57. Bailey, pp. 222-23.

58. Laserson, p. 370.

59. V. I. Lenin, *Polnoe sobranie sochineniy* [Complete collected works], 55 vols. (Moscow, 1958-65), 22:214.

60. Samuel N. Harper, *The Russia I Believe in* (Chicago, 1945), p. 7.

61. Maxim Gorky, "V Amerike" [In America], *Sobranie sochineniy* [Collected works], vol. 4 (Moscow, 1960), p. 21.

62. Philip S. Foner, *History of the Labor Movement in the United States*, vol. 4 (New York, 1965), p. 68.

63. Jeanette E. Tuve, "Changing Directions in Russian-American Economic Relations, 1912-1917," *Slavic Review* 31 (1972): 67.

64. Lebedev, p. 242.

65. Oral History Collection of Columbia University. John C. White, p. 19.

66. Lebedev, p. 263.

67. David R. Francis, *Russia from the American Embassy, April, 1916-November, 1918* (New York, 1921), p. 82.

68. U.S. Department of State, *Papers Relating to the Foreign Relations of the United States* [hereinafter cited as *FRUS*]: *1918, Russia*, vol. 1 (Washington, D.C., 1931), p. 108.

69. G. K. Seleznev, *Krakh zagovora: agressiya SShA protiv Sovetskogo gosudarstva v 1917-1920 gg.* [The collapse of the conspiracy: American aggression against the Soviet nation in 1917-20] (Moscow, 1963), p. 27.

70. A. E. Ioffe, "Missiya Ruta v Rossii v 1917 godu" [The Root mission in Russia in 1917], *Voprosy istorii*, no. 9 (1958), pp. 87-100; M. Boltze, *Die Root-Mission in Russland, 1918* [The Root mission in Russia, 1918] (Munich, 1972).

71. Francis, pp. 97-98.

72. R. S. Ganelin, *Rossiya i SShA, 1914-1917* [Russia and the U.S.A., 1914-17] (Leningrad, 1969), p. 339.

73. Val'kov, p. 14.

74. Robert Lansing, *War Memoirs of Robert Lansing* (New York, 1935), p. 332.

75. Lebedev, p. 295.

76. Seleznev, p. 24.

77. Francis, p. 141.

78. *FRUS: 1918, Russia*, 1:177.

79. Ibid., pp. 181, 187, 190; Francis, p. 145.

80. Ganelin, pp. 350-51, 391.

81. *FRUS: 1918, Russia*, 1:221.

Chapter Two

1. Lenin, *Collected Works*, vol. 25 (Moscow, 1964), p. 359.

2. Ibid., vol. 27 (Moscow, 1965), p. 71.

3. *Dokumenty vneshney politiki SSSR* [Foreign policy documents of the USSR; hereinafter cited as *Dokumenty*], 21 vols. (Moscow, 1957-77), 1:488-89.

4. *KPSS v rezolyutsiyakh i resheniyakh s''ezdov, konferentsiy i plenymov TsK* [The Communist party of the Soviet Union in the resolutions and decisions of its congresses, conferences, and plenary sessions of the Central Committee], 10 vols. (Moscow, 1970-73), 2:122.

5. *Dokumenty*, 2:639.

6. Ibid., 5:191-92.

7. Ibid., p. 385.

8. Pavlovich, p. 46.

9. I. I. Genkin, *Soedinennye Shtaty Ameriki i SSSR* [The United States of America and the USSR] (Moscow-Leningrad, 1934), p. 19.

10. E. A. Kunina, *Proval Amerikanskikh planov zavoevaniya mirovogo gospodstva v 1917-1920 gg.* [The failure of American plans to achieve world supremacy in 1917-20] (Moscow, 1951), p. 230.

11. A. V. Berezkin, *Oktyabr'skaya Revolyutsiya i SShA, 1917-1922 gg.* [The October Revolution and the U.S.A., 1917-22] (Moscow, 1967); L. Gvishiani, *Sovetskaya Rossiya i SShA, 1917-20* [Soviet Russia and the U.S.A., 1917-20] (Moscow, 1970); E. I. Popova, *Politika SShA na Dal'nem Vostoke, 1918-1922* [U.S. policy in the Far East, 1918-22] (Moscow, 1967); V. K. Furaev, *Sovetsko-Amerikanskie otnosheniya, 1917-1939* [Soviet-

American relations, 1917–39] (Moscow, 1964); G. N. Tsvetkov, *Shestnadtsat' let nepriznaniya* [Sixteen years of nonrecognition] (Kiev, 1971).

12. U.S. Congress, *Congressional Record* [hereinafter cited as *CR*], 57 (pt. 2): 1103.

13. Schuman, p. 88.

14. Christopher Lasch, "American Intervention in Siberia: A Reinterpretation," *Political Science Quarterly* 77 (1962): 220.

15. *Nation*. 19 July 1919, p. 67.

16. Hoover Institution on War, Revolution, and Peace. Eugene M. Kayden, A Memorandum on the Political Changes in Russia since the Revolution, 13 August 1918.

17. Sigmund Freud and William C. Bullitt, *Thomas Woodrow Wilson, Twenty-eighth President of the United States: A Psychological Study* (Boston, 1967), p. 234.

18. *Washington Post*, 22 January 1919.

19. This point of view is discussed especially consistently by Pauline Tompkins, *American-Russian Relations*, and John A. White, *The Siberian Intervention* (Princeton, N.J., 1950).

20. Bailey, pp. 236–37.

21. University of Chicago, Joseph Regenstein Library, Special Collection: Samuel Northrup Harper Papers, Box 57, Folder 12. The American-Russian Chamber of Commerce, Russian-American Relationships in 1917, February. 15, 1918.

22. Ibid., box 57, folder 4. An American Policy for Russia, Advocated by the American-Russian Chamber of Commerce, September 1918.

23. Catherine Breshkovsky, *A Message to the American People* (New York, 1919), p. 13.

24. *FRUS: 1918, Russia*, 1:229.

25. Ibid., p. 266.

26. Francis, pp. 173–77. Whether Francis believed in the Russian people is of small interest to us. But for the sake of accuracy and expressiveness we will cite his statement of 21 February 1918: "History shows Russians incapable of great movements or great achievements as whatever creditable has been accomplished can be traced to foreign inspiration and leadership. Now is the time for Allies to act" (*FRUS: 1918, Russia*, 1:384).

27. Francis, pp. 231–32.

28. Jados, p. 43.

29. Lansing, p. 341.

30. *State of the Union Messages*, p. 2584.

31. William A. Williams, "American Intervention in Russia, 1917–1920 (Part I)," *Studies on the Left* 3, no. 4 (fall 1963), p. 35.

32. George F. Kennan, *Soviet Foreign Policy, 1917–1941* (Princeton, N.J., 1960), pp. 29–30. Kennan holds basically to the same line in a more recent article, "The United States and the Soviet Union, 1917–1976," *Foreign Affairs* 54 (July 1976): 671–90.

33. George F. Kennan, *Soviet-American Relations, 1917–1920*, vol. 2: *The Decision to Intervene* (Princeton, N.J., 1958), p. 470.

34. Ibid., p. 471.

35. Ruhl J. Bartlett, ed., *Record of American Diplomacy: Documents and Readings in the History of American Foreign Relations* (New York, 1947), pp. 459–61.

36. *FRUS: 1918, Russia*, 1:395–96. For the Russian translation of the appeal see

Sovetsko-Amerikanskie otnosheniya, 1919–1933 [Soviet-American relations, 1919–33] (Moscow, 1934), p. 12.

37. *FRUS: 1918, Russia,* 1:519.

38. *Istoriya Pol'shi* [History of Poland], vol. 3 (Moscow, 1958), p. 386.

39. William A. Williams, "American Intervention in Russia, 1917–1920 (Part II)," *Studies on the Left* 4, no. 1 (winter 1964), p. 53.

40. *FRUS: 1918, Russia,* vol. 2 (Washington, D.C., 1932), p. 288.

41. Ibid., p. 289.

42. Tsvetkov, pp. 36–37.

43. Ibid., p. 36.

44. William S. Graves, *America's Siberian Adventure, 1918–1920* (New York, 1931), p. 356. The book is available in Russian translation.

45. Ibid., pp. 187, 206.

46. Ibid., p. xxi.

47. Hoover Institution on War, Revolution, and Peace. John F. Stevens, pp. 2–3.

48. Tsvetkov, p. 43.

49. Herbert C. Hoover, *Memoirs,* 3 vols. (New York, 1951–52), 1:411.

50. *The Bullitt Mission to Russia: Testimony before the Committee on Foreign Relations, United States Senate, of William C. Bullitt* (New York, 1919), pp. 89–90.

51. Samuel Northrup Harper Papers, box 57, folder 9. The Russian-American Chamber of Commerce Statement of American Policy toward Russia, 23 December 1920, p. 3.

52. Popova, p. 65.

53. *FRUS: 1920,* vol. 3 (Washington, D.C., 1936), p. 717.

54. Ibid., pp. 463–68.

55. Vera Dean, *The United States and Russia* (Cambridge, Mass., 1948) p. 15.

56. Peter G. Filene, *Americans and the Soviet Experiment, 1917–1933* (Cambridge, Mass., 1967), p. 47.

57. *CR,* 57 (pt. 2): 1392, 1394.

58. Ibid., pt. 4, p. 3377.

59. Ibid., pt. 5, p. 4883.

60. Ibid., pt. 1, p. 342.

61. Ibid., pt. 2, p. 1101.

62. Ibid., p. 1167.

63. E. I. Popova, "1920–1922: Amerikantsy i Sovetskaya Rossiya" [1920–22: The Americans and Soviet Russia], *SShA: ekonomika, politika, ideologiya,* no. 11 (1970), pp. 56–62; D. N. Stashevsky, *Progressivnye sily SShA v bor'be za priznanie Sovetskogo gosudarstva, 1917–1933* [The progressive forces of the United States in the struggle for recognition of the Soviet state, 1917–33] (Kiev, 1969).

64. Ray Ginger, *The Bending Cross: A Biography of Eugene Victor Debs* (New Brunswick, N.J., 1949), p. 382.

65. Ibid., p. 398.

66. Ibid., p. 439.

67. Philip S. Foner, *The Bolshevik Revolution: Its Impact on American Radicals, Liberals, and Labor* (New York, 1967), p. 124.

68. Samuel Gompers, *Seventy Years of Life and Labor: An Autobiography,* vol. 2 (New York, 1925), p. 399.

69. Foner, *The Bolshevik Revolution*, p. 40.

70. Ibid., pp. 260-61.

71. Ibid., p. 189.

72. In Russian the word for *pail* (vedró) rhymes with the name *Woodrow*, pronounced with stress on the last syllable (Vladimir V. Mayakovsky, *Izbrannye proizvedeniya* [Selected works] [Moscow, 1956], p. 259).

73. *Dokumenty*, 1:292.

74. Lenin, *Collected Works*, vol. 30 (Moscow, 1965), p. 51. See also *Chicago Daily News*, 27 October 1919.

75. *Christian Science Monitor*, 17 December 1919.

76. Lenin, *Polnoe sobranie sochineniy*, 40:152. See the English version in *The World*, 21 February 1920.

77. *Dokumenty*, 1:628-30.

78. *Sovetsko-Amerikanskie otnosheniya, 1919-1933*, p. 37.

79. *Dokumenty*, 2:105.

80. Ibid., 3:445.

81. Ibid., pp. 171-77. See the English text in *FRUS: 1920*, 3:474-78.

82. Georgi V. Chicherin, *Stat'i i rechi po voprosam mezhdunarodnoy politiki* [Articles and speeches on questions of international policy] (Moscow, 1961), p. 176.

83. Lenin, *Collected Works*, vol. 31 (Moscow, 1965), pp. 444-45.

84. *FRUS: 1921*, vol. 2 (Washington, D.C., 1936), pp. 787-88.

85. Herbert Hoover Presidential Library. American Relief Administration, Russian Operations 1921-23, 3:133.

86. Ibid., p. 137.

87. Ibid., pp. 169-70.

88. Ibid., p. 169.

89. Ibid., p. 175.

90. Ibid., pp. 50-51.

91. Ibid., p. 447.

92. Harold H. Fisher, *The Famine in Soviet Russia, 1919-23: The Operations of the American Relief Administration* (New York, 1927), p. 553.

93. G. Ya. Tarle, "Ob uchastii rabochikh organizatsiy SShA v vosstanovlenii narodnogo khozyaystva Sovetskoy Rossii v 1921-1925 gg." [On the participation of workers' organizations of the United States in the rehabilitation of the national economy of Soviet Russia in 1921-25], *Mezhdunarodnye otnosheniya, politika, diplomatiya, XVI-XX veka* [International relations, politics, diplomacy: Sixteenth-twentieth centuries] (Moscow, 1964).

94. V. S. Golubtsov, "V. I. Lenin i obrazovanie AIK-Kuzbass" [V. I. Lenin and the formation of the Autonomous Industrial Colony-Kuzbass], *Vestnik Moskovskogo Universiteta* [Moscow University Herald], *Istoriya* [History], no. 2 (1960); "The American at Kuzbass, 1922-24: A Story of Internationalism," *New World Review* 39, no. 4 (fall 1971): 68-103.

95. V. F. Lopatin, *Proval antisovetskikh planov SShA: Genuya-Gaaga* [The failure of the anti-Soviet plans of the U.S.A.: Genoa-The Hauge] (Moscow, 1963), p. 326.

96. *Dokumenty*, 5:579.

97. *FRUS: 1922*, vol. 2 (Washington, D.C., 1938), p. 834.

98. *Dokumenty*, 5:579.

99. Ibid., 6:20, 602.

Chapter Three

1. J. Stalin, *Works*, 13 vols. (Moscow, 1952–55), 10:347.
2. Adam B. Ulam, *Expansion and Coexistence: The History of Soviet Foreign Policy, 1917–1967* (New York, 1968), pp. 136–37.
3. Stalin, *Works*, 7:295.
4. Ibid.
5. *Istoriya vneshney politiki SSSR, 1917–1976. v dvukh tomakh* [History of the foreign policy of the USSR, 1917–76, in 2 vols.) by A. A. Gromyko and B. N. Ponomarev, vol. 1 (Moscow, 1976), pp. 189–90.
6. *Dokumenty*, 10:222–23.
7. Stalin, *Works*, 10:296.
8. M. M. Litvinov, *Vneshnyaya politika SSSR: Rechi i zayavleniya, 1927–1935* [Foreign policy of the USSR: Speeches and statements, 1927–35] (Moscow, 1935), p. 19.
9. Brynjolf J. Hovde, "Russo-American Relations, 1917–1927," *Current History* 27 (1927): 237.
10. *Dokumenty*, 6:155–56.
11. *State of the Union Messages*, p. 2643.
12. *Dokumenty*, 6:547.
13. *FRUS: 1923*, vol. 2 (Washington, D.C., 1938), p. 788.
14. Schuman, p. 235.
15. Oral History Collection of Columbia University. John C. White, p. 69.
16. *Dokumenty*, 7:469–74.
17. Schuman, p. 245.
18. *Dokumenty*, 10:18–19.
19. *FRUS: 1928*, vol. 3 (Washington, D. C., 1943), pp. 822–25.
20. Joan H. Wilson writes: "The original policy of nonrecognition remained essentially the same under the administrations of Wilson, Harding, Coolidge, and Hoover, although it did become more rigidly institutionalized with bureaucratic circles over the years" (*Ideology and Economics: U.S. Relations with the Soviet Union, 1918–1933* [Columbia, Mo., 1974], p. 14).
21. Malbone W. Graham, "Russian-American Relations, 1917–1933: An Interpretation," *American Political Science Review* 28 (1934): 399–400.
22. Foreign Policy Association, *The Recognition Policy of the United States, with Special Reference to Soviet Russia* (New York, 1926), p. 17.
23. Samuel Northrup Harper Papers. Alexeieef to Harper, 18 January 1924.
24. Ibid.
25. Ibid., Harper to Kelley, 19 March 1925.
26. Ibid., Barhmeteff to Harper, 15 April 1929.
27. Hoover Institution on War, Revolution, and Peace. George M. Day, Response to Questionnaires and Record of Interviews with Russians in L.A. Anna Kegeler.
28. Ibid., Glafira Nasedkin (Ossipoff).
29. *CR*, 64 (pt. 4): 4168.

30. Ira S. Cohen, "Congressional Attitudes towards the Soviet Union, 1917-1941," thesis, University of Chicago, 1955, pp. 45-46.

31. Marian C. McKenna, *Borah* (Ann Arbor, Mich., 1961), p. 300.

32. *CR*, 65 (pt. 1): 449.

33. *Vneshnyaya torgovlya SSSR za 1918-1940 gg.* [Foreign trade of the USSR for 1918-40] (Moscow, 1960); *Vneshnyaya torgovlya SShA* [Foreign trade of the U.S.A.] (Moscow, 1965); V. K. Furaev, "O torgovykh i ekonomicheskikh otnosheniyakh mezhdu SSSR i SShA v 1924-1929 gg." [Concerning the commercial and economic relations between the USSR and the U.S.A. during 1924-29], *Problemy istorii mezhdunarodnykh otnosheniy* [Problems in the history of international relations] (Leningrad, 1972), pp. 91-110.

34. *Dokumenty*, 8:474-76.

35. V. I. Kas'yanenko, "Ob ekonomicheskikh i tekhnicheskikh svyazyakh mezhdu Sovetskim Soyuzom i SShA v 20-30-kh godakh" [Concerning the economic and technological ties between the Soviet Union and the U.S.A. during the twenties and thirties], *Novaya i noveyshaya istoriya*, no. 6 (1964), pp. 81-82.

36. Anaslasius Mikoyan, "The Soviet's Advance toward Industrial Power," *Current History* 27 (1927): 159-60.

37. Furaev, *Sovetsko-Amerikanskie otnosheniya*, pp. 139-40.

38. *Vneshnyaya torgovlya SSSR*, p. 37. Here and hereafter sums in rubles are computed at the 1950 rate of exchange.

39. Stalin, *Works*, 13:154.

40. Ibid., p. 151.

41. E. S. Shershnev, "K istorii Sovetsko-Amerikanskikh ekonomicheskikh otnosheniy" [On the history of Soviet-American economic relations], *Voprosy istorii*, no. 1 (1973), p. 23.

42. Schuman, p. 253.

43. Kas'yanenko, p. 85.

44. *Dokumenty*, 6:339-42.

45. Pitirim A. Sorokin, *Russia and the United States* (New York, 1944), p. 14.

46. Hoover Institution on War, Revolution, and Peace. E. Burland, If the United States Should Negotiate a Commercial Treaty with Soviet Russia, 18 June 1925, pp. 49-50.

47. *CR*, 64 (pt. 4):4163.

48. Rurik, if such a person did ever exist, could have been a prince only in the ninth century in the Novgorod territory. Moscow was founded in 1147.

49. Hoover, *Memoirs*, 2:23.

50. *Dokumenty*, 6:408. Senator Borah was a Republican leader.

51. Ibid., p. 239.

52. *Russia after Ten Years: Report of the American Trade Union Delegation to the Soviet Union* (New York, 1927).

53. *Soviet Russia in the Second Decade: A Joint Survey by the Technical Staff of the First American Trade Union Delegation* (New York, 1928).

54. *Report of the First American Rank and File Labor Delegation to Soviet Russia* (New York, 1928).

55. Stashevsky, p. 155.

56. Meno Lovenstein, *American Opinion of Soviet Russia* (Washington, D.C., 1941), p. 61.

57. *Dokumenty*, 12:306.

58. Ibid., 11:446.

59. L. S. Nikol'skaya, "K istorii razvitiya Sovetsko-Amerikanskikh nauchnykh i kul'-turnykh kontaktov" [Toward a history of the development of Soviet-American scientific and cultural contacts], *Amerikansky yezhegodnik, 1973* [American yearbook, 1973] (Moscow, 1973), pp. 208–33; V. K. Furaev, "Iz istorii kul'turnykh svyazey mezhdu SSSR i SShA" [From the history of the cultural ties between the USSR and the U.S.A.], *XXII Gertsenovskie chteniya: Mezhvuzovskaya konferentsiya* [XXII Hertzen readings: The Mezhvuz conference] (Leningrad, 1969); V. K. Furaev, "Sovetsko-Amerikanskie nauchnye i kul'turnye svyazi, 1924–1933 gg." [Soviet-American scientific and cultural ties, 1924–33], *Voprosy istorii*, no. 3 (1974), pp. 41–57.

60. Lincoln Steffens, *The Autobiography of Lincoln Steffens*, 2 vols. (New York, 1931), 2:798–99.

61. *Sergei Esenin* (Moscow, 1958), p. 507.

62. Mayakovsky, pp. 486–87.

63. *Vladimir V. Mayakovsky*, vol. 4 (Moscow, 1968), p. 340.

64. Mayakovsky, p. 224.

65. *Leninskaya vneshnyaya politika Sovetskoy strany, 1917–1924* [The Leninist foreign policy of the Soviet land, 1917–24] (Moscow, 1969), p. 257.

66. Dimitri von Mohrenschildt, "American Intelligentsia and Russia of the N.E.P.," *Russian Review* 6, no. 2 (spring 1947), pp. 59–66.

67. Emma Goldman, *My Disillusionment in Russia* (Garden City, N.Y., 1923) and *My Further Disillusionment in Russia* (Garden City, N.Y., 1924).

68. Filene, pp. 87–88.

69. Francis L. Broderick, *W. E. B. Du Bois: Negro Leader in a Time of Crisis* (Stanford, Calif., 1959), p. 139.

70. Theodore Dreiser, *Dreiser Looks at Russia* (New York, 1928), pp. 9–10.

71. *Vneshnyaya torgovlya SSSR*, p. 14.

72. *Dokumenty*, 16:348.

73. Committee on Russian-American Relations, American Foundation, *The United States and the Soviet Union: A Report on the Controlling Factors in the Relation between the United States and the Soviet Union* (New York, 1933), pp. 209–10.

74. Hubert R. Knickerbocker, *The Red Trade Menance: Progress of the Soviet Five-Year Plan* (New York, 1931).

75. Hoover Institution on War, Revolution, and Peace. Memorandum on the Present Condition of the Union of the Soviet Socialist Republics and Its Population, October 1931; B. W. Sokolov, Soviet Dumping, Paris, April 1931; A. Zaitzoff, Military Aspects of the Five-Year Plan of the USSR, June 1931.

76. Henry D. Baker, "The Five-Year Plan under Fire," *Current History* 33 (1931): 486–92.

77. See, for example, Edgar S. Furniss, "Soviet Economic Disappointments," *Current History* 36 (1932): 616–20.

78. *CR*, 72 (pt 4): 4526.

79. Edmund A. Walsh, *The Last Stand: An Interpretation of the Soviet Five-Year Plan* (Boston, 1931).

80. *CR*, 75 (pt. 1): 930.

81. *Sovetsko-Amerikanskie otnosheniya, 1919–1933*, pp. 66–67.

82. *Dokumenty*, 13:437–39.

83. Ibid., pp. 457–58.

84. Ibid., 14:156–57.

85. Ibid., pp. 522–27.

86. *Vneshnyaya torgovlya SShA*, p. 289.

87. *Vneshnyaya torgovlya SSSR*, p. 37.

88. *Vneshnyaya torgovlya SShA*, p. 289.

89. Stalin, *Works*, 13:136.

90. *Dokumenty*, 15:260.

91. *Istoricheskiy arkhiv* [Historical archives], no. 2 (1960), p. 104.

92. *The United States and the Soviet Union*, pp. 2–4.

93. Ibid., pp. 4–7.

94. Litvinov, p. 62.

95. Joan H. Wilson, *American Business and Foreign Policy, 1920–1933* (Lexington, Ky., 1971), p. 154.

96. Hoover, *Memoirs*, 3:362, 436, 484.

97. *FRUS: The Soviet Union, 1933–1939* (Washington, D.C., 1952), pp. 12–13.

98. Cordell Hull, *The Memoirs of Cordell Hull*, vol. 1 (New York, 1948), p. 297.

99. To be sure, Hull prevailed on Roosevelt to postpone his departure from 5 November, as planned earlier, and left only on 11 November 1933.

100. Donald G. Bishop, *The Roosevelt-Litvinov Agreements: The American View* (Syracuse, N.Y., 1965); Robert P. Browder, *The Origins of Soviet-American Diplomacy* (Princeton, N.J., 1953).

101. Browder, p. 140.

102. *Dokumenty*, 16:608.

103. Ibid., p. 663.

104. Ibid., p. 608.

105. Litvinov, p. 260.

106. *Dokumenty*, 16:609.

107. Bishop, p. 31.

108. Ibid., p. 142.

109. *The Establishment of Diplomatic Relations with the Union of Soviet Socialist Republics* (Washington, D.C., 1948), pp. 7–11.

110. *Dokumenty*, 16:609.

111. Bishop, pp. 149–50; *FRUS: The Soviet Union, 1933–1939*, pp. 26–27.

112. *New York Times*, 18 November 1933.

113. Ibid., 19 November 1933.

114. Ibid.

115. Ibid., 18 November 1933.

116. Ibid.

117. *Dokumenty*, 16:609.

118. *New York Times*, 18 November 1933.

119. Litvinov, p. 259.

120. Stalin, *Works*, 13:310.

Chapter Four

1. *KPSS v rezolyutsiyakh*, 5:335.

2. Ibid., p. 340.

3. Ibid., p. 366.

4. Ibid., 7:111, 181, 119–218.

5. *Izvestiya*, 18 March 1938.

6. J. Stalin, *Problems of Leninism* (Moscow, 1945), p. 601.

7. *KPSS v rezolyutsiyakh*, 5:366.

8. Stalin, *Problems of Leninism*, p. 604.

9. See Soviet research on the New Deal: V. L. Mal'kov, *"Novy kurs" v SShA* [The New Deal in the United States] (Moscow, 1973); V. L. Mal'kov and D. G. Nadzhafov, *Amerika na pereput'e, 1929–1938 gg.* [America at the crossroad, 1929–38] (Moscow, 1967); N. V. Sivachev, *Politicheskaya bor'ba v SShA v seredine 30-kh godov XX veka* [The political struggle in the U.S.A. in the mid-thirties of the twentieth century] (Moscow, 1966).

10. *Dokumenty*, 16:751.

11. Ibid., 17:31.

12. Stalin, *Works*, 13:284.

13. *New York Times*, 19 November 1933.

14. *Dokumenty*, 17:244.

15. Litvinov, p. 278.

16. *FRUS: The Soviet Union, 1933–39*, p. 113.

17. Ibid., p. 114.

18. Ibid., pp. 172–81.

19. Ibid., p. 184.

20. *The Soviet Union and World-Problems*, ed. Samuel N. Harper (Chicago, 1935).

21. Samuel Northrup Harper Papers, box 32, folder 10, p. 2.

22. *Washington Herald*, 9 June 1935.

23. *FRUS: The Soviet Union, 1933–39*, p. 218 and passim.

24. Ibid. p. 248.

25. *Vneshnyaya politika SSSR: sbornik dokumentov* [Foreign policy of the USSR: Collected documents], vol. 4 (Moscow, 1946), p. 58.

26. Edgar S. Furniss, "Soviet World Relations," *Current History* 42 (1935): 105.

27. *Vneshnyaya politika SSSR: sbornik dokumentov*, 4:104.

28. Harper, p. 219.

29. Tompkins, p. 269.

30. Williams, *American-Russian Relations*, p. 241.

31. *FRUS: The Soviet Union, 1933–1939*, p. 193.

32. Ibid., p. 420.

33. Ibid., pp. 429–30.

34. *Vneshnyaya politika SSSR: sbornik dokumentov*, 4:288-89.

35. *Vneshnyaya torgovlya SShA*, p. 291.

36. *Vneshnyaya torgovlya SSSR*, p. 37.

37. A. I. Mikoyan, "Dva mesyatza v SShA" [Two months in the U.S.A.], *SShA: ekonomika, politika, ideologiya*, no. 10 (1971), p. 77.

38. *Dokumenty*, 17:416.

39. *CR*, 79 (pt. 11): 11947.

40. Ibid., 83 (pt. 3): 3120.

41. Ibid., 79 (pt. 2): 1493.

42. *FRUS: The Soviet Union, 1933-1939*, p. 292.

43. Oliver Jensen, ed., *America and Russia: A Century and a Half of Dramatic Encounters* (New York, 1962); Richard H. Ullman, "The Davies Mission and the United States-Soviet Relations, 1937-1941," *World Politics* 9, no. 2 (January 1957), pp. 220-39.

44. *FRUS: The Soviet Union, 1933-1939*, p. 437.

45. Joseph E. Davies, *Mission to Moscow* (New York, 1941), p. 245.

46. Ibid., p. 95.

47. *FRUS: The Soviet Union, 1933-1939*, p. 557.

48. Davies, pp. 414-15.

49. D. G. Nadzhafov, *Narod SShA—protiv voyny i fashisma* [The people of the United States: Against war and fascism] (Moscow, 1969).

50. Basil Rauch, *Roosevelt: From Munich to Pearl Harbor: A Study in the Creation of a Foreign Policy* (New York, 1950), p. 39.

51. The journals of the former head of the European section of the State Department reveal that on 29 March 1939, that is, the day after the fall of Madrid, it was decided that the Franco government would be recognized after two or three days. On 1 April 1939 Hull announced at a press conference that he had already sent a telegram to Franco with news of the recognition (*The Moffat Papers: Selections from the Diplomatic Journals of Jay Pierrepont Moffat, 1919-1943* [Cambridge, Mass., 1956], pp. 236-37).

52. Hull, 2:658.

53. *Istoriya vneshney politiki SSSR, 1917-1976 gg.*, vol. 1, p. 322.

54. *SSSR v bor'be za mir nakanune vtoroy mirovoy voyny [sentyabr' 1938 g.-avgust 1939 g.]: dokumenty i materialy* [The USSR in the struggle for peace on the eve of the Second World War, September 1938-August 1939: Documents and materials] (Moscow, 1971), p. 79.

55. Ibid., p. 81.

56. *FRUS: 1939*, vol. 1 (Washington, D.C., 1956), p. 234.

57. Ibid.

58. Ibid., p. 236.

59. *SSSR v bor'be za mir*, pp. 478-79.

60. *CR*, 84 (pt. 8): 8617.

61. *SSSR v bor'be za mir*, pp. 605-6.

62. *New York Times*, 14 August 1939.

63. Dulles, p. 201.

64. Ibid., p. 203.

65. *FRUS: 1939*, 1:366-67.

66. *New York Times*, 28 August 1939.

67. Samuel Northrup Harper Papers, box 21, folder 21. Curtiss to Harper, 16 October 1939.

68. Rauch, p. 146.

Chapter Five

1. *The Public Papers and Addresses of Franklin D. Roosevelt*, 13 vols. (New York, 1938–50), 8:460.

2. *Vneshnyaya politika SSSR: sbornik dokumentov*, 4:446.

3. *Trial of the Major War Criminals before the International Military Tribunal, Nuremburg, 14 November 1945–1 October 1946*, vol. 15 (Nuremburg, 1948), p. 350.

4. Ibid., vol. 10 (Nuremberg, 1947), p. 519.

5. *CR*, 93:4695–96.

6. Robert Leckie, *The Wars of America* (New York, 1968), p. 709.

7. William L. Shirer, *The Rise and Fall of the Third Reich: A History of Nazi Germany* (New York, 1963), p. 901.

8. *Fal'sifikatory istorii* [Falsifiers of history] (Moscow, 1948), pp. 65–66.

9. Thomas A. Bailey, *The Man in the Street: The Impact of American Public Opinion on Foreign Policy* (New York, 1948), p. 157.

10. Henry S. Commager, ed., *Documents of American History*, vol. 2 (New York, 1960), p. 449.

11. Harry S. Truman, *Memoirs*, 2 vols. (Garden City, N.Y., 1955–56), 1:234.

12. For details, see N. N. Yakovlev, *SShA i Angliya vo vtoroy mirovoy voyne* [The U.S.A. and England in the Second World War] (Moscow, 1961), pp. 103–95.

13. *Istoriya Velikoy Otechestvennoy voyny Sovetskogo Soyuza, 1941–1945* [History of the Great Patriotic War of the Soviet Union, 1941–45], vol. 1 (Moscow, 1960), p. 403.

14. A. M. Vasilevsky, *Delo vsey zhizni* [Things of my life] (Moscow, 1974), p. 119.

15. N. G. Kuznetsov, *Nakanune* [On the eve] (Moscow, 1966), pp. 297, 321–22.

16. Robert E. Sherwood, *Roosevelt and Hopkins: An Intimate History* (New York, 1948), p. 303.

17. *FRUS:1941*, vol. 1 (Washington, D.C., 1958), pp. 766–67.

18. Ibid., pp. 767–68.

19. Sherwood, p. 304.

20. William L. Langer and S. Everett Gleason, *The Undeclared War, 1940–41* (New York, 1953), p. 538.

21. James MacGregor Burns, *Roosevelt: The Soldier of Freedom* (New York, 1970), p. 115.

22. *New York Times*, 24 June 1941.

23. Richard M. Leighton and Robert W. Coakley, *Global Logistics and Strategy* (Washington, D.C., 1955), p. 135.

24. Langer and Gleason, pp. 542–43.

25. For details, see Raymond H. Dawson, *The Decision to Aid Russia, 1941: Foreign Policy and Domestic Politics* (Chapel Hill, N.C., 1959).

26. The whole historical question is analyzed in N. N. Yakovlev, *Zagadka Pirl-Kharbora* [The puzzle of Pearl Harbor], published in the USSR in two editions in 1966–68, totaling more than 100,000 copies.

27. Joint Committee on the Investigation of the Pearl Harbor Attack, U.S. Congress, *Pearl Harbor Attack* (Washington, D.C., 1946), p. 1358.

28. Ibid., p. 1402.

29. Ibid., pp. 1065–66.

30. Louis Morton, *Strategy and Command: The First Two Years* (Washington, D.C., 1962), p. 125.

31. Burns, p. 157.

32. Ibid.

33. Langer and Gleason, p. 893.

34. Samuel F. Bemis, *A Diplomatic History of the United States* (New York, 3d ed., 1950), p. 869.

35. Yakovlev, *Zagadka Pirl-Kharbora*, p. 144.

36. Hanson W. Baldwin, "The Myth of Security," *Foreign Affairs* 26, no. 2 (January 1948), p. 254.

37. Leckie, pp. 737–73.

38. Perry M. Smith, *The Air Force Plans for Peace, 1943–1945* (Baltimore, 1970), pp. 22, 28.

39. M. Matloff and E. Snell, *Strategicheskoe planirovanie v koalitsionnoy voyne, 1941–1942 gg.*, pp. 183–84. This is translated from English, Maurice Matloff and Edwin M. Snell, *Strategic Planning for Coalition Warfare, 1941–1942, 1943–1944* (Washington, D.C., 1953–59).

40. *Proval gitlerovskogo nastupleniya na Moskvu* [The failure of Hitler's attack on Moscow] (Moscow, 1966), pp. 12, 55.

41. Sherwood, p. 497.

42. *New York Times*, 20 October 1955.

43. Leckie, p. 753.

44. See, for example, V. M. Kulish, *Vtoroy front* [The second front] (Moscow, 1960).

45. Elliot Roosevelt, *As He Saw it* (New York, 1946), pp. 54–55.

46. *Vneshnyaya politika Sovetskogo Soyuza v period Otechestvennoy voyny* [The foreign policy of the Soviet Union during the period of the Patriotic War], vol. 1 (Moscow, 1946), p. 285.

47. Franz Halder, *Voennyi dnevnik* [War diary], vol. 3, pt. 2 (Moscow, 1971), p. 282.

48. A. M. Samsonov, *Stalingradskaya bitva* [The battle of Stalingrad] (Moscow, 1968), p. 48.

49. Ibid., pp. 281, 516.

50. *General Marshall's Report: The Winning of the War in Europe and the Pacific* (Washington, D.C., 1945), p. 1.

51. Gabriel Kolko, *The Politics of War: The World and United States Foreign Policy, 1943–1945* (New York, 1968), p. 24.

52. Vasilevsky, p. 270.

53. *Perepiska Predsedatelya Soveta Ministrov SSSR s Prezidentami SShA i Prem'er-ministrami Velikobritanii vo vremya Velikoy Otechestvennoy voyny 1941–1945 gg.*

[Correspondence between the chairman of the Soviet of Ministers of the USSR and the president of the United States and the prime minister of Great Britain during the time of the Great Patriotic War of 1941–45], vol. 2 (Moscow, 1957), pp. 33–73.

54. Vasilevsky, p. 325.

55. Henry L. Stimson and McGeorge Bundy, *On Active Service in Peace and War* (New York, 1947), p. 526.

56. Kolko, p. 22.

57. *FRUS: The Conferences at Cairo and Teheran, 1943* (Washington, D.C., 1961), p. 65.

58. Sherwood, p. 748.

59. Matloff and Snell, p. 282.

60. *FRUS: The Conference at Cairo and Teheran, 1943*, p. 255.

61. W. Averell Harriman, *America and Russia in a Changing World: A Half-Century of Personal Observation* (Garden City, N.Y., 1971), p. 31.

62. Heinz Guderian, *Panzer Leader*, tr. from the German by Constantine Fitzgibbon (New York, 1952).

63. F. Mellentin, *Tankovye srazheniya 1939–1945 gg.* [Tank battles of 1939–45] (Moscow, 1957), p. 236.

64. Arthur Krock, *Memoirs: Sixty Years on the Firing Line* (New York, 1968), p. 216.

65. Kolko, p. 371.

66. *Rokovye resheniya* [Fatal decisions] (Moscow, 1958), p. 363.

67. *CR*, 97:5565.

68. Ibid.

69. *Tegeran, Yalta, Potsdam* [Teheran, Yalta, Potsdam] (Moscow, 1970), pp. 103, 130, 136–37.

70. Ibid., p. 192.

71. *The Public Papers and Addresses of Franklin D. Roosevelt*, 13:580–81.

72. Ibid., pp. 571, 585.

73. Harriman, pp. 68–69.

74. *New York Times*, 8 February 1970.

75. Hans J. Morgenthau, *In Defense of the National Self-Interest* (New York, 1951), p. 110.

76. George F. Kennan, *American Diplomacy, 1900–1950* (Chicago, 1951), p. 76.

77. Williams, *The Tragedy of American Diplomacy*, pp. 223–24.

78. *Washington Post*, 12 April 1970; *New York Times*, 12 April 1970; see also *Sunday Star*, 12 April 1970.

79. Burns, pp. 608–9.

80. *Perepiska*, p. 206.

81. Ibid., p. 207.

82. Shirer, p. 1440.

83. G. K. Zhukov, *Vospominaniya i razmyshleniya* [Recollections and reflections] (Moscow, 1969), p. 624.

84. Harry Truman, *Memoirs*, 1:244.

85. Zhukov, pp. 663–64.

86. Ibid., p. 677.

87. Harriman, p. 38.

88. Joseph C. Grew, *Turbulent Era: A Diplomatic Record of Forty Years*, vol. 2 (Boston, 1952), p. 1446.

89. Vasilevksy, p. 510.

90. A. M. Samsonov, ed., *9 maya 1945 g.* [9 May 1945] (Moscow, 1972), p. 21.

91. P. A. Zhilin, ed., *Velikaya Otechestvennaya voyna* [The Great Patriotic War] (Moscow, 1970), pp. 531, 553.

92. *FRUS: The Conferences at Malta and Yalta, 1945* (Washington, D.C., 1955), pp. 107-8.

93. Matloff and Snell, pp. 523-24.

94. Arthur Bryant, *The Triumph in the West, 1943-1946* (London, 1959), pp. 469-70.

95. *FRUS: The Conference of Berlin (The Potsdam Conference), 1945*, vol. 1 (Washington, 1960), pp. 64-65.

96. Ibid., p. 77.

97. Ibid., p. 73.

98. Ibid., p. 72.

99. Ibid., p. 257.

Chapter Six

1. See, for example, *The Cold War: Origins and Developments; Hearings before the Subcommittee on Europe of the Committee on Foreign Affairs, House of Representatives, 92d Congress, 1st Session* (Washington, D.C., 1971).

2. Hans J. Morgenthau, "Changes and Chances in American-Soviet Relations," *Foreign Affairs* 49, no. 3 (April 1971), p. 429.

3. Richard V. Allen, *Peace or Peaceful Coexistence?* (Chicago, 1966), pp. 178, 184.

4. Dean G. Acheson, *Present at the Creation: My Years in the State Department* (New York, 1969), p. 753.

5. Foy D. Kohler, *Understanding the Russians: A Citizen's Primer* (New York, 1970), p. 10.

6. *CR*, 91:381.

7. *Vneshnyaya politika Sovetskogo Soyuza, 1946 g.* [Foreign policy of the Soviet Union, 1946] (Moscow, 1952), pp. 29, 40.

8. Margaret Truman, *Harry S. Truman* (New York, 1973), pp. 308-9.

9. *The Annals of America*, vol. 16 (Chicago, 1968), p. 309.

10. *Newsweek*, 18 March 1946, p. 30.

11. *Pravda*, 14 March 1946.

12. Harry Truman, *Memoirs*, 1:208.

13. *Public Papers of the Presidents of the United States: Harry S. Truman, 1945* (Washington, D.C., 1961), p. 549.

14. Michael Armine, *The Great Decision: The Secret History of the Atomic Bomb* (New York, 1959), p. 234.

15. Edmund Teller and Allen Brown, *The Legacy of Hiroshima* (Garden City, N.Y., 1962), p. 24.

16. Williams, *American-Russian Relations*, p. 277.

17. Denna F. Flemming, *The Cold War and its Origins, 1917-1960* (Garden City, N.Y., 1961), pp. 282-84.

18. *New York Herald Tribune*, 24 March 1946.

19. William Bradford Huie, "A Navy—or an Air Force?" *Reader's Digest* 53 (December 1948): 63.

20. Flemming, pp. 295-96.

21. *New York Herald Tribune*, 1 May 1949.

22. *Bulletin of the Atomic Scientists*, 1 May 1946.

23. Bernard Brodie, *Strategy in the Missile Age* (Princeton, N.J., 1959), p. 108.

24. Ibid., p. 153.

25. James M. Gavin, *War and Peace in the Space Age* (New York, 1958), p. 103.

26. Cyrus L. Sulzberger, *A Long Row of Candles: Memoirs and Diaries, 1934-1954* (New York, 1969), pp. 307-8.

27. Margaret Truman, p. 347.

28. Krock, p. 427.

29. Ibid., pp. 427, 477-78.

30. Norman A. Graebner, *Cold War Diplomacy: American Foreign Policy, 1945-1960* (Princeton, N.J., 1962), p. 41.

31. Harry Truman, *Memoirs* 2:348-49.

32. Jados, p. 248.

33. Harry Truman, *Memoirs*, 2:355.

34. Cabell Phillips, *The Truman Presidency: History of a Triumphant Succession* (New York, 1966), pp. 306-8.

35. *Vneshnyaya politika Sovetskogo Soyuza, 1948 g.* [Foreign policy of the Soviet Union, 1948], vol. 1 (Moscow, 1950), pp. 195-201.

36. Ibid., p. 28.

37. *Istoriya vneshney politiki SSSR, chast' vtoraya, 1945-1970 gg.* [History of the foreign policy of the USSR, part 2, 1945-70] (Moscow, 1971), p. 145.

38. *Vneshnyaya politika Sovetskogo Soyuza, 1950 g.* [Foreign policy of the Soviet Union, 1950] (Moscow, 1953), p. 27.

39. Bert Cochran, *Harry Truman and the Crisis Presidency* (New York, 1973), p. 335.

40. George F. Kennan, *Memoirs, 1950-1963* (Boston, 1972), pp. 136-37.

41. Ibid., pp. 137-38.

42. Ibid., pp. 142-43.

43. Williams, *The Tragedy of American Diplomacy*, p. 274.

44. John Foster Dulles, *War or Peace* (New York, 1950), p. 175.

45. Jados, pp. 172, 188, 256.

46. Cochran, pp. 398-99.

47. Louis J. Halle, *The Cold War as History* (New York, 1967), p. 234.

48. Rexford G. Tugwell, *Off Course: From Truman to Nixon* (New York, 1971), pp. 233-34.

49. Kennan, *Memoirs, 1950-1963*, pp. 97-99.

50. Dwight D. Eisenhower, *Mandate for Change, 1953-1956: The White House Years* (Garden City, N.Y., 1963), p. 401.

51. N. Vel'tov, *Uspekhi sotsializma v SSSR i ikh vliyanie na SShA* [The achievements of socialism in the USSR and their influence on the U.S.A.] (Moscow, 1971).

52. Sherman Adams, *Firsthand Report: The Story of the Eisenhower Administration* (New York, 1961), p. 455.

53. Dwight D. Eisenhower, *Waging Peace, 1956-1961: The White House Years* (New York, 1965), p. 558.

54. Helen Fuller, *Year of Trial: Kennedy's Crucial Decisions* (New York, 1962), pp. 37-38.

55. John F. Kennedy, *The Strategy of Peace* (New York, 1960) , p. 196.

56. Ibid., p. 195.

57. Ibid., p. 44.

58. Leonard S. Rodberg and Derek Shearer, eds., *The Pentagon Watchers: Students Report on the National Security State* (Garden City, N.Y., 1970), p. 68.

59. Robert F. Kennedy, *Thirteen Days: A Memoir of the Cuban Missile Crisis* (New York, 1969), p. 67.

60. Duane Lockard, *The Perverted Priorities of American Politics* (New York, 1971), p. 304.

61. Arthur M. Schlesinger, Jr., *A Thousand Days: John F. Kennedy in the White House* (New York, 1965), p. 901.

62. Ibid., p. 902.

63. David Halberstam, *The Best and the Brightest* (New York, 1972), p. 601.

64. Arthur M. Schlesinger, Jr., *The Imperial Presidency* (Boston, 1973), p. 184.

65. *New York Times*, 8 February 1970.

66. Adam B. Ulam, *The Rivals: America and Russia since World War II* (New York, 1971) p. 94.

67. O. L. Stepanova, "Istoriki 'revizionisty' o vneshney politike SShA" [The "revisionist" historians on the foreign policy of the United States], *Voprosy istorii*, no. 3 (1973), pp. 105, 107.

Chapter Seven

1. Robert Hargreaves, *Superpower: A Portrait of America in the 1970's* (New York, 1973), p. 371.

2. Raymond Aron, *The Imperial Republic: The United States and the World, 1945-1973*, tr. from the French by Frank Jellinek (New York, 1974), p. 148.

3. Henry Brandon, *The Retreat of American Power* (Garden City, N.Y., 1973), p. 358.

4. Charles E. Bohlen, *Witness to History, 1929-1969* (New York, 1973), pp. 537, 541-42.

5. *Department of State Bulletin* 68 (7 May 1973): 546.

6. *Time*, 3 March 1975, p. 11.

7. *International Conference of Communist and Labor Parties: Document and Materials* (Moscow, 1969), p. 90.

8. L. I. Brezhnev, *Following Lenin's Course: Speeches and Articles* (Moscow, 1972), p. 354.

9. *Pravda*, 30 June 1973.

10. Ibid., 9 April 1975.

11. L. I. Brezhnev, *Report of the CPSU Central Committee and the Immediate Tasks of the Party in Home and Foreign Policy* (Moscow, 1976), p. 25.

12. W. Averell Harriman and Elie Abel, *Special Envoy to Churchill and Stalin, 1941-1946* (New York, 1975), p. vii.

13. *Pravda*, 26 October 1976.

Epilogue

1. A Solzhenitsyn, *Arkhipelag Gulag, 1918-1956* [The Gulag Archipelago] (3 vols.; Pairs, 1973-75), vol. 1, p. 265, n. 12. Trans. here by N. N. Yakovlev.

2. Ibid., p. 548.

3. Ibid., vol. 3, pp. 29-30.

4. Ibid., p. 33.

5. N. N. Yakovlev, *Living in Lie* (Moscow: Novosti Press Agency Publishing House, 1976), pp. 84-85, 92-96.

6. Jack P. Green, *All Men Are Created Equal* (Oxford: Clarendon Press, 1976), pp. 8-10.

7. Richard Hofstadter, *The American Political Tradition* (New York: Knopt, 1948), p. viii.

8. Samuel N. Harper, *The Russia I Believe in* (Chicago: University of Chicago Press, 1945), p. 100.

Index